CULTURE IN THE THIRD REICH

CULTURE IN THE THIRD REICH

MORITZ FÖLLMER

TRANSLATED BY
JEREMY NOAKES AND
LESLEY SHARPE

OXFORD
UNIVERSITY PRESS

OXFORD
UNIVERSITY PRESS

Great Clarendon Street, Oxford, OX2 6DP,
United Kingdom

Oxford University Press is a department of the University of Oxford.
It furthers the University's objective of excellence in research, scholarship,
and education by publishing worldwide. Oxford is a registered trade mark of
Oxford University Press in the UK and in certain other countries

Published in the United States of America by Oxford University Press
198 Madison Avenue, New York, NY 10016, United States of America

British Library Cataloguing in Publication Data

Data available

Library of Congress Control Number: 2019954537

ISBN 978-0-19-881460-3

Printed and bound in Great Britain by
Clays Ltd, Elcograf S.p.A.

CONTENTS

LIST OF ILLUSTRATIONS

Figure 1. A couple at a dance organized by Strength through Joy in Vienna in 1938

INTRODUCTION

'Like a Dream'

'It's like a dream', Joseph Goebbels wrote in his diary in the summer of 1940, while on a trip to see the sights of occupied Paris.[1] The course of the previous few years seemed to justify his comment. On 30 January 1933, after spectacular electoral successes, the National Socialists had come to power in Germany. They had then 'seized' and extended that power. Political opponents and minorities had been uncompromisingly excluded from the new national community. The regime had prepared single-mindedly for war and had been waging it ruthlessly and effectively since 1 September 1939. The ambitions of the Propaganda Minister and of millions of his likeminded compatriots were at first fulfilled—until they became hungry for more. The Third Reich presented itself as a contrast to life during the Weimar Republic, which many Germans regarded as depressing and sordid. The Nazis aimed to be more imaginative than the democrats and 'philistines' they despised. They did not merely indulge in flights of fancy, however; they created a new reality—from the SA rallies in 1930 to the Wehrmacht's victories over Poland and France a decade later. Step by step they were transforming the lives of Germans and of all Europeans in a manner radical enough to fulfil Nazi dreams.

For the real or supposed enemies of the Third Reich, on the other hand, life was not 'like a dream'. Those persecuted spoke instead about nightmares and imagined being free again. Reservations about the Nazis and doubts about the substance behind their promises were not confined to marginalized groups. Nevertheless, millions of Germans not only came to terms with the Third Reich, but hoped it would fulfil their desires. The couple shown in the image preceding this introduction were presumably not thinking about politics, even if a swastika flag is visible in the background. Their dreams for the future may have been purely private. What is certain is that their lives had already undergone fundamental changes, in part because many leisure activities in the Third Reich were provided by the Nazi organization Strength Through Joy and also because they were Viennese and since March 1938, four months before this picture was taken, Austria had been 'annexed' to the German Reich.

The motif of the dream provides a way into the subject of this book, for it was culture that gave expression to the desires and imaginings that were so important to the history of the Third Reich. As early as the later nineteenth century *völkisch* (ethnic nationalist, see Glossary) journalists and writers had envisioned a new world in which Germans rediscovered their supposed Teutonic origins and rose to be the rulers of Europe. Richard Wagner's operas had used an aesthetically innovative form to recount the stories of heroes who rebelled against a hostile world and either triumphed or perished in the process. Such idealized projections were supplemented in the first decades of the twentieth century by new dreams of being able to restructure whole societies by means of modern media, technologies, and scientific methods. These varied phantasies exerted a considerable influence on Adolf Hitler's thinking as well as on that of Joseph Goebbels and many other National Socialists. Between 1933 and 1945 they left their mark on films, plays, journals, posters, and radio broadcasts. Culture was to mediate ideas to their *Volksgenossen* (comrades in the German national community, hereafter 'national comrades') that only a few years before had seemed outlandish and divorced from reality: ideas of Germany as a world power free of Jews and the mentally handicapped.

Culture in the Third Reich had another, less overtly Nazi aspect, however. What was performed on the stage or played in the concert hall or exhibited in a museum derived for the most part from the *bürgerlich* (bourgeois, see Glossary) canon of the nineteenth century and was more conservative than radical. Although the modern media were used for propaganda, each followed the prevailing taste: cinemas showed romances and comedies, the radio broadcast popular music, magazines published attractive features with photos. Bourgeois and popular culture were important precisely because many unpolitical and even many right-wing Germans only partially adopted Nazi ideology. Goebbels himself knew that national comrades on the one hand longed for continuity and on the other sought new opportunities as consumers. Culture, therefore, had the task of promoting renewal and generating willingness to engage. Music, theatre, and film had to be experiences that subtly transmitted Nazi messages, while at the same time reassuring and distracting the more sceptical Germans.

The fact that Nazi phantasies were so ambitious made their artistic realization more difficult. Of course, there were paintings of strapping peasants and fecund women, and *Thingspiele* (historical pageants) were staged that encouraged the audience to identify emotionally with national renewal, but they appealed only to a minority of Germans and thus were fairly useless as propaganda. Efforts to introduce innovation along *völkisch* lines were often frustrated by institutional rivalries or by personal animosities among National Socialists. In addition, influential political figures in the Third Reich, foremost among them Hitler himself, clung to traditional ideas of German culture in part with an eye to national prestige, but also from the urge to present a favourable public image. It was thus hard to define any genuinely National Socialist culture. It gained any distinctiveness it had on the one hand by contrast with 'the' Jews, who were excluded from even the smallest symphony orchestra or theatre company in the Third Reich, and on the other hand from the regime's imperial pretensions. Even before 1939 these pretensions influenced public architecture and went on to set the tone during the war years. For there was now an opportunity to realize a further dream: the dream of German cultural dominance over Europe. The methods used to achieve this included all-out propaganda, economic pressure, and naked violence, particularly aimed at the Jewish minority, whose cultural and physical presence was to be eliminated not only in Germany itself but also elsewhere in Europe.

National Socialism was a product of nineteenth-century German culture as well as of the Weimar Republic. However significant the 'seizure of power' was as a watershed, continuities dating back to the years before 1933 were still important. A 'National Socialist culture' that was distinct from 'Weimar culture'[2] existed only in a rudimentary form. It was characterized less by ideology or formal features than by its close connection with politics, society, and war. Culture was, therefore, more than 'the beautiful surface appearance of the Third Reich',[3] but a crucial part of the dynamic that drove the regime forward. In the process there were many changes of direction and focus (and many of these were unintended). Culture 'in the Third Reich' did not mean the same in 1936 as it had done in 1933 and took a different form in 1944 from 1940. In addition to Nazi innovations, bourgeois traditions, and modern media, we must also include the attempts of political opponents and the Jewish minority to assert themselves among the factors that influenced it. Its reach, moreover, extended far beyond the borders of Germany. Even before the outbreak of war the Third Reich was being subjected to intense foreign scrutiny, and after 1939 it presented Europeans and Americans with a cultural challenge as well as a political one.[4]

Always and everywhere culture is bound up with desires and dreams, and yet it is equally dependent on the concrete circumstances in which it unfolds. Between 1933 and 1945 this tension became acute. How this radicalization came about can best be understood by going back in time to the Weimar Republic, taking into account the Nazi regime as well as German society, and looking beyond the borders of the German Reich. The understanding of culture is deliberately wide, comprising both high culture in the sense of theatre, opera, and classical music and popular culture, namely film, radio, and light fiction. Moreover, neither were separate realms, as they were closely linked to political priorities, scientific visions, and practices of leisure. The dreams the Germans associated with culture had profound consequences for Germany, for Europe, and for the world. They mobilized vast energies—and ended in total destruction.

Figure 2. A mobile newspaper and magazine kiosk on Hauptstrasse in the Berlin district of Schöneberg in 1928.

1

FROM WEIMAR CULTURE
TO 'GERMAN' CULTURE

Berlin, October 1928: A man is looking out at the main street in the Schöneberg district. From his mobile kiosk he serves the dynamic consumer society that has been leaving its mark increasingly on German cultural life since the turn of the twentieth century. People passing by in the city can choose from a wide variety of newspapers and magazines, and the fact that they can do so is not simply a given. Although the economy has recovered from the war years and the period of inflation, the majority of Germans have very limited means. They are unlikely to be able to afford a set, so they have little access to radio programmes. Reading matter, however, can be bought cheaply in the street, obtained via a book club, or borrowed from a library. Access to print, though, can be viewed as an opportunity but also as a danger, for many people at this time see national unity as an ideal. In their view, German identity should be based on an idea of culture as defined by the educated middle classes. From this perspective, newspaper kiosks, station bookshops, and commercial lending libraries present a serious problem, for they enable consumers (and—particularly worrying in the light of traditional gender stereotypes—this means female consumers too) to combine entertainment and information according to their individual tastes. That, in turn, leads to a fragmentation of taste that makes it increasingly difficult to assert any national cultural unity. At the same time, cinemas are showing films that, for worried observers, threaten to trivialize, sexualize, and internationalize German culture.

These trends do not, however, mean that conservative members of the educated middle classes are ready to give up the struggle to define what counts as culture. On the contrary: where content remains under public control they still have considerable influence. The vast majority of theatres and concert halls continue to pay homage to the taste of the *Kaiserreich* (Imperial Germany). State-controlled radio fills its peak-time schedules with Beethoven symphonies or talks on Goethe. In the late 1920s, however, when both the economic situation and the political system of the Weimar Republic seem to have stabilized, the range of cultural events and activities in Germany becomes more diverse. Even the radio provides an outlet for left-wing and modernist views. The idea that adults should be able to decide for themselves what books to read or films to watch is gaining ground. The variety on offer in the kiosk in the illustration is representative of this pluralism. It ranges from the left-liberal *Vossische Zeitung*, aimed at an educated readership, via the tabloid *B. Z. am Mittag*, which has a similar political orientation, to the conservative *Berliner Lokal-Anzeiger*, and from the *Gartenlaube*, a family journal for the educated middle classes, to *Vogue*, the sophisticated fashion magazine.

Nothing about this newspaper kiosk seems to indicate that, in less than five years, the National Socialists will be in power and radically change cultural life in Germany. The culture of the Weimar Republic had a variety of tendencies and possibilities and did not simply presage the Third Reich. And yet closer inspection reveals a number of features that are significant in the light of later developments. For example, the man in the kiosk in liberal Schöneberg does not offer passers-by the opportunity to buy *Vorwärts*, the dry-as-dust official organ of the Social Democratic Party. Clearly the Social Democrats, though the strongest and most reliable republican force, exert little cultural influence beyond their traditional milieu.

There are two copies on display of the *Deutsche Illustrierte*. On its cover is a picture of the airship Graf Zeppelin. Accounts of its successful flights cater to readers interested in technology as well as appealing to people who want to read about prestigious German achievements. In fact, the *Deutsche Illustrierte* developed a line in presenting a wide range of topics from the perspective of national resurgence. Whatever the subject—Martin Luther or Frederick the Great; Germany's technical achievements, gliding activities, or geographical knowledge; the dissolution of the Reichstag or war veterans—the article always ends with the claim that the nation is being subjugated by foreign countries. People must, therefore, unite and strive in each and every field to make it stronger. Even the ruler of Afghanistan's visit to Berlin supplies an opportunity for self-pity. The picture caption reads: 'These are the mock-ups of tanks we are obliged to use if we want to put on a troop inspection for a foreign king.'[1]

Of course, there is no straight line from such comments to the Third Reich. For the whole of 1928 Hitler and the NSDAP (the National Socialist German Workers' Party, which had achieved a mere 2.6 per cent of the vote in the May Reichstag elections) were not even mentioned in the *Deutsche Illustrierte*. Yet the nationalistic tone underlying this and many other publications was a fundamental component of Weimar culture. In the second half of the 1920s it became increasingly prevalent. It was decisive in undermining the superficial stability of the republic as well as in promoting the meteoric rise of the National Socialists from 1930 onwards.

Less than ever could nationalism of any kind be simply imposed from above, and yet it was greatly in demand from the consumers of German media. The family publication *Daheim*, two copies of which are also visible in the Schöneberg kiosk, presented itself as unpolitical and yet in reporting on foreign dances and fashions it conjured up the spectre of 'de-Germanization'. On the 30th anniversary of the death of Germany's first chancellor it said: 'We want to be strong again. We would like to feel we are being led by a true German, as we were under Bismarck.'[2] What in other political and economic circumstances would, in time, have become insignificant developed during the later years of the Weimar Republic into a powerful movement. In 1928 in the metropolis of Berlin the signs were not yet clear, because, although right-wing voters existed, they were in the minority. A newspaper kiosk in Brandenburg, Franconia, or Schleswig-Holstein, where the press was ceaselessly warning of a 'crisis' in the parliamentary system and in contemporary culture and drumming up support for authoritarian political solutions, would look very different. Outside the capital there were early signs of things taking a dangerous turn: from Weimar culture to 'German' culture.

Weimar as 'Crisis': Nationalism v Diversity

The evening was a flop. Elisabeth Gebensleben-von Alten was furious about the performance of Bertolt Brecht's *Threepenny Opera*. While she was prepared to concede that the play itself was a satire, she could see nothing in the stage performance other than a 'glorification of criminality'. She had been forced to witness a laboured 'representation of everything bad that, sadly, exists in the world', while her ears were assaulted by the 'ghastly jazz music that went with it'. Many people in the audience shared her impression—with an important exception: 'Many Jews applauded.' For this woman of 46 they were not merely expressing a different opinion, they were desecrating the long tradition of the Braunschweig Court Theatre, where 'we were used to being edified by the highest and purest art', even more than the performance itself had done. What was worse, their numbers and applause were part of a worrying trend: 'The Jews are at it again, wanting to drag us down as a nation even more.'[3]

That a middle-class woman from Braunschweig with decidedly *bürgerlich* (bourgeois or middle-class, but see Glossary) values did not enjoy *The Threepenny Opera* is not at first surprising, nor was it unusual for the years around 1930. There had been violently negative responses even before the First World War, for example to naturalist theatre or modern music, and these were not confined to Germany. Culture as a kind of broad selection from which people could simply choose, albeit at the risk of the odd failure, was still an alien concept to many in the early twentieth century. Nevertheless, that sort of individualized understanding of art was characteristic of the Weimar period. At that time forms, media, and locations were expanding and the boundaries between genres were becoming more fluid. Yet, because they expected much more from culture than a mere choice of offerings, influential observers did not accept this development. Whereas some were hoping for integration and continuity, others were advocating polarization and transformation. A prime example of the latter is Bertolt

Brecht, whose theatre work was designed to motivate people to bring about a Communist revolution, even though it was enjoyed more as innovative entertainment by the audiences who applauded it. Elisabeth Gebensleben-von Alten is representative of the hope for integration and continuity. She felt Brecht's work dismissed her understanding of culture, and she linked this with a sense of general threat. Thus she diagnosed a crisis in the 'nation' and held 'the Jews' primarily responsible for it. In doing so she was expressing a widespread malaise felt by nationalistically inclined members of the middle classes.

Those interested in Weimar culture usually focus on Berlin rather than on Braunschweig and on what was new then and is still fascinating today. By so doing they overlook something important: namely, that in the 1920s and early 1930s long-established middle-class values did not merely continue to be influential, they were interpreted less flexibly and defended even more vigorously than they had been before the First World War. At that time Germany was exceptional by virtue of its rich and expanding cultural landscape. Theatres, concert halls, and museums were important to local as well as to national identity, which is why they were generously supported even when public money was tight. Many of those who attended performances or visited exhibitions were still able to reassure themselves that contemporary cultural challenges could be met by the nineteenth century's cult of genius or by neo-romanticism as represented by Richard Wagner's or Hans Pfitzner's music. Elisabeth Gebensleben-von Alten too professed her faith in a concept of beauty in which art was a quasi-religion. Thus, in a letter to her daughter about a performance of Wagner's *Die Meistersinger von Nürnberg* she writes: 'Such silly emotional self-indulgence may surprise you, but I was really overwhelmed by it. I couldn't stop thinking the whole time: "Can anything so beautiful really exist! How stupid it is not to enjoy this beauty more often and to let everyday concerns make one forget the intellectual riches of our German nation."[4]

However much Elisabeth Gebensleben-von Alten clung to an ideal of 'the highest and purest art' rooted in the nineteenth century, she was anything but stuck in the past, for she regularly reported attending nationalist and then National Socialist meetings that filled her with enthusiasm and gave her faith in a better future for Germany. In June 1931 she visited her son, who was a student in Heidelberg, and wrote from there of a spectacular event 'to mark a big Nazi rally'. The river Neckar was full of 'boats, big and small, with Chinese lanterns.... Suddenly we heard a cannon fire and the palace emerged from the darkness in all its romantic splendour. It looked as if it was in flames. Then there was a tremendous firework display over the water. But everyone was well-behaved.'[5]

Just as in Heidelberg and Braunschweig, the National Socialist movement in many parts of Germany developed nothing short of an event culture. It enthused and involved the crowds, creating a sense of togetherness and nationalist optimism. The Nazis tapped into middle-class and neo-romantic values but presented them in innovative ways. The result was a dynamic synthesis that provided an escape from the frustration of defensive opposition to the left. Even though the Nazis sometimes adopted a demonstratively anti-bourgeois stance, its impact should not be overstated. Neither the grammar-school teacher's son Heinrich Himmler nor the composer's son Reinhard Heydrich, to name two well-known examples, show evidence of any ideologically motivated rupture with their family.[6] Elisabeth Gebensleben-von Alten's middle-class values were confirmed rather than challenged by her contacts with National Socialism. For her the diagnosis of crisis and the hope of renewal now went hand-in-hand: 'Here in Braunschweig we're deep in crisis. Hitler's coming on Sunday.'[7]

That a 'crisis was looming' everywhere was a commonplace of the later Weimar Republic. Not everyone who spoke in such a way was sympathetic to the radical nationalists, let alone to the Nazis. Social Democrats put the case for overcoming the crisis through gradual reforms—by extending the welfare state and humanizing the education system. Others gave a liberal spin to the idea, arguing, for example, against the conservatism of the judiciary. Communists promoted revolutionary solidarity by painting the economic depression as a crisis situation populated by freezing families, poverty-stricken street traders, and heartless welfare bureaucrats. For quite a few people the cliché of Berlin as the 'world city in crisis' evidently had a certain appeal: a tourist guide even took tourists to welfare offices, closed-down businesses, and political meetings, and engaged young men to act the part of unemployed malcontents and thus generate the 'necessary impression of "crisis"'.[8]

The multi-layered nature of discourse about the 'crisis' was itself part of a varied cultural landscape. When we look back today, we are struck by the coexistence of these varied tendencies in the Weimar Republic: socialists and Catholics moved within their own milieus, in which they sang, took photographs, or went rambling with like-minded people. In the middle classes there were not only opponents of consumer culture but also eclectic metropolitans who went to jazz cafés as well as art exhibitions and were interested in boxing matches as well as theatre performances. There were architects who extended the stylistic range of

Imperial Germany only cautiously at best and built unremarkable detached family homes or public buildings. Others, however, were keen on stylistic innovation in domestic architecture, as exemplified by the clean lines and functionality of the Bauhaus or the sweeping curves of Erich Mendelsohn's Woga complex (today the home of the Schaubühne theatre on the Kurfürstendamm in Berlin). Although most people had not the means to travel or buy a radio, an infrastructure of bus companies, station bookstalls, and inexpensive cinemas developed to suit limited budgets. And advertising was already creating a pictorial world inhabited by motorists and house owners that anticipated later trends in West Germany.

Weimar culture was diverse and thus offered a variety of opportunities. After 1945 Christian Democrat and Social Democrat politicians emerged from the Catholic and socialist milieus. In the German Democratic Republic (East Germany) the top functionaries of the Socialist Unity Party of Germany (the SED) had their formative experiences as Communists during the Depression years. In the Federal Republic (West Germany) skilled workers, white-collar workers, and housewives were able to enjoy what the consumer culture of the Weimar period had promised but never actually delivered. Intellectuals and those in the arts world to this day refer back to the painting, literature, and political theory of that time. The same is true outside Germany: 'Weimar culture' has become an internationally known umbrella term, not least through the influence of German émigrés. It encompasses Bauhaus architecture and design, as well as the compositions of Arnold Schönberg and Paul Hindemith. Even then, Weimar culture was not purely German in character because it shared features with, and had links to, other European countries and the United States.

While acknowledging this great variety, we must not lose sight of an important fact: National Socialism itself emerged from Weimar culture. Its mythic narratives and utopian visions, its pageants and rhetorical figures, belonged to an era attempting to combine loyalty to tradition with looking to the future. However unwilling we may be to admit it, the nationalism that emerged in Imperial Germany and grew progressively more radical in the 1920s was as much a part of 'Weimar' as, for example, the painting and literature of New Objectivity. And it was no less 'modern' for integrating conservative elements. Radical nationalism created the preconditions for the rise of Hitler. Even in the 1920s this worldview made sense to people at the very heart of bourgeois society and was able to win them over years before the Nazis gained electoral victories across Germany. This plausibility was, above all, rooted in the contemporary rhetoric of crisis.

Although this rhetoric of crisis was heard from many quarters, it particularly suited talk of Germany's greatness, destruction, and gradual re-emergence. When people spoke of 'crisis' they were usually measuring the society of their own day against the ideal of a homogeneous nation. From this standpoint cultural diversity amounted to 'fragmentation', a diagnosis that went hand in hand with fears about banks collapsing, mass unemployment, or a supposedly dysfunctional parliamentary system. Being on the one hand so simple and on the other so universally applicable, the blanket term 'crisis' blurred the boundaries between very diverse contemporary phenomena. Of course there were very real problems in the early 1930s, but labelling them a 'crisis' was tendentious. Doing so did not necessarily end in pessimistic visions of total disaster. All or nothing scenarios, according to which a fighting spirit would lead to national renewal, were more potent. When people spoke, for example, about the 'nation's sick body', they assumed that a rapid 'recovery' was possible—providing the necessary drastic cures were administered.

The rhetoric of national crisis offers an explanation why previous outsiders found such broad acceptance for their extreme positions. Contemporaries such as Elisabeth Gebensleben-von Alten were very unwilling to jettison their conservative values, but they clearly recognized that they had to be prepared to accept cultural innovations if they wanted to preserve these values in changed circumstances. Radical nationalists could therefore be assured of middle-class support in their search for starting points for a new national community. They often found them outside or on the geographical margins of the allegedly decadent and fragmented Weimar society. In this context, Germans from the Baltic region and from the territories ceded to Poland were important. The dramatist Arnolt Bronnen, formerly a left-wing expressionist, transformed himself into a *völkisch* novelist and in O. S. (1929) glorified the Free Corps, which had fought against Poland immediately after the First World War to keep Upper Silesia German. German exploits in the lost African colonies also provided models for the present, as many autobiographies, novels, and films emphasized. The search for inspiration in a past moulded to suit the requirements of nationalistic interpretation was shown by the appeal of the mythology of the pseudohistorical Teutons. In addition, Otto von Bismarck was raised to the status of 'Führer', in spite of the fact that his political actions from the 1860s to the 1880s were hardly in line with this. Finally, the soldiers of the First World War were raised to the level of 'heroes', however little this corresponded to the reality of the trenches.

The rhetoric of crisis and the resurgence of German confidence were thus connected. Nationalistic Germans had no interest in other cultures and never questioned their vision of cultural homogeneity. They looked at outsiders through the lens of negative stereotypes, their own need for reassurance, and their claims to dominance. The experience of war and of the post-war period had banished the cosmopolitan outlook that was still very prominent among the Wilhelmine middle classes. Thus Elisabeth Gebensleben-von Alten experienced mixed feelings on a journey to Paris in April 1931. 'A few tears' rolled down her cheeks when she looked around 'for the last time in the Louvre for the Venus de Milo', and she enjoyed the view from the top of the Arc de Triomphe and also her visit to Versailles. But when she looked beyond the journey as a bourgeois cultural pilgrimage, her 'impressions were not all positive' and she considered it a 'blessing to get back to our clean and well-organized country'. She reacted even more negatively to a Russian Jew on his way to the Netherlands who was sitting in her railway compartment and 'appeared very disagreeable and suspect'. She was glad when border guards arrested him because he had no visa, although he 'had not actually troubled her'.[9]

In themselves, dreams of a better future and resentful self-preoccupation had little political traction. To gain it they had to be translated into a vision of German national resurgence. This vision also extended to territories beyond the Weimar state. Nationalists succeeded in keeping the issue of Germany's borders alive in public debate, and even in making it more prominent, at a time when many Germans would have been quite prepared to accept the loss of territory imposed by the Treaty of Versailles. They regarded German minorities, in particular in eastern regions of Central Europe and in Eastern Europe, as levers of future imperial expansion. Quite a number of academics in the humanities and social sciences provided them with the necessary arguments. As 'researchers of the West' or 'researchers of the East', they constructed justifications for German dominance from France and the Benelux countries as far as Poland and the Baltic States, and in doing so they were resurrecting annexation plans from the First World War. They referred to alleged ethnic affinities, for example with the Dutch, and to the assumed racial superiority of the Germans to the Slavs and the Jews. The terms 'cultural territory' and 'ethnic soil' were not terms used only by people on the academic fringe. On the contrary, the geographers, linguisticians, archaeologists, and historians involved enjoyed the support of universities and ministries, to the extent that they could even develop new forms of interdisciplinary cooperation.

Nationalist culture thus offered imaginary escape routes from a present that was felt to be in crisis into alternative worlds—a tendency that also existed in a moderate and apparently harmless variant. Although many popular films and novels seemed conservative in a non-political rather than an openly nationalistic sense, they nevertheless had political consequences. From the end of the 1920s, cinema programmes became increasingly German as a result of the advent of talking pictures. At times Hollywood productions were marginalized because dubbing techniques were still fairly primitive. The adaptations required by cinemas were expensive, and this led to a focus on German film that resulted in the Ufa studios becoming even more dominant. These had been owned since 1927 by the media entrepreneur Alfred Hugenberg, a leading figure in the radical right wing of the German National People's Party (DNVP) and soon to be its chairman. Although

Hugenberg's views did not directly influence the content of films—commercial considerations overrode any crude attempts to use them for propaganda purposes—they nevertheless had an indirect effect, as did the numerous local newspapers he controlled. They pushed left-wing social comment to the margins of Weimar culture.

Musicals such as *The Three from the Filling Station* (1930) with Lilian Harvey, Willy Fritsch, and Heinz Rühmann projected a happy world where differences were resolved in a light-hearted manner and 'a friend' always remained 'a good friend'. The social criticism in Heinrich Mann's novel *Professor Unrat* did not survive the latter's adaptation as the film *The Blue Angel* with Marlene Dietrich, Emil Jannings, and Hans Albers (also 1930). Although the plot still involves an authoritarian grammar-school teacher in the Wilhelmine period who falls madly in love with a cabaret singer on tour and marries her, once he has been dismissed from the school he no longer, as in the novel, destabilizes small-town society by adopting anarchist views and leading the town worthies astray into gambling and using prostitutes. Instead, he returns to The Blue Angel cabaret a broken man, appearing on stage as a clown and dying at the end in his former classroom. The film could be interpreted in an even more conservative way, not as a satire but as a didactic piece about male loss of control and the dangers of female sexuality. For the film critic of the *Göttinger Tageblatt* it was a 'human tragedy' in which the teacher allows himself to be 'wrenched out of his small, well-ordered world and depersonalized' by an 'instinctual creature' until he finally sees 'that he has sacrificed his life to his faith in a whore'.[10]

This interpretation of *The Blue Angel* illustrates how, amid the omnipresent rhetoric of crisis in the late Weimar Republic, 'unpolitical', conservative, and radical nationalist cultures flowed into each other. Illustrated news reports of German battleships, tanks, or fighter planes formed part of media coverage, while gliding was developing into a new, elite form of recreation. Both were highly political in so far as they combined a message of national revival with preparation for a future war. Football emerged as a spectator sport, complete with a distinctive fan culture at regional and local level. At the same time, it was presented as the locus for 'community' and 'struggle'. Such efforts to link attitudes of mind to commerce aroused criticism. For example, the leading publication for radical right-wing intellectuals, *Die Tat*, carried the complaint that the film *Yorck* (about the Prussian war against Napoleon) degraded 'the idea of the nation to a mish-mash of marches'.[11] Yet, in spite of these critical voices, it was precisely the combination of ideology and everyday experience that accounted for the impact of contemporary nationalism.

National Socialism united elements of middle-class conservatism with ethnic nationalist and radical ones, kept the boundaries between them fluid, and brought them together in an overarching vision. The origins of this project can be found in Munich in the early 1920s. The mood there before the First World War had still been liberal and open to experiment but, after the revolution of 1918/19 was suppressed, that mood changed significantly and this, in turn, gave Adolf Hitler the opportunity to come to prominence as the leader of an extreme right-wing culture. He developed his talent as an orator in various beer halls, while using cafés to present himself as an ideological politician and bohemian. He also sought out the company of *völkisch* artists, journalists, and academics. His connections to the circle of Wagner enthusiasts in Munich and Bayreuth gave him an entrée into society and boosted his prestige by association with high culture. The 'Führer' thus secured reliable supporters in the local cultural establishment even before the contours of a real Nazi cultural policy began to emerge around 1930. The NSDAP now had the centrally located Palais Barlow converted at great expense into the 'Brown House' and henceforth had the use of a prestigious headquarters, where Party members could be entertained on their own premises. Its branches in the various districts of the city had their own bands or lending libraries. An amateur dramatics group was started in the local SA branch. The 'Combat League for German Culture', set up by the *völkisch* intellectual Alfred Rosenberg, put on lecture series, film showings, lieder evenings, and cabarets. The League even created its own symphony orchestra, which not only played in Munich but toured Bavaria.[12]

At the same time, National Socialists were extending their cultural presence over the whole of Germany. On the one hand they continued with established perspectives and values. Even in the *Völkischer Beobachter*, which was aimed more at Party members than at a general readership, there were articles about 'Schleswig, the Viking city', Tübingen, 'the pearl among German romantic towns', or 'holidays in the Bavarian Allgäu', which were almost indistinguishable in style from those of the contemporary movement to promote the regions.[13] Local and regional identities were boosted, but placed in a new context. Skilful propagandists emphasized how much they were in touch with rural and small-town voters, while always making the connection with the national community as a whole. On the other hand, the NSDAP presented itself as an innovative force interested in the Zeppelin airship and talking pictures and operating at the forefront of technical development. During the campaign for the presidential election in 1932, Hitler, accompanied by an elaborate propaganda machine, flew round Germany, taking in several speaking engagements every day. In the provinces in particular, the Führer's appearances, like the NSDAP's political rallies, catered to a demand for out-of-the-ordinary experiences—they cost a significant amount in entrance charges, but it was a cost that people were prepared to pay. The Nazis also knew how to cater for the needs of the more individualistic city-dwellers. Thus Joseph Goebbels's newspaper *Der Angriff* offered job application training to its Berlin readers and even promised to widen access to tennis.[14]

Although the Nazi press seemed in many respects open and inclusive, it left no doubt about the imperialist and antisemitic thrust of the movement. It alleged, for instance, that other states and nations posed a threat to the Germans, not only politically but also culturally, by encircling them with powerful radio transmitters. Regular reports presented German minorities in Eastern Europe as feeling that their national identity and use of their own language were being suppressed. Another important theme was the supposed destructive effect of Jewish influence on German culture as typified by Carl Laemmle, the 'film Jew', a naturalized American movie mogul, who was in fact from Württemberg. Laemmle's Hollywood studio Universal had acquired the film rights to Erich Maria Remarque's pacifist war novel *All Quiet on the Western Front*. He was then blamed for the fact that 'nowadays Germans have become the world's dogsbodies, metaphorically spat at and kicked around everywhere'. In the view of the *Völkischer Beobachter*, the threat posed by this aggression from abroad and from the Jews was really brought home by the fact that so many people in Germany were denying their Germanness. Thus Greek and Orientalist archaeologists had, it claimed, spread 'the lie that our ancestors had no culture' and had educated their public 'to look with particular admiration at a small mongrel people like the Jews'.[15]

This scenario of a threat on all sides was designed to force people to act and to lead to a change of cultural direction—if only the Germans would remember their identity as a race. Being part of a project of radical renewal of this kind promised ideological as well as material gains. The Party press appealed to the need for greater security on the part of people in the creative sector, who had to make their way in an unstable market that had been shrunk by the economic depression. Jewish actors or foreign films were blamed for their difficulties. In a future Nazi Germany jobs and commissions beckoned—an argument that gained the NSDAP and the Combat League for German Culture a whole series of new members. These material attractions were boosted by the suggestion that they would be cooperating in a grand venture. During the 1920s there had been frequent complaints that artistic individuals had been pushed to the margins by a purely commercial and technological mass culture. Now artists could hope for an improvement in their social standing, to the extent that they aligned themselves with Nazi ideology and tried to find a link to the 'nation'. In the *Völkischer Beobachter*, for example, there was a call to architects to stand apart from the 'dominance of international, mass norms' in modern architecture by 'gearing materials and technical means to the ideas that emerge from the essence of our landscape and from the natural and intellectual life of our nation.'[16]

The Nazi movement, in other words, owed its success in significant measure to its cultural attractiveness, and this attractiveness in turn derived from the way its agenda overlapped with middle-class nationalist trends. It brought existing tendencies sharply into focus, but gave them a clear direction and invested them with an extra utopian dimension. For precisely this reason, many people at the time could relate to some aspects of the movement and link them to what was already familiar, even while distancing themselves from others. This becomes evident in Luise Solmitz's diary, as it does in Elisabeth Gebensleben-von Alten's. A Hamburg teacher, Solmitz found in National Socialism the grand idea she was looking for, the one 'for which one can make sacrifices and that keeps one going'. As a member of the educated middle class she noted the Führer's 'classic, concise, and penetrating German' and was opposed to his being exploited for commercial gain. She was disgusted by the business instincts of an acquaintance: 'X. is turning out unconvincing Hitler busts and thinks they'll make him rich.'[17]

While the cultural attractiveness of National Socialism was great, it was by no means unlimited. Even in the last years of the Weimar Republic there were those who espoused a liberal version of bourgeois culture and these people were not only found among Jewish Germans. Social Democrats, Communists, and Catholics continued to be strongly influenced culturally by their milieus. Millions of people were consumers of films, sporting events, or theatre performances that made no reference to questions of ideology. In other words, the unquestionable pull of the Nazi movement was not powerful enough to define what was to be considered German. To achieve that it had to demonstrate its own power and marginalize others through violence.

Power and Marginalization: Nazi Violence

'For my part it becomes ever more clear to me how completely useless a creature of over-refinement I am, incapable of surviving in more primitive surroundings....I cannot even be a language teacher, only lecture on the history of ideas, and only in German and from a completely German perspective. I must live here and die here.' The Dresden Professor of Romance Languages, Victor Klemperer, made these grim comments in his diary on 9 July 1933. A few days earlier, friends had spoken with deep pessimism about the future prospects for Jews in Germany and of concrete plans to emigrate. Klemperer himself, however, not only felt overwhelmed by the practical demands of a life in Palestine, he also thought himself incapable of making the necessary cultural adjustments. He was not attracted by a Zionist environment in which he would only be exchanging 'nationalism and narrowness for nationalism and narrowness'.[18] Yet teaching and writing about literary and intellectual history 'in the German language and from a completely German perspective' was proving more and more difficult. In the course of 1933 and 1934 Klemperer found himself increasingly exposed to the antisemitic atmosphere at the Technical University in Dresden. He lost his entitlement to examine and was expecting soon to be dismissed from the university. The publisher of a book he was still writing pulled out of the project, and Klemperer had no enthusiasm for the suggestion that he would have better prospects of publishing if he wrote it in French. As he was now faced with the loss of an important source of additional income that he had been counting on, his material circumstances became ever more straitened, while his career as a scholar was also being held back.

Even before 1933 Klemperer had been watching the rise of National Socialism carefully. At first, being a war veteran himself, he was not a stranger to anti-French prejudices and even to the notion of taking revenge for Germany's defeat, yet he quickly distanced himself from the culture of the radical right. As a Jew, he was marginalized by radical nationalism, even though he had converted to Protestantism in 1912. From the late 1920s onwards Klemperer had been recognizing more and more the ways this culture overlapped with National Socialism. He noted with displeasure, after a walk through Naumburg on the Saale, that the bookshop there had posted news from the local branches of the Stahlhelm ('Steel Helmet', a right-wing veterans' league), the Werwolf (a right-wing paramilitary organization), and the Nazi Party on its door: 'And in the streets too and in the café there were people wearing student caps and also Stahlhelm badges.' Klemperer did not regard these developments as a threat to his existence; he was above all preoccupied with his visits to French Algeria and Turkey, the construction of his house in the suburbs, and the cut in his salary as a state employee. He did, however, identify fear of political developments in others, such as the centre-right Saxon minister of education ('being dependent on and having to tremble before the National Socialists') or an acquaintance whose pessimistic view of the situation caused him to wonder, 'Jewish paranoia? Or something more?'[19]

All this changed when the National Socialists came to power. Klemperer found that political anxieties had become private ones too. Although he was not directly affected by the violence and the publication bans suffered by the left, he regarded them as signalling that the rule of law and a public sphere where criticism could be voiced had been abolished. This change soon had repercussions for life in the universities as well as for his social environment. A young friend for whom he felt almost paternal affection embraced the new regime wholeheartedly. Although other friends made critical comments, at the same time they confessed to feeling helpless. Cultural activities could only partially compensate Klemperer for being marginalized as a university teacher, a humanities scholar, and a German. He read French eighteenth-century literature 'ploddingly and hopelessly' and yet found 'something to hold onto and a degree of consolation' in it. A passionate film fan, he found that going to the cinema gave him temporary escape into a fantasy world: 'It was a real release for me. I felt the effects for a whole day afterwards.' Although he disliked the 'horrible ghetto oppressiveness' he encountered in Jewish acquaintances, he had little to offer to relieve it.[20]

In addition, Klemperer, like many critical contemporaries, found it difficult to make intellectual sense of what was happening. He could imagine Italians, whom he saw as 'illiterates, children of the South, and beasts', putting on displays of ritual violence, but he could not believe that a cultured people like the Germans could behave in that way. And he was underestimating the modernity of National Socialism when he referred to 'gruesome, medieval reviling of the Jews' or to 'a mood of fear such as must have existed in France under the Jacobins'.[21] He then had the idea for a project that afforded him the distanced perspective of an observer, namely an analysis of the language of National Socialism. It was published in 1947 under the title *LTI: A Philologist's Notebook* and to this day has lost none of its analytic power.

Like millions of other Jewish or left-wing Germans Victor Klemperer was excluded from cultural life. The Nazis' use of violence, which was unprecedented in its extent, made public protest, let alone resistance, very difficult. As Klemperer perceptively recognized, the dynamic of power and marginalization had not begun on 30 January 1933. Years beforehand the right had succeeded in reversing the development towards a pluralistic culture such as was emerging in the Weimar Republic.[22] At an early stage Nazis in Munich had taken violent action against members of the left and Jews involved in the theatre—one reason why Bertolt Brecht had decided to move to Berlin. This trend spread beyond the borders of Bavaria at the latest when the Nazis entered the government of Thuringia in January 1930, thereby securing a parliamentary majority for the dominant middle-class parties.

As interior and education minister in this state government the Nazi Wilhelm Frick took advice from Hans F. K. Günther, the racial theorist, and Paul Schultze-Naumburg, an architect on the extreme right. Frick ruthlessly suppressed modernist culture in Thuringia, having works by artists such as Ernst Barlach and Paul Klee removed from the Palace Museum in Weimar and giving instructions that undesirable dramatists and composers be banned from theatres and concert halls. His decree 'Against Negro Culture and for German Ethnicity' was designed to prevent performances by jazz bands through applying a political interpretation of the trading regulations. Social Democrat teachers were dismissed and *völkisch* prayers introduced in schools (even though this innovation was declared to be contrary to the constitution by the state constitutional court). The NSDAP's breakthrough in the Reichstag elections on 14 September 1930 gave new impetus throughout the country to the opposition to pluralism. Capitulating even before they were challenged, the radio boards of control refused to give airtime to left-wing and pacifist voices. Film production companies, which were in any case inclined to caution because audiences were shrinking as a result of the crisis and because the introduction of sound was proving expensive, became increasingly nervous about arousing political controversy. Both Thuringia and Bavaria, which had a conservative government, attempted to reverse positive decisions made by Reich censorship offices and thus exert economic pressure.

Against this background Nazi protests against Lewis Milestone's film *All Quiet on the Western Front* made a big impact. Since the Reichstag elections, the Gauleiter of Berlin, Joseph Goebbels, had been demonstrating the power of his movement through violent acts committed in the very centre of the city. However, smashing the windows of Wertheim's department store and Jewish-owned cafés on the Kurfürstendamm, or attacking Social Democrat students on Unter den Linden had only a limited effect. What Goebbels needed was a cultural event that could be used to mobilize people for weeks and would be rejected by a large proportion of the conservatively minded population. In this way the Nazis could decisively influence the cultural atmosphere even at a stage when they still had no access to the radio network and produced only a few films, which were at best attractive only to Party members. When the film version of Erich Maria Remarque's pacifist novel was shown in Berlin, Nazi activists let off stink bombs in the cinema, released white mice, and assaulted cinema-goers. Meanwhile Goebbels, who was himself in the cinema, took the opportunity to make one of his highly aggressive speeches. In December 1930 Nazis mounted demonstrations against the film almost daily between Nollendorfplatz and Wittenbergplatz. The police had to keep them away from the nearby Kurfürstendamm and protect cinemagoers. In the end *All Quiet on the Western Front*, though it had previously passed the censors with no problem, was banned throughout Germany by the highest Censorship Office. The reason given was that the film might damage Germany's reputation abroad and was provoking unrest at home.

The banning of the film was welcomed by the right, which now clearly saw the value of Nazi shows of strength. In the opinion of the *Deutsche Zeitung*, for the first time since the end of the war 'a decisive demonstration of national *resistance* had broken the presumptuous despotism of foreign and *naturalized Jews*'. Goebbels himself claimed for the movement a breakthrough in the struggle for cultural hegemony in Berlin. 'Those currently in power in Prussia' had been shown 'that the days when they could treat German national pride just as they liked were over.' Members of the 'movement' and sympathizers in provincial towns and cities felt encouraged to adopt similar measures to oppose films they found offensive on the grounds of political tendency, style of presentation, or Jewish involvement. Students disrupted even such harmless products of Weimar culture as *O alte Burschenherrlichkeit* (Oh Those Glorious Old Student Days) and *Ein Burschenlied aus Heidelberg* (A Student Song from Heidelberg). Meanwhile, Liberals and Social Democrats were sharply critical of the decision to censor *All Quiet on the Western Front*; *Vorwärts* not only called it an 'outrage' but also regarded it as one of the 'symptoms of a generally ominous situation'.[23] The republican veterans' league Reichsbanner Schwarz-Rot-Gold demonstrated in large numbers for weeks against the ban, while Social Democrat parliamentary deputies defended the film in heated debates.

Even though in September 1931 *All Quiet on the Western Front* was passed for viewing again in a modified form, there remained a significant degree of legal uncertainty in the cultural sphere. Because films or plays involving social criticism ran the risk of being banned, producing them was economically risky and thus less likely. Although there certainly were still cultural innovations in the final years of the Weimar Republic, they were limited either to fringe theatre performances of Communist agitprop plays or to films such as Brecht's and Slatan Dudow's *Kuhle Wampe or Who Owns the World* (the name of a tent camp on the outskirts of Berlin), which attempted to mobilize (sub)proletarian audiences. At the same time, the popular press owned by the liberal publishing houses Mosse and Ullstein cultivated an outlook in which, even in difficult economic times, private individuals had the right to determine their own pursuits and leisure activities. Yet among the optimistic articles about family days out in the countryside or apartments for bachelors, there was more ominous content. There were reports of political violence affecting not only the residents of proletarian districts, where clashes were common, but also passers-by in the centre of Berlin. In contrast, the Brandenburg lakes, where there was no political strife, where 'only the chirping of mini gramophones' could be heard, and where even swastika tattoos did not cause alarm, were presented as idyllic refuges—even though their tranquillity was constantly at risk of being ended by the National Socialists.[24]

The most important cultural innovation of the later Weimar Republic was the appearance of the extreme right. The Storm Troopers (SA) in particular developed a positive aesthetic of violence that was inseparable from its concrete realization. Their marches through working-class neighbourhoods and city centres engaged several senses at once and produced an impression that they were omnipresent. SA units were also often deployed several times in a row in different places or they would march towards each other in a star formation. The uniformed columns with flags, insignia, and banners produced a visual impression of unity. The marchers' physical posture, facial expression, and outstretched arms suggested conviction and energy. Brass bands and drums reinforced the military rhythm and completed by acoustic means this symbolic occupation of the public space. Without wanting to claim great originality, the SA adapted folksongs and songs from the workers' movement, thus emphasizing their strident assertions of cultural change. When combined with other, more leisure- or hobby-based activities, such marches could dominate the life of small and even of larger towns for days at a time. Thus the President of the Prussian province of the Rhineland reported that the lower Rhine town of Hamminkeln 'was battered for two whole days by Nazi propaganda. A military tattoo, marches, Protestants and Catholics each going to church in one big group on both days of Easter, day-time and evening concerts by the SA band, and a "festival of sport" attracted the population's interest.'[25]

By contrast with this display of cultural and political orderliness, those on the outside were faced with arbitrary outbreaks of violence. The SA decided for themselves when, and in response to what alleged provocations, they attacked Social Democrats, Communists, or unpolitical passers-by. Through such shows of strength they produced a choreography of disorder that displayed their power over the bodies of their opponents. This culture of public violence was distinct from the cult of the secret society that characterized other extreme-right groups and, as a result, it attracted young men looking for a nationalistic cause. Their involvement in the SA enabled not only many working-class men but also members of the aristocracy, apprentices, and students to practise public violence and justify it ideologically. The Sturmführer (storm leader: a rank in the SA) Horst Wessel, for example, was a Protestant pastor's son and was enrolled as a law student at the university in Berlin. In his autobiography, written in 1929, he describes how he was at first attracted by the right-wing Bismarck and Viking Leagues, but then disappointed by their lack of political effectiveness. The SA, on the other hand, gave him ample opportunity to speak and to organize, which he recorded in countless photographs and glorified in the lyrics of the song that was later named after him. 'Street parades, recruitment drives in the press, propaganda excursions to outlying areas', Wessel enthusiastically wrote, 'created an atmosphere of activism and high tension that could only be of benefit to the movement. There were countless clashes. People were wounded, even killed.' The 'high tension' in the Friedrichshain district or the areas outside Berlin was, for him, part of a nationwide 'experience of united will' that he shared with thousands of like-minded people in 1927 at the first NSDAP Party Rally in Nuremberg.[26]

Before long, Horst Wessel was himself one of the SA's casualties. In January 1930 he was shot in the face at his front door and died shortly after of his injuries. The factors leading to the killing remained hard to pin down: among them were a settling of personal scores, the criminal behaviour endemic in the neighbourhood, and communist reprisals. The uncertainty did not, however, stop Goebbels from immediately turning Wessel into a 'new martyr for the Third Reich' and a 'Christ-socialist'.[27] In solemn addresses and in various genres the Sturmführer's biography was deliberately recounted as a Passion narrative. The suffering and self-sacrifice of the protagonist led to a role as exemplar. Horst Wessel thus occupied a central position in the cult of the fallen, in which the movement's dead were consciously exploited. Depictions of their corpses, their names embroidered into SA flags, and specially mounted funeral marches provoked strong emotions in the survivors and committed them to further use of violence. The SA's activism was thus justified as being the existential struggle of a sworn band of brothers that pointed the way to a new German order.

The NSDAP's election rhetoric, almost as much as the SA's marches and orgies of violence, was designed to overwhelm its target audiences and marginalize opponents. Posters carried slogans such as 'That's enough!', 'Make way!', or 'Punch them in the face! Get rid of them! Time to make them pay! Let's show them what's what! We'll clean out the stables!' The Nazis threatened to remove Social Democrat 'traitors' and 'fat cats' as forcefully as they would Jewish 'string-pullers' and 'enemies of the people'.[28] This message was conveyed visually by pictures of peasants and workers clearing out caricatured political opponents with a manure fork or chasing them off with hammers. Although the Nazis could present themselves in more moderate terms—in the election campaigns of 1932, in which they were aiming at a broadly based appeal, they played down their anti-Semitism and emphasized their wish to come to power by legal means—they left nobody in any doubt about their fundamental willingness to use violence. Hitler's image also veered between threat on the one hand and appeal on the other, and his choice of vocabulary and oratorical style, as well as his gestures and expressions, reflected this. He was sometimes pictured with his riding whip or as the Führer of flag-waving Party comrades; at other times he was shown in a more personal light, for instance arm in arm with two blond boys. Both forms of self-presentation appealed to the widespread longing for a saviour who united in himself the normal with the extraordinary, projecting at one and the same time familiarity and distance and, though remaining as far as possible within the bounds of the law, being determined to employ the most radical methods if need be.

Before National Socialism's shock effect and attraction could pass their peak (of which there were certainly signs during the last six months of the Weimar Republic), President Hindenburg appointed Hitler Chancellor on 30 January 1933. The SA and Nazi students, who up till then had been held in check by the police and the criminal justice system, now had a free hand. They celebrated the 'seizure of power' with marches and torch-lit processions. The terror they unleashed in the weeks following was also directed at cultural agencies, institutions, and products. The Nazis destroyed anything they defined as 'un-German'. The Berlin anti-war museum, whose door was broken down with axes and whose exhibits were thrown onto the street, was only one of the institutions affected. Left-wing writers who had not been able to flee Germany at the last moment were arrested and put in one of the many early con-centration camps. The brutality they experienced there was designed in part to overturn differences in cultural status and to humiliate people who had academic titles or were distinguished artists or intellectuals. The anarchist writer Erich Mühsam, who rejected the pressure to commit suicide, had his face and body badly beaten in Sonnenburg, Brandenburg, and Oranienburg. He was forced to lick dirty water from the ground, to pretend to be a dog in 'music hall shows', and to jump over ditches covered in barbed wire. He continued to refuse to kill himself and so was murdered in Oranienburg on 10 July 1934.[29]

Such acts of violence were reinforced by censorship, exclusion from employment, or the process of 'coordinating' organizations (*Gleichschaltung*). The Nazis immediately took control of the radio, which was used for their propaganda in the run-up to the Reichstag elections of 5 March 1933. Even before the Reichstag fire on the night of 27/28 February, Communist and Social Democrat publications with a total print run of around two million were subjected to temporary bans. After it, they were banned completely and their publishing houses and print works taken over. Liberals were affected too, as their newspapers were closed down and journalists no longer allowed to follow their profession. The new Minister of Popular Enlightenment and Propaganda, Joseph Goebbels, made it clear at his first press conference after taking office what consequences were to flow from the ending of press freedom: 'It goes without saying that you will still be given information here, but you will also receive instructions. You will know not only what is happening, but also what attitude the government takes to it and how you can most appropriately convey that to the nation.'[30]

Literary and artistic life were remodelled as fundamentally as the realm of journalism. Threatened by the Nazis with dissolution, the Prussian Academy of Arts forced the writer Heinrich Mann and the artist Käthe Kollwitz to resign. Only a few members of this renowned institution rejected the new measures, among them the historical writer Ricarda Huch, who resigned in protest. Activists from the Combat League for German Culture took over control of the institutions and associations responsible for the theatre, music, the visual arts, and architecture. Where necessary, the threatening presence of SA men reinforced their demands. Immediately after the Reichstag fire the Association for the Protection of German Writers excluded its Communist members. After the governing body had been forced to resign and been replaced by loyal Nazis, commissions set about 'purging' the lists of members during the ensuing weeks. In this manner a professional organization was transformed into one loyal to the regime, the 'Reich Association of German Writers'.

In an effort to secure for itself the regime's recognition, the umbrella organization for German students, the Deutsche Studentenschaft, sent lists of 'corrupting' literature to university towns and cities. It was seeking support for a planned large-scale initiative, while local 'combat committees' applied pressure to bookshops and lending libraries. On 6 May students from the Berlin University for Gymnastics plundered and destroyed the Jewish sexologist Magnus Hirschfeld's institute, though Hirschfeld himself had already gone into exile. The book burning, to which such actions had been the prelude and which had been announced in the press, took place on 10 May, not only in Berlin but also in cities such as Breslau, Göttingen, and Munich, and was meant as a revival of the example set by nationalist students at the Wartburg festival of 1817. The works of many celebrated writers such as Heinrich Heine, Bertolt Brecht, and Erich Maria Remarque and scientists such as Sigmund Freud and Albert Einstein were thrown onto the bonfire. As they went up in flames, the books became yet another symbol of the power of the Nazis over the definition of what was German and what was 'un-German' culture.

In addition to physical attacks on opponents of the regime and book burnings there were a great many less eye-catching acts of violence and measures to marginalize various groups. Jewish Germans suffered, as did the millions of people who continued to feel they belonged in the Social Democrat milieu. Fear was growing in working-class neighbourhoods, and it was reinforced by the fact that even they were not immune to the lure of National Socialism. Karl Dürkefälden from Peine near Hanover noted in his diary how his father, 'who now goes on and on about Hitler and the Nazis', had said that 'we would have to go to church a lot. It would be like the past when if you didn't you were called a heretic.' In the weeks following Dürkefälden recorded visible changes. Swastika flags or (in the case of those who rejected the regime) the imperial black, white, and red flag, which was still tolerated, appeared on the walls of houses. Public squares were renamed. A local singing club prudently left the German Workers' Singing Association. Dürkefälden's own brother was among the workers who marched in SA uniform on 1 May 1933, which was celebrated on a grand scale as a national holiday, and sang the Horst Wessel Song. Resignedly, Dürkefälden noted that people who gave voice to dissenting views were punished—on the basis of newly promulgated laws. Thus the courts imposed a fine of 150 Reichsmarks each on 'four young men who had worn Social Democrat badges while doing gymnastics' and sent a man to 'prison for several months' because he had been flying a black, red, and gold flag (the flag of the Weimar Republic). [31]

What shocked Dürkefälden was accepted gladly by Elisabeth Gebensleben-von Alten. Although she was disturbed by acts of violence such as the smashing of the windows of Jewish shops in the centre of Braunschweig, to her mind these were secondary phenomena 'that Hitler is of course vigorously suppressing' and not an essential part of Nazi rule. When the Social Democrat mayor, whom she knew personally, was beaten up and then dragged through the city streets wearing a red sash, her only comment was that she wished his dismissal had been 'a little less humiliating'.[32] As a declared opponent of the left and of the alleged excessive influence of the Jews, she welcomed the marginalizing effect of torch-lit processions, swastika flags, and the Horst Wessel Song. On the one hand she justified the use of violence because ruthlessness was required, but on the other she denied its extent. To her more sceptical daughter, who lived in the Netherlands, she expressed her indignation at the 'horror stories' put about by exiled opponents of the regime. Her understanding of culture helped her to see Hitler himself as a victim who had overcome obstacles, rather than as the initiator of violence; 'This man has no fear. I thought about him so often recently when I was at a performance of *Siegfried*, for he is supposed to learn to fear but cannot.'[33]

Luise Solmitz too was 'intoxicated with enthusiasm' about a torch-lit procession made up of members of the SA and Stahlhelm and Nazi students in Hamburg. Almost casually she added, 'There were shouts of "May the Jews perish" and songs about Jews' blood spurting from knives.' In the months after, however, she became increasingly sceptical in the face of the rhetorical as well as physical violence directed at this minority, now defined as 'un-German'. She realized that her own husband, a baptized Jew, and their daughter might be affected. In addition, she was troubled by the Nazis' hostility to high culture in the education system and in general to the regime's demand for complete subordination to it. Yet, even for her, Hitler was still 'a man immaculate and unspotted', whose measures against 'red artists' and 'street Muscovites' were all the more admirable as these people had planned 'to destroy all cultural treasures—palaces, museums, churches—as they had in Russia'.[34]

Even though it was unclear how far antisemitic exclusion would go, people at the time could not fail to see the direction Nazi violence was taking. Measures such as burning books and imprisoning prominent writers in concentration camps were designed to force left-wing and pacifist culture out of the public sphere. Jewish Germans saw themselves increasingly excluded from artistic and academic life. The SA men and Nazi students, for whom the use of violence and a sense of cultural mission went hand in hand, played a crucial role. Before 1933 there had been clear resistance to this, but at the same time many middle-class nationalists welcomed the way these shows of power were linked to the marginalization of certain groups. What is more, the Nazi revolution was greeted by many as a means of putting an end to distressing conflicts and as an opportunity for complete cultural renewal.

Decision and Renewal: The Meanings of 1933

For Carl Schmitt, a professor of constitutional law, the Nazi takeover of power at first brought uncertainty. For a good decade he had been making a name for himself as a critic of parliamentary democracy. In doing so, he had not given support to the National Socialist movement but rather to a move towards authoritarian government of a kind practised by Franz von Papen and General Kurt von Schleicher during the complex political constellations of 1932. Schmitt had provided legal justification for the 'Prussian coup', Papen's dismissal of the democratically elected government in the largest individual German state, before the Supreme Court. Now, however, both his political project and his personal ambitions appeared to be in danger. The day after the appointment of the new Chancellor he was 'on edge' and felt 'rage at this stupid and ridiculous man, Hitler'. But it did not take long before it became clear that the Third Reich might even be beneficial to Schmitt's continued professional career, for the regime required academic legitimization. Conversely, Schmitt was flexible enough to discover areas of overlap with National Socialism. 'Bought the newspapers', he noted in his diary in mid-March. 'Hopeful because of the Nazis. Furious with the Jew Kaufmann and the vulgar deceit of these assimilated Jews.'[35]

Schmitt did not content himself with an outburst of private rage against Erich Kaufmann, a Berlin constitutional lawyer who had been baptized into the Protestant Church. He took direct action against him, writing to the Education Ministry to say that to allow any further teaching by such a 'typical example of the Jewish practice of assimilation' would amount to inflicting 'psychological damage' on students. Schmitt not only tolerated and promoted the exclusion of Jewish colleagues, who included Hans Kelsen, to whose support he owed his professorship at Cologne, he also joined the NSDAP shortly after defining the 'legitimacy of the German revolution' in a Party organ, the *Westdeutscher Beobachter*: 'A nation is awakening to consciousness of its own special character and is remembering who it is and those who are like it.' This awakening, he claimed, justified not only the exclusion of Jews as public servants, but also the creation of a new foundation for legality in the Enabling Law. Such formulations do more than testify to Schmitt's ability to adapt quickly to the prevailing *völkisch* rhetoric. Though a constitutional lawyer, he welcomed the defeat of parliamentary democracy and positivist law in favour of a new order. This order, in his view, was based on 'belonging to the same race' and made it possible to distinguish 'friend and foe correctly', that is according to racial criteria.[36]

This was the intellectual basis on which, during the following months, Schmitt increasingly identified with the new regime. His university work and his diverse range of contacts were an integral part of this: 'Then off to the city restaurant at 8 for a flag dedication. Very nice. I was glad to be there. Sang the Horst Wessel Song. Came home tired at 9.30, worked for an hour preparing a lecture.'[37] He soon became a leading member of the Association of German Lawyers and helped in the implementation of the process of 'coordination' in the states and in local authorities. In July 1933, along with many other members of the old elites, he was appointed to the Prussian State Council, whose founding he praised as a 'step towards realizing the National Socialist vision of political leadership and its indestructible connection with the German nation and the German idea of the state.' Schmitt not only hoped to make a concrete contribution to the consolidation of the Nazi regime, he had something more fundamental in mind. He set out to define the nature of the renewal at the start of the Third Reich and simultaneously present it as the culmination of a longer-term Prussian–German development. Thus, in October 1933 at the Lawyers' Conference he contrasted the 'mountain range made up of old habits of thought and concepts' with the 'law of the absolute primacy of political leadership'.[38]

The 'Schmitt case' is still discussed to this day. Yet Germany's most prominent lawyer of the twentieth century was not an exception but rather an altogether typical representative of the German educated elite in the Third Reich. Among their number were academics in the humanities, social sciences, and law, as well as painters and sculptors, writers, and Protestant pastors. Back in the nineteenth century, and even more so during the First World War, they had declared themselves responsible for interpreting the nation as a cultural entity. Although the Weimar Republic had not discouraged or impeded them at all in this task, their claims to authority were hard to reconcile with an intellectual environment characterized above all by a diversity of outlooks and initiatives. Many members of the educated elite saw in the Third Reich an opportunity to further their careers and they were not disappointed. Several of Schmitt's students, for example, were appointed to the posts vacated by dismissed Jewish professors. They were not, however, motivated by opportunism alone. Numerous academics, pastors, and artists were enthused by the atmosphere of decisiveness and renewal that had prevailed since 30 January 1933. They were keen to exercise political, social, and cultural influence, and they found considerable overlaps between their convictions and those of the Nazis. Seen in this light, they were not simply 'coordinated'; rather they made themselves available to the new order and themselves supplied it with content.

What beliefs made up this 'content'? In the 1920s many academics in the humanities and social sciences, but also in medicine and law, held to an ideal of totality, though in a period of growing diversification this seemed harder and harder to realize. Anyone who wanted to become established in these disciplines had to publish in ever more specialized journals. Anyone who, in addition, wrote philosophical essays was in competition with other products on the literary market. The task of combining individual research and overarching interpretation, as had been usual in Imperial Germany, became difficult under the conditions shaping the university and publishing worlds in the Weimar Republic. Modern scholarship and research were developing in a systematic and formal direction and this was in conflict with the contemporary demand that scholars should bridge the gap between science and 'life'. At the same time, the provisional and 'relative' character of all scholarly knowledge was distasteful to the many professors who hated ambiguity and yearned for authority, in particular in an age when Einstein's theory, though not widely understood, was nevertheless being widely referenced. Younger academics also found themselves having to take up a stance vis-à-vis an older generation that had won favour among nationalists in the First World War. They could opt for other political outlooks and even advocate left-wing or pacifist views, though that rarely happened and carried a serious risk to their careers. Alternatively, they could outdo the older generation in nationalism, a strategy that had led many to sympathize with the radical right long before 1933.

An answer to this immense challenge facing younger academics was suggested by the overarching idea of 'the nation'. It promised wholeness, lack of ambiguity, and closeness to life experience. At the same time, its vagueness gave the younger generation of academics an opportunity to join the revolution from a number of different directions as it was happening. In 1933, however, even established academics tried to build bridges to the thinking of the new regime. What role did their attitude to 'the' Jews play in this? Why did scholars, among them people who, like Carl Schmitt, had routinely had dealings with Jewish colleagues, now resort to antisemitic arguments? It was more than a case of professors taking advantage of new methods to settle old disputes in their favour. During the Weimar Republic antisemitism had been, as it were, latent in the academic world. There were certainly anti-Jewish prejudices, though it was not the done thing to express them in public. Even so, these prejudices made it simple to identify this intellectually successful minority with the nuanced, formalistic, and relativist character of modern scholarship and thus with a trend that contradicted the dominant principle of 'the nation'.

From the spring of 1933 onwards it was evident that science and scholarship would be overhauled and that left-wingers and Jews would in future be excluded. Antisemitic statements were now not only tolerated but encouraged and applauded. Beyond that, however, the direction this 'renewal' would take was still undefined, a situation that made many people ambitious to shape develop- ments and seek advancement through them. Medical experts hoped that the Nazis' racial policies would increase their influence and they thus regarded the passing of the Law for the Prevention of Hereditary Illness in July 1933 as an indication that their polit- ical engagement had been successful. Right-wing physicists saw the opportunity to get rid of the 'Jewish' theory of relativity and reverse the general trend for mathematics to dominate their subject. Their like-minded colleagues in the sister subject of mathematics wanted to see it resting once again on an intuitive and descriptive basis rather than on a purely 'formalist' one of the kind that had been developing since the turn of the century. Those who turned their own field of work into a form of 'combat' often did so for tac- tical reasons, but they were also responding to a strong urge to make a significant contribution to consolidating the nation. They thus fitted into the vision of achieving a new, post-individualistic concept of freedom through 'leadership' and 'decision'.

For Carl Schmitt, this development resulted in overlaps with his authoritarian and statist thinking and also with his view of politics as the clash of friend and enemy. 'There is no such thing as free science and scholarship in a nation dominated by alien influences and there is no scholarly or scientific struggle without this political freedom,' as he put it in his inaugural lecture in Cologne, 'so let us put all our efforts into coming through the great struggle in the realm of academic scholarship too, so that we do not become slaves but rather free human beings.'[39] Meanwhile, the Nazi revolution reminded the Freiburg philosopher Martin Heidegger of the origins of Greek thought. He believed the opportunity had arrived finally to overcome 'the division of the sciences into rigidly separated specialties' and the 'arbitrariness of intentions and inclinations of different aims and preferences' and instead to focus on the 'world-shaping powers of human being' and on the 'honour and destiny of the nation': 'All faculties of will and thought, all strengths of the heart and all skills of the body, must be unfolded *through* battle, heightened *in* battle, and preserved *as* battle.'[40]

Quite often this rhetoric of renewal employed by academics took on (neo-)religious features, especially when being used, as at the book burning, in ceremonies of a cultic and ritualistic nature. Rhetorical language was used to celebrate the passage to a new state of redemption made possible only by Germany's ecstatic reawakening and the messianic figure of Adolf Hitler. This revolution seemed to offer academics the chance to connect with the younger generation and with the working population. As a Göttingen university tutor in German Literature put it, these groups had not yet become 'arrogant and sterile' as a result of self-consciousness, intellect, and the atomizing effects of individualism and thus could respond 'most completely and fervently to the forces of rebirth'.[41] This perspective brought him close to the large and active section of the Protestant clergy that did not simply cautiously welcome the Nazi seizure of power but actually promoted and helped to shape it. Even before 1933 the National

Socialist 'German Christians' had increased in influence and could now emerge as the dominant force. The clergy belonging to this group were on the whole relatively young, came from a lower-middle-class background, and had grown up in parts of Germany particularly affected by the Treaty of Versailles, such as border areas or territory now lost. Instead of theological debate they sought contact with the people advocating 'action'. As well as offering career opportunities within the Church, this new direction promised to be a counterweight to consumerist culture, with its materialism and secularism, and to the labour movement, with its Marxist ideology.

In Berlin, where both consumerist culture and Marxism had been particularly evident, the German Christians were in the ascendant after 30 January 1933. They conducted services of thanksgiving and remembrance in, among other places, the Church of St Mary, the Kaiser Wilhelm Memorial Church, and the cathedral. Swastika flags and SA standards now adorned the chancel and formed the backdrop to *völkisch* sermons from the pulpit. The liturgical range was extended to include ceremonies to mark the Führer's birthday. Later there were mass weddings and baptisms. Meetings of German Christians took place in parish halls decorated with portraits of Hitler, where Nazi anthems were sung in addition to traditional Protestant hymns. The political revolution seemed to fulfil the longstanding hope of religious renewal in a nationalist spirit. For Joachim Hossenfelder, a pastor from the Kreuzberg district in Berlin and Reich leader of the German Christians, God had sent Adolf Hitler to rescue 'the German nation from despair and to restore its faith in life'. That, in turn, would lead to the creation of an 'army of millions' that could build on the self-sacrifice and the 'heavenly sentry duty' of the fallen of the World War and the SA's dead. Using similar high-flown language, a pastor from Friedenau in Berlin described the first year of the Third Reich as 'the victory of faith': 'The last year gave us back heroism and greatness. It made us all combatants on a common front, both externally and internally, and touched the very core of our lives.'[42]

Just as in the case of academics, the Nazi revolution was welcomed by pastors for many different reasons. Whereas in the capital the chief bogeymen were materialism and Marxism, in those parts of Germany with a mix of Protestants and Catholics there was hope that the new regime would support Protestants against the influence of the Catholic Church. In addition, antisemitism, which was strong among Protestants, played a key role. In congregations where German Christians were particularly influential, they pressed for the dismissal of 'non-Aryan' pastors, organists, or kindergarten teachers. The new regime gave them an opportunity to advance the anti-Judaism familiar for centuries among Christians as well as the antisemitism that had developed in the later nineteenth century. Christianity's origins in Judaism were to be forgotten. In their place 'nation' and 'race' were elevated to the status of central, God-given points of reference in matters of faith, thus providing the German Christians with a means of opposing the fundamental rejection of Christianity by the influential neo-pagan movement.

Although many Protestant pastors and churchgoers were not prepared to follow the German Christians' line—the oppositional movements the Pastors' Emergency League and the Confessing Church quickly formed—this opposition was more concerned with defending institutional freedoms and the Church's central spheres of activity than with challenging the regime on principle. The exclusion of baptized Jews and presumed Jewish influences from the Church and from German culture in general was broadly welcomed. The reason for this, in addition to traditional prejudices, was that many Protestants associated Jews with the real or supposed consequences of secularization. They were seen as symbols of both capitalist and Marxist materialism and could be linked with such things as moral relativism, social pluralism, and intellectual abstraction. Even Martin Niemöller, the pastor in Dahlem in Berlin who criticized the policy of exclusion and later resisted Nazi attempts to control the Protestant Church, believed that the Jews were 'cursed' because they had crucified Christ. As a result, he urged them to give up any Church posts voluntarily.[43]

Many artists, musicians, and writers also welcomed the Nazi revolution because it brought with it an explicit boost to 'German culture'. Anyone who joined in had the prospect of jobs, commissions, or awards. Moreover, this renewal presented itself at first as more open and complex than it may seem when viewed in the light of the subsequent development of culture in the Third Reich. On the one hand, the Combat League for German Culture was active at a local level as early as the spring of 1933. It put on orchestral concerts and lieder performances and made moves to gain control of municipal theatres and musical associations. Modernist styles were denounced in exhibitions with titles such as 'The Art of Government 1918–1933', 'The Spirit of November', or 'Art's Chambers of Horrors'. On the other hand, the League's activism met with resistance within Party and state, in particular in the NS League of Students and in Goebbels's newly created Propaganda Ministry. The latter insisted that culture should remain to some extent autonomous and through this be enabled to contribute more to the renewal and prestige of the Third Reich. Their standpoint was that expressionist art should not just be silently tolerated but exhibited in public—as long as the subjects were German landscapes and not urban scenes. Goebbels made no secret of his admiration for the work of Ernst Barlach and Emil Nolde. In the summer of 1933 the Berlin National Gallery set up two rooms exclusively for Nolde's work. This was not altogether surprising, for the famous artist had made very positive statements in private correspondence about the National Socialist renewal, contrasting the rural, North German elements in his work with what he claimed to be the excessive foreign influence on the work of Weimar-era artists. And he intervened against his rival Max Pechstein by falsely denouncing him as a Jew to the Propaganda Ministry.[44]

Apart from the obvious self-interest motivating these words and actions, they were also the product of essential components in the self-image of artists of the time. Their self-conscious status as outsiders was combined with a desire to belong and, even in 1900, this mix had often expressed itself in right-wing attitudes. The rise of a popular mass culture with unmistakable American elements had made many artists anxious about their own role in society. These anxieties were now combined with nationalist resentments. Even during the Weimar period, 'New Objectivity', a trend in which art found inspiration in an urban, mechanized society, was not only greeted with enthusiasm but also met with vehement rejection. It was against this background that expressionists such as Nolde or the writer Arnolt Bronnen were searching for ways of revitalizing their art. They wanted to be committed to a larger whole but not in the way that many people on the left in the cultural scene during the late 1920s and early 1930s had been. Gottfried Benn was part of this group, alongside second-rank authors and *völkisch* hardliners such as the leading functionary for Nazi literature, Hanns Johst.

Benn's poetry and prose writing were experimental, exploring the borders between mind and body. However, by 1933 he was already part of the literary establishment. He was on the radio regularly and was a member of the Poetry Section of the Prussian Academy of Arts. Unlike many other writers, Benn considered both pacifist utopias and socialist egalitarian demands to be equally pointless. He was as much at a loss when faced with American culture ('standardized idols, spectral dancing formations, staple goods') as he was when confronted with the reality of republican politics ('parliaments endlessly being dissolved, crises, party bickering, customs disputes, two flags, three religions'). In place of these he insisted on the gulf between literature and the world and on an anti-rationalist understanding of mythical greatness. It earned him painful attacks from the left and later made him welcome the Nazi take-over of power as a 'new epoch in history'. When Klaus Mann wrote to him from exile in France to express his bewilderment at Benn's attitude and to challenge him, as a writer he admired, to make a moral decision, Benn responded vehemently that he was happy to be on public record as saying he regarded emigration as nothing more than a misguided gesture. In making it, cosmopolitan literary types had estranged themselves completely from their own nation and relinquished the right to pass judgement on recent developments. He portrayed the seizure of power in visionary language as a historically inevitable step that opened up the possibility of the 'emergence of a new bio-logical type' and thus of one of the 'greatest ever realizations of the World Spirit'.[45]

Thus 'renewal' was a powerful rhetorical topos, but at the same time more than that. A process was in train whose effects had a drastic impact on universities, the Protestant Church, and the artistic world, while also stretching far beyond them. Gala performances and massed rallies, reaching out far and wide by means of radio broadcasts and newspaper reports, presented the popular face of 'renewal'. The introduction of the Hitler salute took it to the residential districts. In photo spreads and speeches on the radio Hitler personified the energy and 'decisiveness' that had produced the new national community. This was all very attractive, though it also conveyed to people a sense of having no alternative. The Germans were compelled, even in their family relations and private thoughts, to adopt an attitude to the Nazi revolution. In most cases this meant adjusting their understanding of themselves, insofar as it was not already influenced by National Socialism, to fit the new circumstances.

Karl Dürkefälden's barber, who for many years previously had spoken openly about having deserted from the army in the World War, now claimed he had returned to the front, been wounded, and been decorated. After the revolution Dürkefälden's brother became 'more interested in tradition' and suddenly asked where his war diaries were, though he had not looked at them in years. And the local pastor, now a member of the German Christians, visited him 'to find out what sort of impression the changes had made on me'. Responding to his carefully formulated scepticism, the pastor said that 'the intellectual aspect, not the economic one' was the main thing; 'there was a progressive idea in it'.[46] Elisabeth Gebensleben-von Alten joined the German Christians. Their blend of Protestant and National Socialist ideas comes through again and again in the quasi-religious expressions she uses to interpret her experiences, for example in response to the processions, flags, and garlands for 1 May 1933: 'No nation has ever experienced anything so tremendous and uplifting.' Her admiration for

'Germany's saviour' prompted her to ask whether it was 'at all possible for such strength to be found in one human being'. In her opinion, this strength accounted for the 'solid support' among the German population 'for Hitler's act of deliverance'.[47]

This element of 'decision' that formed part of the Nazi revolution was expressed in powerful mass rituals and celebrated by the press, which had already to a great extent been coordinated. Many of his contemporaries welcomed Hitler's and his adherents' regime because now internal enemies could be neutralized and social conflicts resolved. Everywhere there was palpable relief at the end of the mood of tension and strife associated with the Weimar Republic. Luise Solmitz was not only pleased that, thanks to the 'saviour', Hitler, there could finally be 'strong measures' to deal with Communists and dangerous criminals. She was also prepared to confess: 'I personally feel very comfortable under the dictatorship.' In spite of her growing anxiety about the future of her Jewish husband and their daughter, she was 'really impressed with coordination' because it brought clarity and certainty: 'For once I just want to have a sense of one united will.'[48] Her very choice of words brings the Hamburg teacher close to Martin Heidegger, who had the 'experience and pleasure of seeing that the Führer has created a new reality that gives real direction and impetus to our thinking'.[49]

Thus the Nazi revolution was not only the work of an aggressive minority; it was welcomed by large sections of the German population as a trailblazing decision that they could help to shape. This upheaval signified a profound discontinuity in that it drastically curtailed the range and variety of German culture, far beyond the censorship and violence that had already occurred in the early 1930s. Many people, including numerous churchmen and intellectuals, justified this break not only out of opportunism but from conviction. Since 1930 there had been sufficient voices conjuring up the image of the Weimar Republic in 'crisis', taking up positions ranging from authoritarian to far right, and tacitly accepting the movement's violence, to secure a position of dominance for National Socialism in the cultural realm as well. For people such as these, the renewal led by Hitler provided an answer to the fundamental challenge of the modern, from mass culture via secularization to the progress of science. In an apparent paradox, this answer simultaneously promised innovation and continuity. The mission of establishing a national culture, which the German educated elites had seen as their task since the nineteenth century, now appeared once more achievable.

In committing to this, virtually nobody simply wanted to turn the clock back and only a very few people looked for a restoration of the culture of Imperial Germany. Rather, the Nazi revolution was welcomed in part because it promised something fundamentally new. What was to constitute this new thing was still an open question, though it would be defined within the limits imposed at the outset by the dictatorship. It was precisely this lack of clearly defined content that made it possible to tap into the desires and dreams of Germans at that time, as much as to appeal to individual or institutional interests. A National Socialist framework allowed Heidegger to see connections with the origins of Greek thought, Schmitt to find confirmation of his friend–foe thinking, and quite a few clergymen to hope for a resurgence of the Protestant faith. All of them wanted not only to be integrated into the culture of the Third Reich but also to influence it. Precisely what shape this culture would take, however, would only become evident during the years following.

Figure 3. A winter holiday in the Alps in 1937, courtesy of Strength through Joy.

2

NATIONAL SOCIALISM AS
A CULTURAL SYNTHESIS

Somewhere in Bavaria, 1937: Three young people are sitting on folding chairs in the sun and looking out onto snow-covered mountains. The two men are sitting casually with their feet up, while the woman sits unselfconsciously between them. What appears to be an unremarkable holiday snapshot has great symbolic meaning, for it represents a new era in which all Germans have—or will shortly have—access to alpine scenery and bracing winter air. The picture suggests health, though the idea of strengthening the 'body of the nation' is at most a passing one. The dominant impressions are of recuperation and relaxation in the company of good friends or new acquaintances as a well-deserved antidote to the concentrated work of the rearmament years. There is a clear contrast to the later years of the Weimar Republic with its abundance of stories of the 'little man', impoverished, exhausted, and worried by the all-embracing crisis. Even though we cannot see their facial expressions, the two holidaymakers with their feet up seem to be confident in their masculinity, but also prepared to be good sports and make room between them for the woman—as befits the relatively modern clothing and hairstyles worn by the three of them.

The photo was used by the press office of the German Labour Front to exploit a winter holiday offered by 'Strength through Joy', the Front's leisure organization, for propaganda purposes. It is one of a whole series of pictures of similarly relaxed situations: perfectly normal people are shown swimming in a lake, reclining on the deck of a ship, or walking in Madeira after docking there. It is not evident that Jews, political opponents, and 'asocials' are excluded from such activities. Pictures such as these are similar to those created especially for foreign visitors, who, since 1933, have been coming in ever larger numbers to Bavaria in particular. In the main, the mountain scenery shown in them conveys an unpolitical image of Germany. From time to time, however, Nazi rhetoric is used to stimulate the curiosity of potential tourists and to make them aware of a sense of new beginnings in the Third Reich. A leaflet commissioned by the Propaganda Ministry from the British travel agent Thomas Cook & Sons bears the heading 'Heil! Summer!'[1]

Pictures of mountains can be used and interpreted in a variety of ways. While winter holidays were offered by Strength through Joy, they could also be booked, as before, through private travel agencies. Adolf Hitler himself often withdrew to the Obersalzberg near Berchtesgaden, where his Berghof, with its central heating and private cinema, was surrounded by a huge, restricted 'Führer zone'. Hermann Göring and Albert Speer also had houses close by. The Security Service set up premises there and the SS built a barracks. Hitler's *Volksgenossen* (national comrades) did not enjoy the same luxury, but they too could enjoy the mountains by going on hikes, watching films set in various German regions, or dreaming of driving on modern motorways through forested hills.

What is striking in all this is the proximity of apparently contrasting things: the normal and the extraordinary, continuity and renewal, the everyday and the political world. *Völkisch* (ethnic nationalist) ideas and dictatorial interventions exist alongside bourgeois traditions and modern trends. Extending far beyond the example of the mountains, this was the most important characteristic of culture in Germany in the mid-1930s. This culture manifested itself in concrete terms on a variety of levels. The leadership of the regime was keen to acquire cultural prestige and emphasize its power in this area as well. New leisure opportunities and entertainments offered Germans new experiences and stimulated their imaginations—though this did not by any means apply to all. Dissidents in the Third Reich were excluded, for example. Through underground networks or in exile they attempted to overcome their cultural isolation. That their efforts were ultimately unsuccessful can be explained, on the one hand, by the state's system of surveillance and repression but also by the attractive synthesis that National Socialism created from a variety of *völkisch*, bourgeois, and popular sources.

Prestige and Patronage: The Political Control of Culture

For Joseph Goebbels January 1935 was as enjoyable as it was successful. The Minister for Popular Enlightenment and Propaganda attended a 'magnificent performance' of Wagner's *Tristan* at the Deutsche Oper in Berlin. He also approved of a production of Shakespeare's *King Lear* at the Staatstheater and praised the 'brilliant depiction of milieu' at the Komödienhaus.[2] He confidently attributed these cultural pleasures to the Nazi revolution. 'In Berlin we have a theatre again. That's something we've done.'[3]

Goebbels at first made criticisms of the set of *Tristan*, but soon after attending a second performance he was able to record with satisfaction that improvements had been made: 'My stage directions have been carried out. It's a wonderful production, both visually and musically. Führer enthusiastic.' The Propaganda Minister did not always confine himself to such 'stage directions'. When he considered the staging of a comic opera from the late nineteenth century to be mediocre, he made it the occasion for imposing new 'guidelines' on the theatre director: 'Bocaccio [*sic*] was a dud. It has to be put right.' Goebbels also prevented a film that he found to be 'unbearable' and 'sending out the wrong message' from being shown in cinemas. At the same time, he not only supported larger subsidies for radio, theatre, and film, he even contributed a number of ideas of his own to the cultural development of the Third Reich: 'Film meeting: Cromwell material ready in outline. Will be really good. My idea.'[4]

Goebbels's diary entries illuminate the thinking behind his cultural politics. He had completed a doctorate in literature, had written a novel, and, since the 1920s, had risen to be the leading Nazi propagandist. He saw being a minister as conferring immense personal prestige because it gave him institutional power and enabled him to lead a life of luxury. Goebbels rapidly expanded his ministry's range of responsibilities. He took personal control of the Berlin Philharmonic and of a whole series of performance venues, including the Deutsche Oper. Utterly convinced of his own understanding of culture, Goebbels felt qualified to pronounce judgement after every theatre or film performance he attended. If a production was to his liking, he regarded himself as deserving praise because he had approved it, promoted it, or simply made it possible in the first place. Shortcomings that he perceived in no way shook his self-confidence, for his overwhelming sense of power allowed him to identify them and bring pressure to bear on, or intervene directly in, productions with respect to both form and content. Thus Goebbels exerted considerable influence on the theatre world and the politics of film. In addition to boosting his personal prestige, his main concern was to increase respect for the Third Reich at home and abroad. For that reason he considered it opportune to keep the boundaries of legitimate culture quite fluid. He liked to distinguish himself in this from other leading figures in the regime. The Gauleiter of Saxony, Martin Mutschmann, seemed to him provincial ('his home is a monument to neo-German culture. Dreadful!'), while he considered the *völkisch* ideologue Alfred Rosenberg to be 'obsessively pigheaded': 'If he had his way there would be no more German theatre but only cultic pageants, *völkisch* open-air performances, myth, and all that nonsense.'[5]

Goebbels's outlook was consistent, in so far as he considered the past and contemporary cultural achievements of the Germans to be immense. 'What tremendous prestige German musical life enjoys! And what riches we have in the Berlin Philharmonic and Furtwängler', he wrote in his diary: 'A primitive race can be musical. In the case of the Germans, the Nordic element adds creative talent.' He did not wish to do anything to suppress this potential, but rather wanted to exploit it for the Third Reich. In addition, as a seasoned propagandist he was aware of the importance of popular entertainment in ensuring the stability of the regime. Hence he avoided scaring off film and theatre audiences by giving them too much propaganda. Goebbels himself liked to see established performers as well as new stars on the stage. He also enjoyed their company because he found them 'stimulating and responsive':

'They're like children, but so endearing.'⁶ Rather than imposing strict rules on them, he preferred to gain their friendship and keep them dependent on his tokens of personal favour and interventions in cultural politics. Leading conductors and actors approached him with their concerns and asked for his support, which he often gave. At the same time, he had the power to reprimand them or even to bring their careers to an abrupt end.

Adolf Hitler was and remained his point of reference. Even by Third Reich standards Goebbels's relationship with the Führer was extraordinary. The close, normally daily contact between them not only formed the basis of Goebbels's power but of his private life as well. Always gratified by Hitler's renewed attention, he would note in his diary that he had had another long 'chat', watched films, or attended an opera with him. For him, the Führer was a visionary, able to achieve an ideal combination of artistic intuition and cultural insight. A typical example is to be found in his entry during the Nuremberg Party Rally in 1935: 'The Führer speaks. Clear statement of his position on current cultural problems. Tremendous display of authority and artistic engagement. He is a master builder not just in the realm of statecraft.'⁷ Thus he was also prepared on occasions to bow to Hitler's judgement. Fearing disapproving comments, he had the paintings by Emil Nolde that he had acquired in 1933 for his private residence taken down again.

When Hitler supported his jealously guarded position and his relatively moderate approach, Goebbels was delighted. Thus Hitler strongly opposed 'efforts to devalue German history through petty-minded attempts to split it into good and bad'. Goebbels's arch-rival Alfred Rosenberg, whose *völkisch* view of history was the target of the Führer's barbs, could only listen 'in silent resentment'. Yet Hitler took care never to let Goebbels feel completely confident of his support, thus spurring him on to greater efforts and renewed protestations of loyalty. After Hitler made a critical comment about the current artistic policy, Goebbels resolved to improve matters 'by making a few changes in personnel': 'I can't allow a few useless people to destroy the Führer's confidence in my work.' Even so, from time to time he had to put up with Hitler deciding against him in cases of disagreement or giving some rival a token boost. Thus Goebbels noted after a discussion of suitable candidates for the German National Prize for Art and Scholarship: 'And then he suggested — Rosenberg. O God! That was a bit of a shock.'[8]

Goebbels's successes, as well as his occasional failures, point to an important feature of cultural politics in the Third Reich: the leading figures in the regime exploited culture as a means of creating a public image. Many of these Nazis had a high opinion of their own artistic sense, but they reacted above all to stimulus from the top. Hitler, the erstwhile painter and opera lover, had declared culture to be at the heart of the Nazi regime. Those in his close circle were constantly competing for personal prestige and political influence, while the Führer in part accepted and in part deliberately stoked this rivalry. In order to assert or even improve their position his satellites constructed entire institutions. These quickly grew and expanded their range of powers, though in the process tensions could arise between an institution and its originator's own ideological and interventionist self-understanding. Goebbels, for example, complained that the Reich Chamber of Culture, which was subordinate to him, was 'so bureaucratic'.[9] In the end, however, it was this very mixture of ideology, bureaucratic procedures, and arbitrary interventions that determined the development of cultural policy. There was never a clear programme. Even Goebbels was only one of a number of key influences and he himself offered no unequivocal guidance on the limits of what was permitted. Sometimes his public statements suggested that art should to some extent remain autonomous. Then at other times he would go back to using a threatening tone to insist on ideological conformity and refer to cultural freedom as outmoded.

In November 1933 Goebbels, with Hitler's support, succeeded in establishing the Reich Chamber of Culture, thereby resisting Robert Ley's attempt to force all those engaged in the cultural sector to join the German Labour Front and securing the superior position of the Propaganda Ministry. At first, this new institution regarded artists as having the status of a 'free' profession, though one that was also under state supervision. In order to be able to work professionally at all, orchestral musicians, painters, actors, and writers had to belong to it. For the most part, this was not felt to be a problem because, after 1933, the various professional organizations were absorbed into the Chambers of Literature, Theatre, Film, Music, the Visual Arts, Radio, and the Press. Artists were also reassured by the fact that among the presidents and committee members of these various Reich Chambers were not only activists from the Combat League for German Culture but also established artists such as the composer Richard Strauss. He, for example, campaigned for composers to be given a larger share of the profits from their works and to raise the level of musical life. Because Strauss contributed to boosting the cultural prestige of the Nazi regime both nationally and internationally, he was at first able to fend off ideological interventions by promoting a sort of corporate self-regulation. So, for a time, the Reich Chamber of

Music enjoyed the freedom to take the view that 'in principle' it could not 'forbid works of an atonal character' but must rather leave it 'to the audience to judge such compositions'.[10]

The Reich Chamber of Culture's efforts to regulate admission to the profession and the laws of copyright, and to introduce work-creation schemes and a social insurance system for members at first seemed promising to many artists. After all, the crisis-ridden free market of the Weimar Republic had been a difficult time for them. Yet in the long run all of this could not blind them to the fact that cultural life was now subject to dictatorial interventions. From 1935 onwards Goebbels took a more repressive line and accused Strauss of making too many concessions to the Jewish members of the Reich Chamber of Music. In addition, he was annoyed that the Reich Chamber of Theatre had not taken decisive enough steps against Berlin cabaret artists who had made fun of several regime bigwigs. Institutional changes were the result. The specialist subdivisions within the various Reich Chambers, particularly those for music hall or cabaret performers, ceased to be partially autonomous. They were transformed into so-called 'associations' and subjected to supervision by ideologically sound Nazis. Parallel to this, the Ministry of Propaganda secured direct influence over culture at regional level by constructing a network of heads of culture in the various states.

Why did Goebbels adopt a more radical approach to cultural matters? The explanation lies in the rivalry between individuals within the leadership of the Third Reich. Alfred Rosenberg's hostile measures were threatening to undermine Goebbels's position. Rosenberg came from a Baltic German family, had studied architecture, and had become a *völkisch* journalist in Munich in the post-1918 period. He had made his name as the author of a (little-read) doorstop entitled *The Myth of the Twentieth Century*, which identified the roots of the German nation in a Teutonic race that had later been subjugated by the Judeo-Christian tradition. Although Rosenberg laid claim to being National Socialism's chief ideologue, he was unable to fulfil that role in reality, for in the cultural 'tug-of-war', as he himself called it, he could not ultimately win through. All the same, he exerted significant influence. Hitler tasked him with monitoring 'intellectual and ideological training and education' in the Party and in its mass organization Strength through Joy, and Rosenberg exploited this to mount campaigns to ensure everyone toed the *völkisch* line. Although incapable of making any fundamental change in the 'vacuous speeches by Goebbels' and 'the Reich Chamber of Culture's lack of direction', both of which he detested, he was able to bring about changes of course in many individual instances.[11] In addition, the National Socialist Cultural Community, which was directly subordinate to him, made efforts to give practical expression to a *völkisch* radicalism by offering the public concert evenings, cheap theatre season tickets, several journals, and a cycle of recordings, until in 1937 it was taken over by Strength through Joy, and hence by Rosenberg's rival Robert Ley.

Strength through Joy already had an 'Office for Leisure' and an 'Office for German Further Education' and had organized various cultural events. As the German Labour Front had taken over the trade union publishing houses of the Weimar period, its leisure organization could also produce and market books and journals, thus gaining an influence over cultural content as well as expanding economically. Other Nazi institutions and individuals also tried to gain prominence on the cultural scene. Hermann Göring exploited his office as Prime Minister of Prussia to satisfy his notorious love of putting himself in the public eye. To this end he gained control of the theatres in Prussia, which enabled him, among other things, to present himself as more tolerant than the other leaders of the regime. For instance, he protected the actor Gustav Gründgens whose homosexuality would otherwise have created problems for him sooner or later. Bernhard Rust's Reich Ministry for Science, Training, and Education took on the responsibility for textbooks, libraries, and museums. Max Amann, who as Reich Leader of the NSDAP press published many specialist journals and periodicals (including Hitler's and Rosenberg's books and the official Nazi Party newspaper, the *Völkischer Beobachter*) via the Franz Eher publishing house, soon extended his influence to what remained of the bourgeois press. A great range of Party organizations, such as the NS teachers' organization and the Party's Official Censorship Board, applied themselves to overseeing and promoting publications, including regional calendars and novels for teenagers (in which the leaders of the Hitler Youth also had an interest). The practical surveillance of authors, publications, and bookshops was the task of the Gestapo and the SS Security Service. Just how far the cultural sphere was affected by this general impulse on the part of individual leaders to gain more extensive powers is shown by a diary entry by Goebbels: '[SA Chief of Staff Viktor] Lutze wants to make SA films as well. I'll put a stop to that, or else a load of incompetents will be invading my turf yet again.'[12]

What were the implications of this complicated cultural scene, where institutions coexisted, cooperated, or competed with one another from one case to the next? The theatre provides an example of the significance of isolated arbitrary decisions. Paradoxically, this also applied to decidedly Nazi plays, which were banned at various times. It was feared that negative propaganda would result from particularly daring scenes, sexual scenes in particular, or from Jewish characters making an unintended sympathetic impression. Playwrights might, in spite of their *völkisch* convictions, not toe the party line sufficiently, or they might come to grief simply because of the hostility of a powerful Party functionary. By contrast, theatre directors who kept a low profile politically and shied away from aesthetic experiments enjoyed considerable advantages. They benefited from the economic recovery at a time when there was a shortage of affordable consumer goods and leisure activities became more important as a consequence. Festivals, expensive productions, refurbishments of performance spaces, even the creation of new theatres were made possible by generous subsidies. The amount and conditions of work for actors improved. Directors of theatres could live off the fat of the land and were frequently given the title of Director General or Professor—which made it easier for them to fit into the new ideological framework. Thus, although Gustav Deharde was forced to fend off a number of attacks from *völkisch* circles, as Director General of the Württemberg Staatstheater in Stuttgart he nevertheless saw his profession boosted ideologically by the Third Reich and entrusted with the task 'of rescuing what is good from the past, while seeking out and recognizing the new, and imbuing the theatre as a whole with an attitude befitting the new age'.[13]

There was a general expansion in opportunities for artists, because the various Party and state organizations themselves offered concerts, theatre evenings, and art exhibitions. In 1938 Strength through Joy alone organized a good 12,000 opera performances, 20,000 theatre performances, 11,000 variety shows, and 5000 concerts in the Reich as a whole. A total of 54 million tickets were sold. Ambitious individuals such as Herbert von Karajan benefited. In 1935 he had the opportunity to conduct a performance of Beethoven's *Fidelio* at an opera evening organized by Strength through Joy. Throughout the Reich, buildings and art works were being commissioned and competitions announced, and architects and artists profited. Writers could take advantage of a positive flood of literature prizes. The wave of lecture series and book readings grew to the extent that the *völkisch* author Bruno Brehm complained that almost every day he received 'requests, in fact even contracts for lectures'. What is more, they were often scheduled for the same date.[14] And even though the system of fixed minimum wages and honoraria introduced by the individual Reich Chambers remained as patchy in practice as old-age provision for artists, both measures still represented a significant improvement for less prominent theatre employees and orchestral musicians.

This general support for artists by the regime had its limits, however. Musicians playing popular music went on being poorly paid and visual artists continued to make only very modest sums. Nevertheless, these disadvantaged groups, who had, in any case, not exactly been spoilt under the crisis conditions of the later Weimar Republic, could hope for a gradual improvement in their situations. Well-known artists, on the other hand, ran the risk of conflict with the censor. Persecutions, purges, and book burnings put an abrupt and definitive end to the cultural politics of the Weimar Republic, which had offered openings to modernists, left-wingers, and Jews. In the years that followed, though there were occasional signs of easing, there was no return to greater tolerance. Conscious of the regime's power, publishers or theatre directors were disinclined to take any risks. If in doubt, they put out feelers to the appropriate authorities in the regime's institutional jungle, a course of action that appeared advisable above all because the boundaries of the permissible were always unclear, even though lists of forbidden writers and composers were circulated. To impose censorship, to refuse to grant licenses, or to exclude an artist from his or her particular Reich Chamber on the grounds of unreliability was therefore almost never necessary.

This complex web of cultural measures and regulations was almost impenetrable from the outside. The case of Hans Fallada can serve to illustrate this. As a former Social Democrat, Fallada (real name Rudolf Ditzen) was a problem for the Nazis, and yet he was significant to them because of his popularity. From 1933 onwards he showed that he was prepared to make compromises. In the foreword to his novel *Who Once Eats out of the Tin Bowl* (1934) he distanced himself from the humane punishment regime of the Weimar Republic, and in revising his next novel he was largely amenable to interventions from the censor. In spite of this he was attacked on several occasions by Nazi reviewers and even for a time labelled an 'undesirable author'. Fallada began to learn English with a view to emigrating. 'We have discussed the matter with some very experienced people', he wrote to his parents in September 1935, 'and have been given the clear advice to go completely legally—for this is possible—to London or Copenhagen'. Yet he could not get used to the 'thought of living in a foreign country', so he first of all changed to writing stories for children. He succeeded in rehabilitating himself as an artist with his novel about the period of hyperinflation in the early 1920s, *Wolf among Wolves* (1937), which was read as a criticism of the Weimar Republic and admired by Goebbels. Fallada was now in a position to sign contracts for translations and film versions. At the same time, the

Propaganda Minister now expected him to produce a positive presentation of the Nazi seizure of power in his next novel *Iron Gustav*. Intimidated by his earlier experiences and troubled by money worries, Fallada acceded to this demand.[15]

The surveillance exercised by the Nazis over literary life thus left people room for some flexibility in their own attitude to the regime, but to what extent is hard to judge. In some isolated cases, for example, authors who were married to 'half-Jews' were given special permission to go on publishing. Some of their politically less sound colleagues were able to keep themselves afloat with self-evidently harmless works or film scripts. The vital factors in this regard were literary success, the protection of someone influential in cultural politics, or simply the good fortune of being overlooked by the authority responsible. In other cases, even writers and academics more positively disposed to the regime than Fallada could find that real campaigns were mounted against them. Thus Gottfried Benn was expelled from the Reich Chamber of Literature after his poems were called 'unnatural filth' in *Das Schwarze Korps*, the SS publication. Although Carl Schmitt remained a professor in Berlin, he lost his position as the Third Reich's pre-eminent legal expert as a result of SS hostility. Martin Heidegger was similarly disappointed in his hopes of a leading role in framing Nazi ideology, which led him to resign as Rector of Freiburg University in April 1934 after only one year. Anyone who, like Benn, Schmitt, or Heidegger, was suspect as a result of prestige acquired before 1933 or who asserted a right to express a personal view was targeted by Nazi rivals or activists. The consequence was not loss of life or freedom but the curtailment of opportunities to publish or reach the public in other ways.

Those who challenged the regime—and only artists who felt their position was secure dared to do this—had to be prepared for more severe consequences. Ernst Wiechert, whose novels and stories had been recommended for acquisition by public libraries, voiced opposition to the prevailing cultural policy for the first time at a reading in Munich organized by the National Socialist Cultural Community. He also read his story 'The White Buffalo or On the Great Justice' on several occasions in public. This tale tells of the resistance of an Indian peasant's son to a despot and clearly implied criticism of the Third Reich's claim to total power. When, in 1938, Wiechert also protested against the arrest of the Protestant pastor Martin Niemöller, he was no longer simply isolated and kept under surveillance with his opportunities for publication restricted, as he had been before; he was now arrested and sent for several months to Buchenwald concentration camp.

In his autobiographical story *The Forest of the Dead*, Wiechert describes how he was filled with 'a chilling feeling of being abandoned and hopeless'. He experienced being treated 'worse than cattle', yet, not least because of his self-perception as a member of an elite, he did not attempt suicide. 'You had to stand like a stone in the dirt, like a milestone on a dark road'.[16] Goebbels had Wiechert brought before him and did not disguise his glee at being able to show off the power he had over life and death. 'I'm on top form and cut him down to size intellectually. A final warning!' He was gratified to note the result of this one-sided interview—an agreement that Wiechert would cease criticism, though the writer never admitted it later. 'By the end the delinquent has become very small and declares his detention has made him think and get the message. That's exactly how it should be. Any further transgression and he will be physically destroyed. We both know that now.'[17]

Hans Grimm, the popular nationalist writer, who was more useful as a poster boy for the regime, was spared a similar experience. He had, after all, published the novel *A Nation without Space* in 1926 that attributed many of Germany's problems to a lack of living space (*Lebensraum*). But he overestimated the strength of his own position by founding a circle for critical writers. After this initial act of rebelliousness, he distanced himself from further dissenting comments and activities when Goebbels impressed Wiechert's fate vividly upon him.

The leading conductor Wilhelm Furtwängler also thought himself as secure as Wiechert and Grimm. In 1934 he published a newspaper article in the *Deutsche Allgemeine Zeitung* in support of Paul Hindemith, who had been attacked by the music magazine of Rosenberg's National Socialist Cultural Community. This was already unusual enough, but Furtwängler went beyond what could be tolerated when he used the opportunity to level general criticism at the practice of denunciation in cultural life. That same evening the audience at the Staatsoper, many of them readers of the middle-class newspaper in question, gave him a particularly lengthy ovation—in the presence of Goebbels and Göring. Furtwängler was now in a precarious position. He had not only alienated the radical *völkisch* camp, but also challenged the authority of the leadership of the Third Reich. That even an artist of his standing found himself forced to yield to pressure from the regime was widely noted. Luise Solmitz mentioned Furtwängler's chastening in her diary. 'He says he is regretting the fact that his support for Hindemith has had political consequences. How will a great artist like him be feeling?[18] Although Furtwängler escaped with a warning, he had done the controversial composer a disservice. It had seemed for a while as though Hindemith's moderate modernism might find a home even in the Third Reich, but now, in addition to dogmatic *völkisch* nationalists, he had the Reich Propaganda Minister lined up against him—unlike his less exposed colleague Carl Orff. In 1938, after the performance of his works was banned, the composer emigrated to the United States.

A situation that, from an artist's point of view, represented in part latent repression and in part new opportunities offered National Socialists a prominent stage on which to present themselves. Only a few years before, they had not necessarily been taken seriously as a cultural movement, even by their voters. Moreover, their opponents often accused them of being uncultured. Now the Nazis were able to give advice to prominent artists and even issue instructions, to provide them with opportunities, or, if they put a foot wrong, to threaten them with being banned or worse. By attending art exhibitions, appearing in the foyers of opera houses, receiving birthday greetings from leading actors, or conferring some distinction or other on artists, they gave a public demonstration of their power over cultural life. Even the functionaries of Strength through Joy or the Reich Chamber of Culture were boosted in their status, as were Gauleiters and activists in the National Socialist Cultural Community. Whenever they made a speech, wrote an article, or made a recommendation, people took note. They were the ones who established cultural guidelines (or deliberately left them vague), issued arbitrary bans, and took decisions about artists' careers.

The leadership of the regime was constantly in search of new ways to project itself in public and in doing so appropriated public assets without scruple. This became most evident in their art collections. This was the means Hitler himself used to emphasize his claim to personal greatness and dominion over a nation that was, he believed, culturally superior to all others. The Führer acquired nineteenth-century Austrian or Bavarian genre painters such as Carl Spitzweg, also Renaissance old masters, as well as politically and aesthetically congenial contemporary artists. Through his own predilections, which influenced other buyers, Hitler exerted considerable influence on the art market in Germany, thereby boosting trade for a whole series of dealers and auction houses, mainly in Munich and Berlin but also in Chemnitz and Cologne. Hitler also acquired works of art from museums, including from the Haus der Kunst in Munich. On five visits in 1938 he bought 202 works for 582,000 Reichsmarks. The money came from sales, boosted by state provisions, of *Mein Kampf*, from donations, and from the sale of commemorative stamps. In addition, Hitler had to pay only a little for paintings formerly owned by Jews, if these had not already simply been confiscated.

The leading figures in the regime took Hitler's taste as a guide when they bought and displayed paintings themselves. Göring adopted the pose of a Renaissance man and adorned his various residences with appropriate German and Italian paintings. After an initial interest in Expressionism, Goebbels in his collecting concentrated on the kinds of works favoured by his Führer, while Joachim von Ribbentrop, besides Hitler's favourite genres, favoured French Impressionists. He also borrowed works by Lucas Cranach the Elder and Arnold Böcklin for his ambassadorial residence in London. Owning and displaying works of art also played a role in the way rivalries were expressed between the powerful figures in the regime. Hitler received numerous and regular gifts of carefully selected paintings, which lent symbolic weight to his absolute pre-eminence as the Führer. He reciprocated by presenting his most important followers with works of art and his own drawings. The leading protagonists in the Third Reich also exchanged gifts of art works to smooth relations between them, for, in spite of their rivalry, they were always at pains to reassure one another of their mutual support and shared cultural ambitions.

The culture that emerged from this combination of needs, predilections, and rituals remained unmistakably bourgeois. Although the *völkisch* movement made an impact on book catalogues and theatre programmes in the Third Reich, the works it produced did not meet with a positive response. Pseudo-Teutonic open-air pageants (*Thingspiele*) soon became a niche genre after audiences found them uninteresting. Hardly any conductors or theatre directors owed their position to a commitment to National Socialism prior to 1933. Given that the leaders of the regime were using culture to make a public show and to appear to have artistic taste, established works, which could be given a Nazi spin if necessary, seemed to be the wise choice. In practice, therefore, the culture of the Third Reich consisted of the paintings of Albrecht Dürer, Carl Spitzweg, and Arnold Böcklin, the plays of Friedrich Schiller and Shakespeare (who was regularly claimed to be a 'Nordic' poet), and the music of Beethoven or Verdi. In this the Nazis were not obviously different from the majority of middle-class lovers of culture, who still focused primarily on nineteenth-century works and had few regrets about modernists, left-wingers, and Jews being excluded. Wagner's operas too were as important for the cultural legitimacy of Hitler and his adherents as they were for the affective responses of the bourgeoisie. Elisabeth Gebensleben-von Alten told her daughter of enthralling radio experiences: 'Afterwards we'll all switch on Bayreuth for the third act of *Die Walküre*. Yesterday *Das Rheingold* was wonderful and was our special treat for the whole of Sunday.'[19]

Precisely because of this overlap between Nazi and bourgeois culture the majority of theatre bosses, conductors, and museum directors were allowed to carry on undisturbed after 1933. By contrast with the Weimar Republic, however, the financial provision was now generous—and Brecht's epic theatre and Schönberg's twelve-tone musical system were no longer a threat. In addition, thanks to Strength through Joy and other organizations, it now seemed possible to make the desired connection with 'the people'. Yet, in spite of all apparent continuity, culture was above all 'an essential expression of political leadership', as Hitler himself put it at the 1936 Nuremberg Party Rally.[20] Political pressure determined what plays were performed, what books were published, what paintings were exhibited, and what reviews could be written, even if that pressure amounted to no more than Goebbels advising the conductor of the Leipzig Gewandhaus Orchestra to play more 'sure-fire standards' in future, and 'always some Beethoven' in particular.[21] Films and newspapers, radio broadcasts, and travel advertising were, however, at least as important for culture in the Third Reich as Wagner's operas, Shakespeare's plays, or Beethoven's symphonies. For it was, above all, the modern media that gave expression to Germans' desires and dreams.

The Power of Imagination: Media and Consumption

As a result of chance encounters and feminine wiles, a newly married racing driver finds himself the rival in love of his best friend. His wife has been carried off to the Côte d'Azur; he speeds off in his sports car to fetch her back. He finds unexpectedly that he has to take part in the Monaco Grand Prix, wins it—and all misunderstandings are resolved amid general rejoicing. A banker's wife threatens to leave her husband because he is so dull and dependable. He then adopts a forceful, masculine attitude and contrives to be caught in his own home with a female neighbour—at which point his wife falls in love with him again. A vacuum cleaner salesman will inherit millions from his dead uncle in America—but only if his marriage to a cabaret singer can be shown to be stable in the face of any temptation. A couple of crooks trick him into going to New York and, without his realizing it, make it look as if he is an errant husband. In spite of this, he is able to explain everything at the end and embraces his wife once again. In 1930 a head waiter moves from his home town, a seaside resort, to Berlin in order to get ahead and enjoy a new kind of life. There he meets the daughter of a Reichstag deputy from the 'Liberal Business Party', an encounter made possible by his being mistaken for the son of a Westphalian industrialist. When his true identity is revealed, he realizes that his snobbish new friends do not really want to know him. So he leaves Berlin and returns to his fiancée.

All these film roles were played by Heinz Rühmann, in *Allotria* (1936), *The Model Husband* (1937), *Five Million in Search of an Heir*, and *The Roundabouts of Handsome Carl* (both 1938). Rühmann was one of the most successful German actors of the twentieth century. Although his films are not set in a recognizably Nazi Germany, he was one of the pre-eminent leading men in Third Reich film. Even as the racing driver he was the embodiment of the little man who is both youthful and thoroughly good and pursues his own path single-mindedly. He is open to the achievements of the modern world without threatening the cohesion of marriage, family, or nation. He enjoys success, but does not show excessive ambition and cannot be corrupted. Only in *The Roundabouts of Handsome Carl* does Rühmann's character have to rediscover his true self after he has flirted with the morally disreputable big city world of the Weimar Republic. Rühmann was a total contrast to the heroic fighters and Aryan supermen, with whom few beyond the confines of Party, SA, and SS could identify. Yet he never gave the impression of being 'un-German' or 'effeminate'. He overcame difficulties with good humour and without ever seeming materialistic, not even as a vacuum salesman or banker. So he was able to represent both the prevailing optimism and the still modest consumption opportunities that prevailed in the mid-1930s.

Both as an actor and in real life, Rühmann was a symbol of how seeming opposites could be reconciled. He was normal to the point of being banal, but at the same time his face was familiar throughout Germany and he was a passionate recreational pilot and wealthy villa owner. Film and theatre audiences found it easy to identify with him, and this made him the object of a real personality cult. In June 1938 a journalist described how the inhabitants of Wittenberge in Brandenburg were waiting for the great actor at the local airport, but Rühmann landed in a field 'where he made friends with a shepherd tending his flock there and ate his breakfast while cheerfully chatting with him'. His combination of pragmatic individuality and warm-hearted approachability was successful because it fulfilled the emotional need for a star who was also a human being 'like you and me'. Although a *völkisch* theatre critic saw in Rühmann an actor who had 'turned away from individualism and subjectivism in favour of portraying in monumentalized form a character drawn from the people', such strained attempts to inject ideology into his acting style are less significant than the fact that he represented the entertaining, humorous, occasionally daring, and harmlessly erotic side of the Third Reich. This connection was made explicit in 1936 by a film magazine that praised another Rühmann comedy in the following terms: 'Three years ago many people in Germany thought "that laughter was over now". And that particular kind of laughter *was* over!...In those days, jokes were uptight, humour was slick, light-heartedness was ambiguous. In the new Germany people can laugh again!'[22]

Though his fans at the time had no idea of it, the Third Reich was in fact far from straightforward for Rühmann himself. He had already been a success during the Weimar Republic, working with Jewish actors and directors. In addition, he was subject to hidden pressure because, although they had separated, he remained close to his wife, who was classified as a 'full Jew'. In order to be able on the one hand to protect her and on the other to advance his career in Germany (and earn large amounts of money), he first sought Hermann Göring's protection against attacks by the SS publica-tion *Das Schwarze Korps*. On Göring's advice, Rühmann eventually divorced his wife and arranged a sham marriage for her to a for-eigner from a neutral country so that she could remain in Berlin for the time being. Even then, he continued to give her financial support. Admired by Goebbels and Hitler, he was shown appearing before a smiling Führer with a collecting box for Winter Aid in his hand. Looking back, Rühmann described himself as an unpolitical person with a sunny temperament, who was at the mercy of those in power, whether they were hostile or admiring: 'None of my friends tried to ingratiate themselves with the gentlemen in brown, but if there was a reception for the arts world we had to go.'[23] In saying this Rühmann was failing to see the impact of his performances and of his personal popularity: whether consciously or not, in his own way he was helping to promote a sense that National Socialism was largely morally acceptable and pleasingly modern.

Heinz Rühmann's role can be understood only within the context of a large group of stars with whom audiences could identify in a variety of ways. The rugged masculinity of Hans Albers, a blond Hamburger, the exoticism of the Hungarian dancer Marika Rökk, and the seductive sensuality of the Swedish actress Zarah Leander seemed to promise eroticism and authenticity. Their actions and characters gave wings to the audience's imagination. Though their films drew on the repertoire of the Weimar period and were often set in the pre-1914 German past (thus, in contrast to the relatively few Nazi propaganda feature films, suggesting continuity), at the same time they stood for the widespread hope of renewal because unsettling ambivalence and overt social criticism were now banned from the screen. This is evident not only from looking at the films produced after 1933 but also at those that were not made at all and at the people who were no longer in front of or behind the camera: directors such as Fritz Lang and actresses such as Marlene Dietrich, whose work and roles resisted unambiguous interpretations. In the Third Reich the public sphere remained under surveillance, and that oversight extended to foreign influences. Audiences could admire selected foreign stars, watch Heinz Rühmann's film characters make excursions to Monaco or New York, and thoroughly enjoy Hollywood films even—without ever risking being disturbed by anything unfamiliar.

The most important fiction mediated by film was that of the Third Reich as a normalized and cohesive society. Gender conflicts had been resolved, economic problems overcome, and cultural differences did not arise. The remilitarization that became increasingly apparent, from the newly built armaments factories, via the reoccupation of the Rhineland, to intervention in the Spanish Civil War, appeared to the majority of Germans to pose no threat to their lives. In spite of all the economic and cultural restrictions, Germany after 1933 was a place where people could 'laugh heartily'. Actually going to the cinema was not the only thing that provided guaranteed entertainment; there were posters and fan magazines, autograph cards, and picture calendars that created what seemed like a direct link between the public and its stars. The primacy of entertainment also made it easier for the regime to draw in new sections of society, as the idea of a national community suggested it should. In rural areas Party organizations were successful with their film shows only if they took account of the needs of the local population. Thus peasants in smoky pubs could pass comments on comedies or sports films in their local dialect instead of listening to lectures by *völkisch* activists.[24]

Like the theatre, film in the Third Reich also satisfied a demand for meaning on the part of nationalist members of the educated bourgeoisie. Although people in these circles occasionally criticized popular comedies and highly paid stars, at least German films offered an alternative to the cultural dominance of Hollywood. And although this development had been on the horizon since the coming of talking pictures in the late 1920s, it was now credited to the new era. The film industry profited from state subsidies. Screen writers and actors were made members of the Reich Chamber of Film or the artistic committee of the Ufa film studios, which raised hopes of artistic considerations being given greater weight in relation to purely commercial ones. The educated middle classes had long had a sceptical attitude towards the new medium. Now they were won over by the fact that there was an emphasis on aesthetic norms or on 'personalities' who felt a connection with their 'nation', because they saw a link to the values of the nineteenth century. Spectacular acting careers and entertainment as a commodity could be tolerated because they were clearly distinct from 'America'. The process of rapprochement between the aesthetics of the educated bourgeoisie and the film industry was crowned by the founding of the German Film Academy. It developed training for actors that was independent of the theatre. Lectures provided an academic flavour, and there was also an emphasis, at least rhetorically, on the selection of roles.

Film in the Third Reich was thus not shaped by a specifically National Socialist ideology and its mode of rule alone. Hidden continuities with the Weimar period, international trends, and bourgeois traditions were also influential. The same was true also of leisure and popular culture as a whole. People whose taste was not opposed to the prevailing culture from the outset might imagine themselves in a society that offered a largely free choice from a broad range of cultural possibilities. Although radio was able to be brought particularly quickly and easily under complete dictatorial control, once the wave of political broadcasts during 1933/34, when propaganda and military marches were transmitted almost without a break, was over, entertainment programmes soon became dominant. Most of the time was taken up with light music, with even some occasional jazz thrown in despite its being loathed by the Nazis. Apart from this, the radio offered advice programmes, live commentary on sports fixtures, and folksy radio plays. There were also comedy programmes such as *Three Jolly Fellows*, in which a Rhinelander, a Hamburger, and a rather conceited 'cosmopolitan' were always crossing swords in mock rhetorical battles and then setting them aside to end on a harmonious note. Musical requests and interviews with ordinary Germans, who were recorded by means of mobile transmission vans, gave an impression of popular participation in a medium genuinely expressive of the national community. At the same time, programmes with a *völkisch* tinge and focusing on people's home regions and the peasantry, as well as broadcasts of Hitler's speeches to whole factories, restaurants, and public squares, left no doubt that the content of this medium was ultimately controlled by the dictatorship.

For the regime, and particularly for Propaganda Minister Goebbels, it was important to make radio, previously dominated by the middle classes, accessible to 'the whole nation'. For less affluent sections of society the radio licence fees were lowered or even abolished. The production and distribution of the 'people's wireless' was particularly important. The idea of making a simple radio with built-in speakers and a plastic casing had been conceived during the Weimar Republic and reflected international developments, but putting it to effective use in the public sphere did not come until the Third Reich. The people's wireless was mass-produced and sold in millions, many purchasers making use of the payment plan on offer. The fact that a battery-powered model was obtainable and could be combined with an aerial meant that it was usable beyond the range of the still patchy electricity grid. Alongside the introduction of the people's wireless, radio reception was improved in many rural areas.[25] By these means ownership of radios had more than doubled by comparison with the Weimar Republic on the outbreak of war, even if only 57 per cent of households possessed a set. In addition, there was an intensive advertising campaign for the people's wireless in shop windows and magazines, in pictures and at radio exhibitions. Even those who could not afford one, in spite of the modest price set by the state, became conscious of it as a desirable future acquisition and a means of being part of the national community.

The abundance and variety of popular literature further demonstrate the importance in the Third Reich of the demand and opportunity for entertainment. Though many books were nationalist and conformed to Nazi ideology, there was still a wide range of publishing houses. One of the literary bestsellers was Margaret Mitchell's *Gone with the Wind* about the southern states of America during the Civil War. Novels by prominent British or French writers were as easy to obtain as the popular crime fiction of Edgar Wallace or 'The Adventures of Billy Jenkins', a series of Wild West stories for young people. There were militaristic publications harking back to the First World War. However, the war also featured in the love story *André and Ursula*, published in 1937, which promoted understanding between Germany and France and sold in hundreds of thousands.

Ultimately, however, there were limits to this variety. Publications were now supposed to communicate nationalistic values. The successful comic novels of Heinrich Spoerl may have been unpolitical and made fun of authority figures, but they transported their readers to an imaginary, non-specifically German small-town world of the early twentieth century, free from social or cultural conflicts. To Goebbels's mind, they were perfect for film adaptations. Karl May, whose books had first been published in Imperial Germany, was also popular, including with the Propaganda Minister and his Führer. In them 'Yankees' were treated negatively, while Native Americans were romanticized, and the most important characters were Old Shatterhand and his companions, most of whom came, like him, from Saxony. Non-fiction books with fictional elements emphasized German achievements and capabilities in science and technology, from *Anilin* or *Robert Koch* to *Oil War*, which raised awareness of the struggle to make Germany independent of foreign raw materials. Anyone looking for guidance in his or her own life could find it, combined with Nazi principles, in such titles as *The German Mother and Her First Child*. Biographies of Hermann Göring and his wife Carin, who had died young and whom he presented in an idealized light, gave the regime's leaders a human face, as did *Germany Awakes*, a picture album produced by the cigarette firm Reemtsma on the history of the Nazi movement (which was in reality initiated and overseen by the Propaganda Ministry).

While radio and film made an impact, it was still newspapers that were the medium with the broadest reach. They too combined a degree of variety with what was ultimately a clear political message. Left-wing and Jewish journalists had been excluded in 1933, and many publishing companies had been taken over by the Nazi press empire. Permission to set up new ones was granted only sparingly. In addition, even before the war publishers had problems with paper shortages. Reporting and comment were controlled by censorship and rules regarding content. Nevertheless, many newspapers that catered for other readerships than that of the *Völkischer Beobachter*, which was aimed primarily at Party members, were able to stay afloat. Editors and journalists of the bourgeois press had quickly fallen into line with the requirements of the Third Reich. The local sections and miscellaneous general news stories in particular were designed for fairly unpolitical readers, who were defined as ordinary Germans. From such sections one could tell most clearly what the consensus was with regard to what could be seen as part of normal life and what could not. This consensus had already shifted markedly by the mid-1930s. Closer inspection reveals that Nazi ideology was all-pervasive, yet it was conveyed in subtle ways and linked to many apparently unremarkable pieces of information and reports.

The *Berliner Lokal-Anzeiger* provides a telling example of this. Before 1933 this paper had been aimed at the capital's conservative middle classes; now its accessible content was clearly contributing to the city's Nazification. The metropolis no longer appeared as a scene of social conflicts, cultural ambiguities, and existential crises. Neither, conversely, was it the scene of a massive restriction of freedom. Advertisements, readers' letters, and reports of everyday occurrences in the city suggested that Berliners enjoyed more opportunities as individuals than they had previously in areas that mattered to them: clothes shops, sports stadiums, or family homes on housing estates, as well as within the nuclear family. The new atmosphere of communality was presented as not so much challenging as supportive. It could even give rise to expectations regarding public institutions: 'The railway's view that the only thing the public can claim is the right to be transported somewhere no matter how', as one reader wrote to complain about packed suburban trains, 'is no longer appropriate in this day and age'.[26] Above all, however, it was insinuated that the ideal of community had had positive effects on Berliners' hitherto notoriously rough behaviour. They were now, apparently, more polite and helpful, and their relations with the police were characterized by mutual respect. The image projected was one of a city finally at peace with itself, one that made it easier for the paper's readership to believe that compulsory sterilizations took place voluntarily, that civil defence exercises were designed purely for a war started by a foreign aggressor and that Jews had innately criminal tendencies—provided, of course, that readers had not had personal experience of the regime's repressive side.

The newspaper's view was that Berlin was in the happy position of being constantly renewed from the outside or the periphery. The city dwellers there showed 'toughness in struggling and winning through' by planting fruit trees along a railway line. A collection of allotments showed the 'German's delight in having a little plot…that he can cultivate and tend'. When taking part in water sports on one of the lakes surrounding the city, others discovered a sense of freedom similar to 'those old pioneers of the savannah, who set off under the western stars to live and fight there'. In this way criticism of the city was woven into the way urban life was presented. Though this had happened before 1933, it now served to legitimize the regime. Thus it was asserted that Berlin's being linked to the autobahn network would enable people to relate to nature in new ways: drivers would enjoy a 'picture of the landscape of the Mark Brandenburg', whose 'variety and beauty would make their journey a happy memory'.[27]

It was not only in the *Berliner Lokal-Anzeiger* that the building of the autobahn was presented as strengthening Germans' sense of belonging. It was said to extend people's experience by revealing regional characteristics rather than making them disappear. Emblematic of this were the motorway services on the Chiemsee, built in the style of alpine farmhouses, the 'gate to Thuringia' on the Saxon border, or the city coats of arms visible at the entrance to the Berlin ring. Panoramic viewpoints were positioned to allow people to see not only the landscape but also the autobahn viaducts. The autobahn's route in some places fitted itself into the German terrain of forests and hills and in others cut through them in order to create spectacular vistas. All of this was designed to underline the Third Reich's claim to have created an organic and holistic form of the modern. Even an otherwise marginalized Jew and critic of autobahn construction such as Victor Klemperer, who had only just got his driving licence, was attracted by the prospect of travelling on roads like these: 'Always straight, fine, smooth, near empty roads through forest. When the road was shut off on both sides, the effect was almost dangerously soporific; when a view over meadows and plantations appeared, I became more wide awake.'[28]

Only a small section of the population could experience the autobahns for themselves. The regime's economic priority was rearmament, and even fewer people owned private motor vehicles in Germany than in France or Britain. This also meant, of course, that the potentially sobering effect of long journeys on a road network that was more functional than aesthetic and also incomplete was rare. Experiencing the autobahn was primarily a matter of reading reports, novels, or poems, or looking at picture books, documentaries, paintings, photos, or stamps. It was even the subject of a board game. All this made the autobahn into a total work of art composed of stories and pictures. It fascinated planners and engineers, who for some time had been searching for 'German technology'. Above all, it answered the middle classes' dreams of being mobile, besides being linked to concrete hopes for the future—at least for the 170,000 people who before the outbreak of war had begun to save for a Volkswagen, a 'people's car'.

Leisure in the Third Reich was thus not just a matter of self-realization in the here and now. By the mid-1930s the economic depression had been sufficiently overcome for the Nazi regime to claim loudly and disingenuously that it deserved the credit. This claim gave credibility to the promise that people's individual circumstances, often still very modest, would soon noticeably improve. The expansion of the range of experiences available to people and the acceleration of the pace of life were fascinating rather than threatening, for they were softened by association with community, regional identity, and the natural world in a way already familiar in German culture, despite now being communicated with the concentrated force of the modern media. Even Victor Klemperer could at times banish the knowledge that all this was part of the National Socialist project. Anyone who was neither Jewish nor a dissident took a mostly positive view of the new era as offering a constantly growing, though not troubling, variety of options. As before, people could spend their holidays walking in the Black Forest, sunning themselves on a beach on the North Sea coast, or visiting Goethe's house in Weimar. At the same time, many visitors showed a genuine interest in seeing sights connected with politics: the New Reich Chancellery in Berlin or the Feldherrnhalle in Munich, where Hitler had mounted his attempted putsch on 9 November 1923. Even his private address in Munich and a Weimar hotel where he liked to stay became tourist attractions.

The stated aim of the leisure organization Strength through Joy, modelled on the Italian fascist Opera Nazionale Dopolavoro, was to give more national comrades than ever the opportunity to enjoy a holiday. With a market share of over 10 per cent of all accommodation booked, it was soon competing with private travel agencies and threatening to flood established resorts popular among the middle classes with noisy tour groups. Admittedly, many people could not afford a Strength through Joy holiday, as the contribution required from customers was still considerable and getting a place often depended on personal or political connections. For that reason, the holidays were booked mainly by the middle classes (including many hard-drinking Party members) and a minority of relatively well-paid skilled workers. From a social point of view, there was clear continuity in the development of tourism from the Weimar period onwards, but propaganda naturally misrepresented this. The prospect of one day seeing the Bavarian Alps or the Harz region with one's own eyes, or perhaps even taking a cruise to Madeira or Norway, appealed to the imaginations of many Germans, and at the same time the country's rapid recovery made such journeys seem within reach. Though in fact never completed, Prora, the gigantic holiday complex on the island of Rügen, held out the promise of a future in which every 'Aryan' family would go on a package holiday to the Baltic coast.

Even the correspondents of the Social Democrat exile organization, normally more interested in reassuring themselves about the cohesiveness of their own milieu and inclined to regard the regime as being in crisis, were forced to concede the attractiveness of Strength through Joy. As early as September 1935 an informant reported from Bavaria: 'Although workers are often unable to come up with the modest cost of these trips, all the same, many proletarians get the chance to see something, which used not to be the case.' At the end of the same year workers seemed to be divided into those who were still unable to afford holidays and excursions and those who had already taken advantage of them or planned to do so soon. What was disturbing was that only committed comrades on the left were able to recognize the political side to the Third Reich's use of leisure to achieve integration. One informant from the Rhineland complained somewhat resignedly that the comparison between the achievements of the Third Reich and those of the workers' movement in the Weimar period was simply not a fair one: 'We wouldn't be being objective if we did not acknowledge that Strength through Joy organizes quite a few good holidays. But didn't we have those in the past? There just wasn't such a song and dance made about them.' And a Berlin Social Democrat commented that Strength through Joy had to be seen as a whole set of leisure possibilities and people should 'not only focus on the holidays. There are many events of every kind: sport, hiking, swimming, skiing, gymnastics, theatre etc. etc. and it's really cheap for people to take part.'[29]

In spite of the rhetoric of community, Strength through Joy's activities could be exploited in a thoroughly individualistic manner. Depending on their financial means, people could make their own choices, and once on a trip they could wander off on their own every now and then. That reflected a leisure culture that most Germans experienced as very varied, for, as well as those spheres that were under political control (even if they were not always perceived as such), there was still a market for entertainment and consumption. People could buy local beer, traditional fizzy drinks, or the fashionable new drink Coca-Cola. There were German comedies and Hollywood films, there was 'traditional' as well as functional furniture. People could even listen to jazz in city pubs or at home on imported records. They felt that they determined their leisure activities themselves, from swimming lessons provided by Strength through Joy to photography as a hobby or to driving a car, real or imaginary. Even where what was offered to consumers was influenced by ideology, people could still set their own priorities. They could go into the cinema after the newsreel and its political content was over, ignore the main section of the newspaper they subscribed to or, to the horror of sport functionaries with their glorification of 'community', they could get into fights with opposing football fans.

The secular and international trend towards expanding leisure and consumption was thus evident in the Third Reich and was in line with Goebbels's thinking in particular. He judged that the nation's acceptance of the regime would grow if the latter did not attempt to infuse everything with ideology, and to all intents and purposes he was right. As the example of the people's wireless shows, there were many opportunities to appropriate developments dating from the Weimar Republic and exploit them politically. The fact that, in spite of the Nazi promise of equality, it was a new middle-class culture that began to emerge caused no real problem of legitimization for the regime. Rather this culture created scope for the still influential educated bourgeoisie. Its members had to say goodbye to the long radio talks they used to enjoy and felt powerless in the face of quite a few aspects of modern life (Luise Solmitz was, for example, indignant that the saxophone, 'this degrading wind instrument that has nothing to do with music and art, destroys and suffocates everything, an American invention', had been adopted in the Luftwaffe's bands[30]), but, then again, film criticism, local journalism, and travel writing gave middle-class writers new opportunities and the chance to gain some prominence. In addition, the Third Reich's bourgeois culture motivated ambitious members of the working class to rise as individuals and thus contributed to the disintegration of proletarian milieus. Although first and foremost it enabled people to come to terms with the present, it was ultimately designed to go on mobilizing desires and dreams. Even if people were not always aware of it, this process was linked to the exclusion of the politically persecuted and the lonely state of those who did not belong. The power of the imagination in the Third Reich had a dark side: the isolation of the dissidents.

The Isolation of the Dissidents: Anti-fascist Culture

In a prison cell Peter Pagel awaited his trial. The young socialist passed the time by writing stories, poems, and letters to his partner. But these were not enough to overcome the social and cultural isolation of solitary confinement: 'Only in his imagination could he take part in the pleasures enjoyed by those outside. Walks in the parks or through the town. Buying some sweets. A good cigarette. Drinking a cup of aromatic coffee. Going to the cinema or the theatre.' Sentenced in a show trial to several years in prison, for a time Pagel shared a dirty cell with political prisoners and criminals. Then he was moved to Brual-Rhede camp in the Emsland, where he was exposed to an entirely new level of brutality and deprivation. He was made to toil to the point of complete exhaustion at cultivating the surrounding moorland. Among the daily humiliations meted out were vulgar insults, intimidating physical exercises, and frequent beatings. In addition, the prisoners were forced to sing 'The miller's joy is to go wandering' (a poem by Wilhelm Müller set to music by Schubert) on their morning march to work. When a new arrival discovered the lack of hygiene facilities and exclaimed, 'Good heavens! What's happened to our much vaunted German culture?', Pagel replied, 'It's certainly not here among German prisoners!'[31]

Peter Pagel was the alter ego of Wilhelm Henze. Henze was from Hildesheim, had trained as a motor mechanic, and was a commercially unsuccessful writer. He was arrested in August 1933 for distributing anti-fascist pamphlets and from May 1934 he spent a year and a half in Brual-Rhede. Like his semi-fictional counterpart, Henze was one of the 'politicals', who 'even during their suffering are sustained by ideas', because the workers' movement has given them a 'more thorough knowledge and a sharper insight into how things in life are connected'. Hungry, exhausted, and ill, he still dreamt of personal happiness and a future with his girlfriend, whom he could write to only seldom. He got on well with other prisoners and talked to them about everyday matters as well as political issues. Sometimes they sang songs and even practised Esperanto. He attempted to compensate for the intellectual barrenness of camp life through his own creativity. He wrote in his diary: 'I have started to carve wooden moorland figures. I made the male and female figures as comical as possible. It gave me a lot of pleasure. The days here on the moor are so boring and empty. There's nothing to read.'[32] Henze also drew and wrote poetry, though he had to do these things in haste and unobtrusively. After his release he was once again active in the resistance before escaping from the Gestapo into exile in Sweden. There he used his camp experiences as the basis for his stories about Peter Pagel who, in spite of tribulations, remains true to his political and moral vision.

Henze's drawings show emaciated figures digging up the inhospitable moorland or pushing heavy carts. They are constantly under threat from exaggeratedly tall guards before spending the evening behind barbed wire. There are also moments of relaxation, however, when they stretch and gaze into the distance or meet as socialists for a study group. Henze's poems express this tension too. They speak of feelings of isolation, when the poet identifies with a tree on the moor, standing alone but free: 'It is an image of my longing, as I stand in the morning and see it through my wire cage standing free.' They also illustrate the absence of civilized standards, for example in his praise of his shabby 'face cloth, nothing more, that serves me every day'. Another poem captures in penetrating language the Nazi project of dehumanization: 'We're hungry, we toil, a good few have dug their own graves; the guards curse endlessly, the slaves are animals, not humans; cruelty taken to a new height; culture? Of course, it's the Nazi norm.' But the following lines propound the dream of a socialist society: 'Then we shall control our own destinies and build our own happiness; the economic model is clear and good, the people bright and hopeful; then the nation thrives, the people thrive (*das Volk* in the socialist sense, in the original) and culture blossoms, in technology, science, and nature.'[33]

Henze's poetry, prose, and drawings are among the anti-fascist reactions to the revolution of 1933. For its opponents the Third Reich brought persecution that reached into people's homes, violent oppression, and in many cases death. Dissidents' cultural activities brought home to them and to others how completely inhumane Nazism was, while at the same time keeping the hope of a better future alive. In the camps writing poems, singing songs, or discussing socialist ideas could bring relief from the daily humiliation and intimidation. Strict supervision, however, meant that these activities were limited to individuals or at most small groups and so could not really overcome the dissidents' isolation. In addition, some of the camp supervisors and guards permitted cultural activities or even promoted them, with the result that they became part of the system of repression. In exchange for small privileges, functionaries in the Emsland camps commissioned art objects from the prisoners, giving them as presents to the initially suspicious inhabitants of the surrounding villages. Significantly, Henze, for whom culture and resistance were inseparable, could not in retrospect imagine large-scale events being staged, although there is evidence that in the neighbouring camp of Börgermoor a cabaret evening was put on with official permission.[34]

Functionaries and guards in any case had complete control of those aspects of cultural life inside the camps that, as in the case of music, could not be carried out in secret. They forced the inmates to sing songs with Nazi, chauvinistic, or obscene lyrics and in so doing to demean themselves. Camp choirs and orchestras were created to accompany the rituals of daily life or to drown out the screams of those being tortured. The choirs and orchestras were also aimed at occupying and re-educating the inmates. They could be wheeled out when journalists and official visitors came to the concentration camps. They were also there quite simply to entertain the staff, sometimes putting on whole 'evenings of entertainment' and 'cultural events'. While some performances did take place covertly, most were overseen by the camp authorities. Permission to organize or attend an event could be treated as the equivalent of being granted a privilege. And even the 'moor soldiers" own songs, which continued the traditions of the workers' movement, or those of the inmates of Lichtenburg, Esterwegen, and Sachsenburg were tolerated and sometimes welcomed. The camp administration had an interest in encouraging each camp to develop its own distinct identity. For this same reason the SS in Sachsenhausen and Buchenwald commissioned its own songs and even established whole orchestras. The extent to which the opportunity to engage in cultural activities was dependent on the camp commandant in question, however, is shown by the example of Dachau. There there was neither an orchestra nor a camp song, and the Sunday variety shows were soon banned.[35]

Social Democrat and Communist dissidents felt isolated, whether outside or inside work and concentration camps. When, after his release, Wilhelm Henze returned home by train, he was sitting in a compartment with members of an acting troupe whose 'vanity, conceit, and stupid pride' gave him a feeling of hopelessness: 'No character. And these are the people who are supposed to be keeping our culture alive! It's both sad and frightening.'[36] Although his new resistance group had been assembled with care, one member betrayed it to the Gestapo after only its second leaflet. By the mid-1930s surveillance, denunciation, and the threat of a concentration camp had deprived the previously strong workers' movement of its ability to engage in political struggle or express itself culturally. Only small groups still existed, which could support each other in their beliefs but were unable to develop any plan of action. In March 1935 a Social Democrat observer travelling through Germany found almost no sign of resistance. He saw it as an encouraging sign that quite a number of young workers exchanged socially critical novels and memoirs from the Russian Revolution, but, disillusioned by the mainly passive attitude of the 'masses', he described how people remembered with sadness the earlier public presence of the left: 'When I told them about socialist life outside, about marches with red flags, the Children's Friends and Socialist Workers' Youth [*Kinderfreunde* and *Arbeiterjugend*, two Social Democrat organizations] in blue smocks and so on, some female comrades started to weep.'[37]

Otherwise hard-headed Social Democrats were constantly expressing astonishment at the attraction exerted by National Socialism, both in popular culture and intellectually. 'Where are the academics, now that it's vital to protest?' asked an informant from western Germany in 1935. 'They have coordinated themselves, knuckled under, and left the fight yet again to the anonymous masses, the unsophisticated workers.' But the latter were not a reason to be optimistic either. Their frequent dissatisfaction with tough working conditions and meagre take-home pay was not translated into active opposition, for the preconditions for it did not exist. The workers' gymnastics, singing, and cremation associations, which had been politically suspect from the outset, had been banned for years, while any new attempt to organize was highly risky. Although the working class's rough culture could not simply be abolished, it was subjected to strong discipline, with young men being recruited into the Reich Labour Service. Neighbourhoods such as the 'wild estates' on the outskirts of Berlin or the alley district (*Gängeviertel*) near the Hamburg docks had been cleared. How difficult the situation seemed to the left-wing opposition is shown by a pessimistic literary comparison drawn by Social Democrats in Saxony: 'In gloomy moments a few comrades are starting to think: "Is Socialism not just a noble illusion? Aren't we just Don Quixotes?"'[38]

Middle-class opponents of the Third Reich were in a slightly better position, in so far as they preserved a few areas of cultural autonomy. They could afford occasional trips abroad, find independent information and critical comment in the Swiss newspaper, the *Neue Zürcher Zeitung*, which was freely available up to the outbreak of war, and they could read foreign writers in the original or in translation. In the arts sections of some previously liberal newspapers, in particular the *Frankfurter Zeitung*, people could tell by reading between the lines that they were not alone in their reservations about Nazi policies. And, thanks to the continuing abundance of publishers and journals, it was still possible to read the latest writing by German authors who were unsympathetic to National Socialism. Among them were moderately modernist writers as well as traditional ones. The former could certainly publish, as long as they were too young or too obscure to be associated with Weimar culture. Protestants had access to congregations led by pastors who defended traditional beliefs against the encroachments of the German Christians. That people could find these niche circles to move in was not necessarily seen by the Nazi leadership as detrimental to its plans for domination, for if they could not win over sceptical Germans, they could neutralize them politically by employing a strategy of qualified restraint. Thus it was not a dissident act to write or read literature that was unpolitical and had nothing to do with the regime or to be a sympathizer with the Confessing Church, contrary to what is implied by the terms 'inner emigration' and 'Church struggle', which only came into use after 1945.

Even for the middle classes, however, it was extremely risky to express criticism of the regime outside very limited circles of like-minded people. There was too great a danger of denunciation, a practice that itself had only arisen as Hitler and his policies gained broad acceptance. While some people took the view that the regime was betraying the ideals of a 'nation of culture' on a daily basis, that view was held only by a silent minority. Middle-class opponents of National Socialism were depressed by their sense of isolation. Looking back, the writer Joachim Fest describes how his consistently pro-republican father instructed him never to repeat outside the home anything said at mealtimes about politics. As more and more neighbours in Karlshorst, a suburb of Berlin, succumbed to the inducements offered by National Socialism and, for example, spoke approvingly of cheap theatre tickets, the family drew strength from the motto: 'Even if everyone else joins in, I won't!'[39] This sense of isolation could, however, also emerge as anxiety. Thus a Berlin woman told the Jewish journalist Charlotte Beradt of dreaming about being at a performance of *The Magic Flute*: 'After the words "That is surely the Devil" a police unit marches in with lots of noise and heads straight for me. A machine has told them that when the word "Devil" was used I had thought of Hitler. I look round beseechingly at all the formally dressed people. They stare straight ahead, silent and expressionless; there is not even the slightest trace of pity in anyone's face. But no, the old gentleman in the box at the side looks nice and kind, but, when I try to look into his eyes, he spits at me.'[40]

The dissidents found it hard to distinguish between the pressure of real and imagined persecution, and this was precisely what the Nazi regime intended with its repressive policies. In a poem Wilhelm Henze expressed how, when on the run, he had known 'nothing but tension' because of the numerous people who might denounce him: 'And every house grimaces, staring at you with an evil expression. And every person is like a cat, so sly that no-one can be trusted.' The drawing that goes with it shows him running off, looking back as he goes at a sign on a wall that says, 'German Customs Border'. Behind it there are prison walls in the shape of swastikas.[41] In fact, Henze only narrowly escaped being shot by the guards as he fled across the Dutch border. In exile in Sweden he could feel safe and also had the advantage of being able to speak the language because of an earlier stay there. Yet he was forced to keep himself and his family afloat with casual work and hand-outs. Regular wages and independent work, still less political activity, were out of reach. As his parents suffered repression at home he could only watch helplessly from afar. His camp experiences stayed with him and although he could give them literary expression and attach to them a message of anti-fascist solidarity, there was no opportunity to publish them. Even in exile as a dissident, Wilhelm Henze remained isolated.

Henze's situation in Sweden was only one among many experiences of exile. Thousands of writers, painters, sculptors, and academics emigrated because the Nazis deprived them of the scope to work or even put them in imminent danger. In particular in Paris, Prague, Amsterdam, and Zurich, the centres for exiles before the Second World War, a German culture flourished that was fundamentally different from that of the Third Reich (and also from that of Catholic and authoritarian Austria). Here there was a critical mass of artists together with prominent figures such as the painter Max Beckmann, the writer Alfred Döblin, and the cultural theorist Walter Benjamin. Visual artists, architects, and musicians could hope to interest gallery owners, construction companies, and concert impresarios. Political conviction as well as their ambition as publishers prompted a number of cultural mediators native to those cities, such as Emanuel Querido in Amsterdam, to support the German-language writing of dissidents. And a range of newly founded journals provided a public forum for their perspectives and views, which could also be shared openly with like-minded people in clubs, cafés, and private homes.

For the opponents of the Third Reich, exile was both a liberation and a burden. In May 1936 Irmgard Keun wrote from the Belgian resort of Ostend to her Jewish lover, who had already emigrated to the United States: 'I still just can't believe that I'm not in Naziland any longer and really can write, speak, and breathe. I'll have to get used to it slowly.' In the later Weimar Republic Keun had risen to be the literary figurehead for modern ideas of femininity and had even tried at first to bring a court action after her novels *Gilgi, One of Us,* and *The Artificial Silk Girl* were banned. When she realized that both her marginalization in the regime's cultural life and her estrangement from her conformist husband were irreversible, she decided to emigrate. In the Netherlands and Belgium there were not only publishers interested in producing new editions of her books, she also discovered a group of German editors and authors among whom she immediately felt at home. She commented with irony: 'I hope there won't be an outbreak of anti-Christian persecution. I couldn't spot any Aryans apart from me.'[42]

While pursuing her own writing career, Irmgard Keun also wanted to take part in the 'fight against Nazism, human stolidity, lack of backbone, and barbarity' and not forget those being perse-cuted back in Germany: 'What's happening in Germany concerns the whole of humanity. One mustn't become complacent and close one's eyes.' But soon she was expressing doubts about the point of literary resistance in exile: 'You only have to open a newspaper to feel idiotic for still writing at all.' She also wrote about difficulties with her divorce, about the underlying threat of being expelled, and the permanent shortage of funds, which in turn was connected with her penchant for hotels, cafés, and bars. She was not, on the other hand, open with her lover about her intermittent relationship with the brilliant writer Joseph Roth, an alcoholic who was seriously ill and retreating ever further into the Habsburg past. None of this stopped her from giving literary expression to the themes of life under a dictatorship and as a refu-gee in her novels *After Midnight, Third-Class Express,* and *A Child of All Nations.* Yet in the summer of 1938 she described the mood among the exile community in Amsterdam as positively 'hysterical': 'Some friend or colleague is always committing suicide and there's a general suicide panic. Everyone has grown terribly sentimental and they even show it. Nobody hides behind a mask of cynicism any more. Everyone is dissolving in noble feelings of friendship, just like the characters in *Werther*.'[43]

Irmgard Keun's experiences provide a good example of how, for all its variety and quality, the influence of German-speaking exile culture abroad was ultimately limited. It had a sustained impact above all in countries that were still secure places of refuge after the outbreak of the Second World War. Exiled Germans thus left their mark on architecture in what would later become Israel, on the academic discipline of art history in Britain, and on the natural sciences in Turkey. They had the greatest impact in the United States, from the director Fritz Lang and actress Marlene Dietrich in Hollywood to the Bauhaus architect Ludwig Mies van der Rohe in Chicago, the theoretical physicist Albert Einstein at the Institute for Advanced Studies at Princeton, or the social philosopher Hannah Arendt at the New York School for Social Research. The situation in Paris, Prague, or Amsterdam differed from that in America. Although exiles in Europe could preserve some aware-ness that there was another German culture apart from that of the Third Reich, the community of emigrants was very fragmented. As well as the famous, there were many whom nobody had ever heard of. There were political and artistic differences, exacerbated by personal conflicts and jealousies. In addition, theatre directors, writers, and journalists, all of them important in convincing people to oppose fascism, remained dependent on the German language. Even though a few could speak French or reached audi-ences or readerships in the Netherlands or Czechoslovakia who understood German, they frequently felt themselves to be in an alien culture. They moved exclusively in their own circles, while also suffering financial difficulties and problems with their residency permits.

These exiles came to very different conclusions about their situation, for, although it offered them temporary safety, they remained isolated. Those who stood for culture as defined by the educated middle class tended to stay out of politics. Quite often they turned to historical subject matter, which was also most likely to appeal to an international readership. They had virtually nothing in common with the doctrinaire Communists, trying from Moscow to work towards an international revolution. In between were the anti-fascist humanists. They attempted to mobilize public opinion in western Europe by publicizing Nazi violence in all its gory detail. The *Brown Book about the Reichstag Fire and Hitler Terror* was translated into fifteen languages and sold over 600,000 copies. The 'Library of Burned Books', founded in Paris to commemorate the barbaric acts in May 1933 and offer a meeting place to exiled intellectuals, was a powerful symbol of those parts of German literature that had been ostracized. But the international shock effect soon wore off. Hopes of seeing the Third Reich collapse were also soon disappointed. The rise of the left in France and Spain created for a time the new prospect of Europe-wide cooperation, which appeared to be taking concrete shape in 1935 at the Paris conference 'In Defence of Culture'. All the speeches and resolutions were nevertheless powerless to alter the fact that, from abroad, Hitler's regime was hard to analyse, let alone combat effectively.

Why did politically engaged exiled Germans find it so difficult to mobilize the international public sphere in opposition to

Hitler's regime? The political and cultural climate in the countries they had sought refuge in was not in their favour. In Austria, Switzerland, and Belgium, and also in France (though less so in the more tolerant Netherlands and more generous Czechoslovakia), the enduring economic crisis created an environment where people were less open to foreign influences and competition. In addition, right-wing radical movements were gaining strength in these countries and even conservatives were looking to Nazi Germany for strategies with which to overcome their own national crises. Even those who did not share those sympathies often admired bourgeois German culture. The German pavilion at the Paris World Exhibition of 1937 with its display of handsomely produced books was very popular. The novels of the exiled writer Thomas Mann were admired, but less so the politically engaged culture of the left. When Kurt Weill performed a composition in Paris based on texts by Bertolt Brecht, the audience reaction was negative, in complete contrast to Wilhelm Furtwängler who, along with his Berlin Philharmonic, enjoyed an enthusiastic reception.

In Britain and the United States anti-fascists, whether exiled or home-grown, found it difficult to impress their view of the Third Reich on others. In both countries culture was very geared to commercial interests, and this limited people's openness to political controversy or artistic experiment. Although British intellectuals were unhappy with this situation, quite a number regarded National Socialism for this very reason as 'a passionate crusade for a regeneration from within', 'a profoundly spiritual movement' or 'a display of biological forces' that could point the way forward for their own country.[44] In the United States severe criticism was levelled at the Nazi regime by, among others, the early civil rights movement, which pointed out parallels between German and American racism. Yet the regime was also greeted with considerable sympathy by right-wing and, in particular, antisemitic groups, as well as and above all with a pragmatic interest in cooperation. Although in Hollywood the Anti-Nazi League was very active, it was overshadowed by a variety of corporations that wanted to go on marketing romances starring Clark Gable or Greta Garbo, children's films with Shirley Temple, and cartoons featuring Mickey Mouse to Germany. Finally, the still significant German-speaking minority in the United States guaranteed the Third Reich a certain degree of cultural influence that reduced the impact of anti-fascist protests. Although films from Germany as a whole enjoyed limited success, they were shown in the 1930s in Chicago, in Cleveland, and on the Upper East Side of Manhattan in the original language.

German dissidents could expect even less support from foreign travellers to the Third Reich than from the people of the countries to which they had emigrated. Alongside the critical observers, there were many visitors who made positive comments about the 1936 Berlin Olympic Games, the new social policies, and even the concentration camps, which were shown to various delegations, albeit always in the best possible light. The regime's leadership took great pains to present international tourists with an attractive image of a peaceful and progressive country with a peasantry rooted in the land and a culture-loving citizenry. The advertising literature made no attempt to hide Nazi ideology and symbols, although clearly antisemitic statements were omitted for image reasons. Even travellers who did not regard the Third Reich as any kind of model still mostly regarded it as a legitimate regime and could not be persuaded to give up their positive view.

John F. Kennedy, as a young visitor to Europe, spent an evening at the Hofbräuhaus in Munich. The following day the future President of the United States had a conversation with the owner of his hotel, who indicated he was a 'Hitler fan'. Kennedy concluded from these personal impressions that as a result of 'effective propaganda' the dictator had clearly gained recognition from his own nation. After visiting the German Museum with its focus on technical achievements he noted: 'A great job and shows the German sense for detail.'[45]

Kennedy was not interested in the victims of National Socialism, and in many other ways the contrast between the dazzlingly handsome Harvard student from a wealthy background and the emaciated working-class writer Wilhelm Henze could hardly be greater. The attempt by anti-fascist humanists to make audiences inside and outside Germany identify with tortured concentration camp inmates was ultimately doomed to failure. Their backgrounds, perspectives, and interests were too different. For most observers the situation in Germany appeared less negative and clear-cut than it did for Henze and his small group of fellow dissidents. There continued to be some flexibility in the cultural sphere, with the result that people could go on being reassured that the influence of *völkisch* dogmatism was still limited. One consequence of this lack of clarity was that a decision to emigrate was not a foregone conclusion. Fritz Lang commuted between Paris and Berlin for a few months in 1933. Marlene Dietrich received a lucrative offer from Goebbels to try to induce her to return. Before she emigrated, Irmgard Keun applied to be a member of the Reich Chamber of Literature. With some justification the architect Ludwig Mies van der Rohe and the composer Paul

Hindemith were able for a while to entertain the hope of practising their versions of modernism even under the new regime. In the mid-1930s it was evident enough that culture in the Third Reich was subject to arbitrary political decisions. For the time being, though, the precise implications of that were not yet clear.

Figure 4. A float waiting to join a parade celebrating the Day of German Art in Munich in 1938. The theme was '2000 years of German Culture'.

3

TOWARDS A 'PURE' CULTURE

Munich, 8 July 1938: A group of men in pseudo-classical costume are leading a horse-drawn carriage on which the goddess Athene is standing. In the background is the Feldherrnhalle, where on 9 November 1923 the Bavarian police crushed the Hitler putsch. Since the National Socialists have been in power those putschists who were shot have been honoured every year with great pomp as 'blood witnesses of the movement'. Their names are inscribed on a memorial plaque on the east side of the building. Anyone who passes is obliged to give the Hitler salute. When Hitler's personal photographer, Heinrich Hoffmann, took this photo, however, not only the Feldherrnhalle but the whole of the centre of Munich had become a stage for the summer parade, which aimed to present the Third Reich's view of German history in a way that would appeal to the public. Its slogan was '2000 Years of German Culture'.

This spectacle had taken place for the first time the previous year, when the monumental 'House of German Art' was opened. It followed on from 'Glorious Eras in German History', a parade that in October 1933 ushered in the 'new era' and underlined Munich's status as the 'capital of the movement'. The ideas underlying this performance were diffuse. Hitler himself often referred to the Greeks and Romans, seeing the Germans as their successors: 'Immense efforts are being made in countless areas of life to elevate the nation,' he proclaimed. 'In appearance and in its sentiments the human race was never closer to the ancient world than it is today.'[1]

Although the sculpture on the float was an embodiment of this idea, at the same time the procession amounted to a Germanization of the past: 'Tall, weather-beaten, blond-haired people, who lived around 1800 BC on the North Sea and Baltic coasts', so the spectators were told, were passing in front of them. Groups of actors celebrated German achievements from the 'Gothic Age', the 'Age of the Renaissance', and the 'Age of Classicism and Romanticism'. There were floats presenting Charlemagne, the Emperor Frederick Barbarossa, and Henry the Lion as Teutonic figures. These historical clichés had been absorbed into the National Socialist view of history and appeared as staging posts on the way to the 'new age', which was depicted by horsemen in costume, by sculptures of thrusting youths and the movement's fallen 'victims', and not least by models of the Führer's future 'monumental buildings'. It was, however, present-day successes that determined the view of history presented here: A few months after the Anschluss, a group of Austrians symbolizing Carinthia, Vorarlberg, and Styria bore 'the parade's most historic and venerable treasure', the imperial insignia brought from Vienna.[2]

The cost of '2000 Years of German Culture' was immense, the result of intensive activity in studios and workshops to make floats, sculptures, replicas, and costumes. Thousands of people were recruited from various Nazi organizations and gymnastics clubs and schools to act as common people, grooms, and horse-women. The centre of Munich was closed to traffic, decorated with flags and plaster figures, and illuminated in the evening. The parade itself was framed by a programme of concerts, theatre, and opera, and by a variety of artistic festivals. As often happened if the leadership of the Third Reich was pursuing a political project, money was no object. As an experience, '2000 Years of German Culture' greatly impressed many of the spectators and participants. For one fifteen-year-old girl the parade turned into a 'terrific adventure': while on horseback she became a Valkyrie 'with an iron breastplate and a helmet with wings'. The American journalist Ernest R. Pope, on the other hand, noticed the pressure that the Party had exerted in the lead-up. Shop windows had to be dressed and every building in the city centre had to be 'decorated and illuminated': 'A week before the big event local Party stewards rang people's doorbells and palmed off candles, candleholders, and coloured lampshades at inflated prices on every household.'[3]

The parade in Munich was part of a culture that, by the end of the 1930s, increasingly focused on inner 'purity' and outward 'strength'. This culture still bore recognizably bourgeois and nationalist characteristics, new comedies starring Heinz Rühmann were still being shown in cinemas, and light music was still being played on the radio. But the Nazis were no longer content with exercising political control over a culture that, apart from being 'dejewified' and purged of left-wing and modernist influences, had hardly changed. Their aim now was to remake Germany fundamentally and eliminate any awareness of alternatives. At the same time, they intended to recover the revolutionary energy that had powered change in 1933 but had lost some of its impetus since the mid-1930s. Although the Party Rallies remained attractive, this quality was hard to communicate and thus remained limited to the city of Nuremberg and the membership of the NSDAP. What was needed was a new set of cultural assets, but finding them was proving difficult. In January 1936 Goebbels noted impatiently: 'We don't have the people, the top performers, the Nazi artists. But they must emerge in time.'[4]

Even in the following years, the number of loyal Nazi 'top performers' was limited, and this had consequences. The leadership took their cue from Hitler's own interests and from areas in which results were particularly visible, namely in large-scale public architecture. The newly planned buildings, which were only partially completed before the outbreak of war, were a synthesis of neoclassical and modernist influences. These apart, it is difficult to pinpoint any positive, long-lasting expression of Nazi culture. It went on being defined instead in negative terms, as being 'purged' of any Jewish influences and of traces of Weimar culture, and as permitting only limited foreign input. That seems to fit a set of policies that were increasingly overt in their racism and imperialism. In 1938 Austria and the Sudetenland were annexed and later that year the November pogrom against the Jews occurred. Thus what counts as 'German' had been established politically. Hitler's interventions, the increasing influence of Heinrich Himmler's SS, and the frequent acts of antisemitic violence made this only too evident. The quest for 'purity' was omnipresent in the late 1930s and increasingly determined how culture could be experienced and moulded.

The Primacy of Race: Science, Art, and Antisemitism

The married couple were hugely enjoying their stay in Italy: 'The day began at 10.00 with a visit to the Capitol. Then we went on to the forums. It was Mussolini who excavated all the splendid buildings. H's historical knowledge was amazing.' Margarete Himmler's diary entry is written in the traditional style associated with the educated middle class, and her respect for the Duce's achievements was by no means unusual even before 1933. The subsequent visit to Sicily also conformed to the patterns of middle-class tourism. She went swimming, played tennis, and paid visits with her husband to monasteries, museums, and Roman excavation sites. The only element that was out of the ordinary was the couple's intense interest in finding traces of the Hohenstaufen emperors and remains of the Teutons, just as earlier in Rome it had been the grand reception they were given by the German embassy. One reason Margarete Himmler took such pleasure in her Italian journey with her husband was that she felt worn down by her everyday life. The family commuted between his official residence in the exclusive Grunewald district of Berlin and Lindenfycht, their alpine-style home on the Tegernsee in Bavaria. The result was endless packing to fit in with her husband's wishes: 'But H. likes it.'[5] Though she valued the social contact with the wives of diplomats and other Nazi bigwigs, she found the frequent separations difficult: 'Though I enjoy being married, I have had to forgo many things in my married life. For H. is almost always away and does nothing but work.' In addition, she felt that her personal happiness was compromised by an already marginalized minority: 'This business with the Jews', she noted shortly after the November pogrom, 'when will we be rid of this riff raff and be able to enjoy life.'[6]

Margarete Himmler's diary entries throw much light on the life and career of her husband, Heinrich, for in the late 1930s he left almost no record of his personal life. The son of a Munich grammar school teacher, he had studied agricultural sciences and taken part in his twenties in political agitation by the extreme right. In the Third Reich he quickly rose to be ruler of an empire, controlling the police, the Gestapo, the Security Service, and the SS. In private the 'Reichsführer SS' led a luxurious life and had an extramarital relationship with his secretary. This did not, however, prevent him from exercising minute control over the selection, professional demeanour, and personal conduct of his subordinates. Under his leadership the concentration camp network was systematically extended, from Dachau via Buchenwald and Sachsenhausen to Neuengamme. Himmler's political programme and method of ensuring his continued rise consisted in finding more and more groups of people to define as political 'opponents'. In addition, he entertained wide-ranging cultural ambitions. As early as the mid-1930s the SS, in conjunction with Alfred Rosenberg and his fellow *völkisch* supporters, had been agitating against alleged Jewish influence and disloyal artists and academics. Now that Rosenberg's power was waning, Himmler had the chance to extend his influence over ideological matters and give definitive shape to the Nazi world view.

What were the ideas underlying this extension of his power? Himmler represented Nazism's racial views in their most extreme form, but his ideological convictions are inseparable from his strategic motive, which was to justify the expansion of the concentration camp network. Between early 1935, by which time left-wing opposition was already smashed, and 1938, when homosexuals, 'asocials', and 'career criminals' were targeted, the number of inmates in German concentration camps rose from 3000 to over 20,000. In January 1937 Himmler claimed that these prisoners were 'the dregs of criminality, of people who have taken the wrong path': 'There are people there with hydrocephalus, people who squint, people with deformities, half-Jews, a mass of racially inferior material.' The definition of 'opponents' was significantly influenced by his personal obsessions. In the past the Catholic Church had killed millions of 'fighters for justice, champions of the faith, heretics, and witches'. Its priesthood was 'for the most part a homosexual, erotic male society'. Same-sex love was a threat to the Germans' vigour and so it was important to prevent it by bringing boys and girls together 'at dancing classes, evening get-togethers, or in some other way'.[7] Himmler saw a wellspring of renewal in Teutonic identity, stretching back to early history, which he wanted to trace and recreate. Hence Nordic–Teutonic ornaments decorated the Wewelsburg in Lippe, where SS Gruppenführer were sworn in, gathered for their annual meetings, and were immortalized by death's head rings when they died. Further sites connected with the mythology of the SS lay in the vicinity of this renovated Renaissance castle: the memorial to Hermann the Cheruscan, in the place where in 9 AD he had defeated three Roman legions, and also a sandstone formation that Himmler believed had been a Teutonic religious site. Also not far away was the area that the Saxon King Henry I had come from. The fact that he had conquered Slav lands around 900 AD made him a suitable figure with whom the Nazis could identify.

The cult of the Teutons helped underpin the exclusivity and inner cohesiveness of Himmler's 'order', the SS. It was exemplified in the contemporary world by tall, blond men and reinforced by runic emblems, black leather coats, and high boots. The SS's own porcelain factory at Allach near Munich produced figurines of SS men, soldiers, and animals, as well as pseudo-Teutonic vases, bowls, and candlesticks. The journal *Das Schwarze Korps* and the publications from its own publishing house, Nordland, were vehicles for its world view. Central to it was the image of a race that had been threatened and enslaved by inferior opponents. Becoming aware of one's own ancestors was the precondition for overcoming the legacy of Christianity and mobilizing entirely new capabilities. For, as Himmler declared in 1938, if the German nation elevated the 'law of blood' to be the criterion for selection and recognized 'the eternal circulation of all being, all activity, and everything else in life on this earth', it could 'always have children' and thus become 'truly immortal as an Aryan–Nordic race'.[8] Even before the Second World War these efforts to renew the nation had turned into imperialism. A vision arose among the SS of a Greater Germanic Empire that would build on the legacy of the Hohenstaufen emperors and the Teutonic Knights in East Prussia.

Himmler disseminated his Teutonic cult with great political skill. A network of agencies, institutes, and commercial sponsors powered the search for the origins of the German race. Academics whose research was linked to SS ideology were showered with money. Although some projects, such as archival research into the early modern witch hunts, got bogged down in spite of extensive preparatory work, the German Ancestral Research Association (*Forschungsgemeinschaft Deutsches Ahnenerbe*) controlled by Himmler was highly active. In dozens of institutions work went on into philological, ethnographic, and prehistoric topics. Many employees were tracing the 'clans' of SS leaders. Others were engaged in archaeological excavations or investigating Indogermanic–Finnish cultural links. Research was even taking place into astrology, geology, and botany. The *Ahnenerbe* communicated its research findings, however dubious they might be, in its own series of publications, in popular science journals, and at numerous conferences.

Within this sprawling network, which in many respects was driven by Himmler's private interests, the boundaries between serious scholarship and pure ideology became blurred. Without the appeal exerted by *völkisch* ideas since the Weimar Republic and before this would have been impossible. But the disciplines focusing on the Teutonic past were also pursuing pragmatic interests of their own. Himmler's priorities might lead to advancement for their institutions, career opportunities for individuals, and the chance to make a broad cultural impact. The specialists in pre-history and early history, for example, gained posts in research projects, departments for the preservation of monuments, and museums, while also feeling that they had improved their academic standing. The hectic construction of autobahns, military facilities, and concentration camps made for emergency excavations that uncovered the 'Teutonic legacy' in a way that was inexpensive and interesting to the public. Excavations of the early medieval trading settlement Haithabu near Schleswig were carried out under Himmler's aegis and with more abundant resources than ever before. In western Germany an extensive research programme promised to 'solve the key problems in ethnography arising from the pre-history of the Rhineland'. In addition, permanent exhibitions were overhauled, open-air museums created, excursions organized, and documentary films made, all of which gave people an opportunity to pass on their specialist knowledge in a new way.[9]

While specialists in pre-history and early history were taking advantage of the boom in all things Teutonic, other disciplines contributed to the symbiosis of modern scholarship and racism.

Under the particular influence of the SS, the target groups for the regime's policy of marginalization and persecution were constantly being extended. This explains the emergence of a comprehensive and multi-layered image of the racial 'opponent' that the 'Aryan', who was kept under close supervision and mobilized by social policy, was facing. Medical and legal experts contributed to the realization of these goals, as well as demographers, sociologists, and ethnographers. They were in demand as specialists who were prepared not only to work in interdisciplinary teams but, in particular, to provide state institutions with the information they wanted. One example of this is town and country planning, which only became established as a discipline in the Third Reich. It combined local data on towns or rural areas with large-scale plans. Thus Nazi visions of renewal could be presented visually on maps and be translated into concrete proposals, for example to relocate industries or particular sections of the population.

Racist ideology, economic productivity, and a focus on practical applications were all factors in these developments. And there was always an emphasis on the 'purity' and efficiency of the national community. In school textbooks and popular sex education films links were made between biology and society, ensuring that the regime's ideology had a broad cultural resonance. The scientists involved enjoyed the political and social recognition that ensued, though they were not usually simple opportunists but rather racists by conviction. So, they elevated the ideology's principles to the status of premises that shaped their research projects and consequently had to be confirmed by the research results. Many had been socialized in the 1920s in the *völkisch* student movement and now regarded themselves intellectually, in practical research terms, and politically as bang up to date. To contribute to the racial renewal of German society while also advancing their own specialist and career interests was for them an attractive prospect and it could be made a reality at the point where research institutes, state and Party institutions, and SS networks intersected.

This appeal of racism for academics also explains their willingness to take part in Nazi persecution. Acting as supposed experts, clinicians recommended the sterilization of hundreds of thousands of men and women. After the outbreak of war, a number of them promoted the euthanasia programme, which claimed the lives of at least 70,000 mentally handicapped children and adults. 'Gypsy researchers' provided forensic definitions of Sinti and Roma and on this basis ultimately denied them the right to life. In so doing they were contributing to the increased radicalization of Nazi policy towards this largely unpopular minority. The withdrawal of trade licences and welfare provision for travelling tradespeople, police repression, and violent assaults by members of the Party or the SA were only the start. After Himmler had taken over control of the police in 1936, 'gypsies' were recorded on a central register and sent to one of the quickly extended or newly created concentration camps as a 'crime prevention measure'. Academics such as Robert Ritter claimed that Sinti and Roma were subject to the 'power of heredity'. They were thus, he said, impervious to any educational intervention and were also a threat to the national community, so that it was necessary to resort to 'terminating procreation in order to reduce petty criminals of this type'. As director of the Research Unit for Racial Hygiene in Berlin, Ritter was the driving force behind anthropological research into Sinti and Roma as well as behind the compulsory sterilization of 'gypsy mongrels', even if they had permanent homes and had never been in trouble with the police.[10]

In addition to the quest to find the origins of the Teutons and to define various marginal groups, racist academics devoted themselves to researching Jewishness. At first Himmler had been less interested in this, even though he and his SS were power-hungry enough to adopt this trend as well. Academic studies were important to the extent that they promised findings on the alleged destructive influence of the Jewish minority in society, business, and culture. That fitted the Nazi agenda, for they were looking for rational foundations for the emotionally driven antisemitism of their supporters. These studies also provided arguments to underpin legal definitions of 'half-Jews' and 'quarter-Jews' and justify their marginalization, which were being increasingly called for from the mid-1930s onwards. Thus antisemitic measures were given a broader and seemingly scientifically attested legitimacy. This was important to the extent that the middle classes looked askance at the use of violence, in particular against a minority that on the whole was also middle-class.

A number of different disciplines were involved in research into the Jews and Jewishness. Historians described the development of the Jewish race and its antagonism towards other races. From this perspective both the Jewish emancipation in nineteenth-century Germany and the multi-ethnicity in Eastern Europe necessarily appeared to be negative developments, because they undermined the prospect of national ethnic unity. Theologians insisted on category differences between Judaism and Christianity and on this basis supported 'pure' versions of the Bible and even the exclusion of the Old Testament. Biologists and anthropologists defined Jewishness with reference to hereditary predispositions. These, it was claimed, had affected Jews' physical and physiognomic characteristics and made any racial mixing dangerous. Finally, social scientists connected all these factors with contemporary problems such as criminality, class conflict, and migration, the conclusion always being that the Jewish race was destructive and must therefore be eliminated from German society.

The 'researchers into Jewishness' could build on developments dating from Imperial Germany and the Weimar Republic. In the Third Reich they also had the benefit of newly established chairs and institutes outside the university system. However disparate the disciplines and individuals involved were, their studies all shared one approach: they created links between supposed racial characteristics, cultural prejudices, and scenarios that posed a threat to society. Against this background, basic assumptions about Jewish genes, facial features, and behaviour patterns were inevitably and constantly reconfirmed. Thus people could be complacent in their assurance that their own antisemitism was grounded in scientific evidence. According to a detailed study of 1938, which was allegedly based on the ideal of 'the strictest objectivity', the antisemitic movements in Eastern Europe were determined by economic conflict as well as emotional and religious hostility. By contrast, the Third Reich possessed 'a consistent "world view" that sees the Jews as a racially defined group and requires a very specific approach to dealing with them'.[11]

Such judgements fulfilled Nazism's demand for ideological clarity, guaranteeing their authors professional kudos as well as public acclaim. Encouraged by Hitler, at the end of the 1930s the combination of 'research into Jewishness' and legally backed marginalization became even more systematic and destructive, with a tangible impact on those categorized as part of the oppressed minority. Thus the exclusion of 'half-Jewish' artists, which had previously been only patchy, was stepped up. In May 1938 Goebbels noted smugly what great strides had been made in 'purging the Chamber of Culture of Jews': 'The only resistance now is in the Chamber of Music, but I'll crush it.'[12] A few months later Victor Klemperer noticed that antisemitism had again increased, and that it included not only new forms of harassment but presented itself in a more academic form than before. In public lectures professors attributed 'cruelty, hatred, violent emotion, adaptability' or a 'materialistic psychology' to the Jewish minority. In addition, Klemperer was constantly faced with 'the repulsive poster for the political touring exhibition, "The Eternal Jew"'. The newspapers made 'daily reference to the need to visit this exhibition: the most odious race, the most odious bastard mixture'.[13]

A third strand in antisemitism was blended with the process of academic definition and deliberate marginalization: religious hostility to Judaism. This feature had been present in both Christian denominations for centuries. In the Third Reich it represented the lowest common denominator between Nazis and Roman Catholics, who were otherwise very suspicious of each other. There was antisemitism in the Oberammergau Passion Play, just as there was in the Cologne or Mainz carnival processions, whose floats now made fun of the Jewish minority rather than the authorities. Similar prejudices were prevalent in Protestantism too. The German Christians stepped up antisemitism and made their hostility absolute and independent of any individual's religious belief. For National Socialists, whether affiliated to a church or not, the dream of a Germany without Jews brought together both religious and racist elements. This dream needed only to be communicated to the majority of the population, which was in part accepting and in part hesitant.

In propaganda competitions SA men held up placards containing such slogans as 'What the Jew believes is irrelevant, for in his race lies his rascal character' or 'Knowing the Jew is knowing the Devil'.[14] Hatred was mixed with a religious longing for the Germans to be liberated from any kind of Jewish heritage. Although this cultural legacy had long since been marginalized, it continued to be felt by Nazis as an intolerable burden, the more so because it provided the foundation for Germany's Christian traditions. For that reason their violence was directed particularly at Jewish religious institutions. From June 1938 onwards synagogues in Berlin, Munich, and Nuremberg, among others, were demolished. During the night of 9/10 November around 1400 more synagogues were burnt down throughout the Reich, accompanied by staged events that gave spectators a direct personal experience of what was happening: Party members and SA men publicly burned Hebrew Bibles and Torah scrolls or, as in Emden, Emmerich, and Frankfurt am Main, forced Jews to do it themselves. Elsewhere children and young people trampled on these religious objects, used them as footballs, or tossed them in the nearest river or stream.

The November pogrom was the expression of an antisemitic aggression that had been building up over years. The culture of public spectacle—street marches, intimidating songs, and choreographed rioting—had already been significant components in the Nazis' rise and takeover of power. Since July 1934, however, they had been less prevalent. After the murder of Ernst Röhm and other high-ranking functionaries, the SA could no longer take independent action. By this time it had also served its purpose by smashing the Left. Even local initiatives such as book burnings had become rare as a result of the increased control exerted by the

Propaganda Ministry. Yet these shows of aggression did not disappear from the public arena, but rather found an outlet in increased attacks on the Jewish minority. Specially erected show-cases displaying slogans and articles from the *Stürmer*, the most radical Nazi newspaper, inflamed the atmosphere. Party members and SA mounted demonstrations and boycotts, smashed windows, or dragged people through the streets who were accused of sexual relations between Jews and Aryans. Such initiatives resulted from an urge on the part of convinced Nazis to demonstrate their beliefs openly and gain acceptance for them in the face of sceptics. In particular in places that offered few leisure opportunities, they exploited people's morbid curiosity and invited other Aryan inhabitants to participate by shouting out slogans or committing acts of violence themselves.

Jewish communities had already been decimated by emigration and marginalized in their local social environment by legal measures. In 1938 Nazi antisemitism intensified. The dream of a Germany without Jews was allegedly now nearing fulfilment. Consequently, attacks on Jewish religious identity and physical assaults on Jews increased markedly. One of those affected later recalled how he was forced to carry a coffin through a jeering crowd in Gelnhausen in southern Hesse because Jews were no longer permitted to use vehicles: 'Upon reaching the cemetery we said certain prayers for the dead according to ancient Jewish customs. The persons assigned this task and the few congregational members had stones thrown at them from all sides.' Another Gelnhausen resident described what happened when two members of the congregation reopened the door to the synagogue, which had been bricked up overnight: 'The work had hardly been done when hundreds of screaming people gathered in the courtyard and bombarded it by throwing stones, destroying all the windows in the synagogue and the windows of the room in the community center that was still being used by the congregation.' Whereas this small town was already 'free of Jews' by 1 November, in Emden in East Frisia an organized pogrom led to hundreds of Jews being arrested and abused. The SA forced them to bark like dogs and to fight each other like cocks, before they took their victims to a prison in Oldenburg: 'The town was a cordon of school children and other people; they spat upon us and threw stones at us.'[15]

The radicalization of antisemitism in the years just before the outbreak of war reveals once again the cultural power of racism in the Third Reich and how it resulted from a blend of academic scholarship and law with popular prejudice and naked violence. This blend was made possible by patterns of speech and images that found their way into ever more areas of life. The keyword 'cleansing' promised that negative hereditary tendencies and Jewish influences would be stripped away from the Aryan core. Before the advent of National Socialism, this would have sounded utopian, but now it seemed achievable. The visions of 'sickness' and 'degeneracy' conjured up a perpetual feeling of threat: they gave the impression of denoting both causes and symptoms and blurred the distinction between the individual body and the 'national body'. All these terms gave support to the notion that racism could explain any problem and open up ways to solve it. They were even used when it was hard to connect 'degenerate' phenomena with the persecuted minorities. In such cases bridging arguments had to be employed, as can be illustrated by the example of 'degenerate art'.

This term already existed at the beginning of the twentieth century, but it was the influence of *völkisch* campaigns and Hitler's own statements that caused modernist paintings or sculptures to be exposed to public condemnation. Although before and immediately after the seizure of power there had been some mutual understanding, by the mid-1930s the gulf between Nazism and expressionist art was established. The 1937 Munich exhibition 'Degenerate Art' was Goebbels's initiative; its aim, once again, was to cement his position of power in the ongoing competition for influence in cultural policy. Adolf Ziegler, a long-standing member of the NSDAP and president of the Reich Chamber of Visual Arts, was put in charge. The 'degenerate' aspect of the art displayed was, it was claimed, the distorted representation of faces, bodies, and landscapes, which was in direct contrast to the idealized depictions on show at the nearby 'House of German Art'. It was less the artists themselves who were blamed for this than the allegedly excessive influence of Jews in the art world, both as dealers and as critics. This influence was documented in accompanying material and denounced in slogans such as 'German peasants seen through Jewish eyes' or 'Museum bigwigs called this "German National Art"'. There was thus no contradiction in Emil Nolde, who belonged to the German minority in Denmark and had greeted the Nazi take-over of power in 1933 enthusiastically, becoming the most represented 'degenerate' artist. In addition, the exhibition's creators presented modernist pictures as degenerate by placing slogans above them such as 'Madness becomes Method' or surrounding them with photographs of the mentally handicapped.

The 'Degenerate Art' exhibition in Munich was seen by two million people. It then toured a whole series of German cities, though without achieving comparable visitor numbers. In ideological terms it was closely linked to anti-Bolshevist and antisemitic exhibitions such as 'Degenerate Music', which was first shown in Düsseldorf in 1938. While 'Degenerate Art' was very extensive, only a small proportion of the works that had been removed from numerous German museums was put in the show. Adolf Ziegler, assisted by various art dealers made arrangements for the majority to be exchanged for valuable foreign currency. Thus these hated modernist works were, for the most part, not destroyed but rather benefited the acquisitive Nazi elites and contributed to the Third Reich's rearmament programme.

The use of the term 'degeneracy' indicates yet again that, although Nazi culture was searching for some kind of original 'purity' it was defined above all negatively. Heroically proportioned bodies, monumental landscapes, and idealized peasant scenes were abundant in the 'Great German Art' exhibition running alongside 'Degenerate Art'. Ziegler himself contributed a number of female nudes. Hitler and Goebbels, however, were unhappy about the choice of pictures. In his speech at the opening of the exhibition the Führer hardly mentioned the 'true new German art'. In rather vague terms he called for art that expressed 'Aryan humanity' and looked back to the example of the Romantics. He commented at much greater length on the link between the national and cultural 'decay' that had been promoted by 'successful Jewish art dealers' and 'earlier Jewish journals'.[16] Beyond that the boundaries between 'German' and 'degenerate' art were arbitrary. A number of artists were admired in some quarters but removed from galleries in others. One artist was even accidently displayed in both exhibitions.

How the public viewing 'Degenerate Art' responded is hard to establish. Some may have been horrified, as the creators of the exhibition had intended; some may have felt some deeper fascination or even nostalgia for the cultural freedom of the Weimar Republic. Only a small minority shared Hitler's extreme antisemitism. The crucial issue was that the Germans were obliged to take up a position with regard to the omnipresent racism. That was the case even if they were not interested in it, were not involved in imposing it violently, and did not belong to any of the persecuted minorities. Reading about the marginalization of Jews in the newspaper or experiencing it in their own neighbourhood gave no pleasure to many Aryans. At the same time, such events made them conscious that in maintaining friendly relations, let alone making public gestures of solidarity, with those persecuted they were taking a risk. Anyone looking at images of the mentally handicapped, 'gypsies', or 'career criminals' was constantly reminded of his or her good fortune in being on the right side of the divide. If people had to produce a record of their ancestry, for example in order to become a civil servant, they were obliged to engage in their own genealogical researches, to which was added the fear of discovering hitherto unknown Jewish roots. To that extent being a member of the Teutonic race was on the one hand reassuring and on the other always fragile.

From a foreign perspective the radical nature of the Nazi project became abundantly clear at the latest by November 1938. At first, by no means all international observers had taken this view. After all, at this time racism existed even in the democratic United States. African Americans were systematically discriminated against, Jews excluded from many hotels, and the mentally handicapped compulsorily sterilized. World-wide, in radical right-wing movements the Third Reich's racial policies even enjoyed some approval. Thus Indian Hindu nationalists regarded the Germans as descendants of Aryan Brahmins.[17] However, international news reports about the November pogrom had the effect of making previously neutral commentators distance themselves from Nazi antisemitism. While the claim to racial superiority was shared by the Brazilian–German journalists who urged people to 'ethnic self-assertion' and warned of the day when 'the last German blood is mingled with the blood of negroes and Indians',[18] most people in Europe and the world felt it as menacing. For since the annexation of Austria and the Sudetenland the Third Reich's assertion of its power had been linked to a project of continental expansion. Because consent and loyalty had to be manufactured for this, public displays of imperial ambition played an increasingly prominent part in German cultural life.

Imperial Power on Display: Public Architecture and Propaganda for War

At the end of January 1937 Albert Speer's career reached a temporary zenith. Adolf Hitler appointed him as General Building Inspector for the Reich Capital. The son of an upper-middle-class liberal in Mannheim, Speer had become a member of the NSDAP in 1931 while he was a junior academic at the Technical University in Berlin and a self-employed architect struggling with the economic crisis. Soon he was completing his first commissions for alterations to buildings owned by the Party. His efficient methods and his style of architecture made him popular. In the wake of the seizure of power, Goebbels secured him more commissions. Speer was to remodel the eighteenth-century Leopold Palace as the headquarters of the Propaganda Ministry and also renovate Goebbels's official residence. In addition, the ambitious architect decorated the Tempelhof Field with enormous swastika flags for the demonstration on 1 May 1933. Soon he was designing buildings and light installations for the Nuremberg Party Rally ground as well as the German pavilion at the Paris world exhibition of 1937. Hitler declared him to be his favourite architect. His regular encounters with the Führer made a deep impression on Speer and gave him increased kudos. 'I mean, architecturally I was still a nobody', as he put it later. 'But all of them began to treat me, who at twenty-eight was younger than any of them, like "somebody"....' He had the prospect of a 'wonderful life, wonderful beyond any dreams'.[19]

From then on Speer's home with his wife and children was on the Obersalzberg close to Hitler's Berghof, though he was mostly in Berlin, where, as General Building Inspector, he had huge powers and his own agency and staffing. Thus he could make a start on planning the 'Reich Capital of Germania'. The aim was to give a comprehensive display of the Third Reich's power. At the same time, he had the task of giving a more open architectural shape to the crowded city with its many tenements, which aroused the hope of finally overcoming the social conflicts of Imperial Germany and the Weimar Republic. To realize the project of a Nazi metropolis, a North Station was to be built in Moabit and a South Station in the Tempelhof district. Hitler and Speer intended to link the two stations by creating a north–south axis. Various government agencies and institutions were to be built along this grand boulevard, as well as a triumphal arch. The Museum Island was to be extended and there were also plans for an 'indoor swimming pool in the Roman style and as large as the baths at the time of the Roman emperors'.[20] The point of intersection of this axis with the east–west axis also being planned was envisaged lying north of the Reichstag. There the 'Great Hall', a rough plan of which Hitler had sketched in 1925 and which would accommodate 150,000 people, would be crowned with a dome 300 metres high. The plan was to extend both axes beyond the city centre and into the suburbs.

Speer was given opportunities of this kind to shape new projects because personal ambition and ideological conviction made him willing to contribute to his Führer's public staging of his own power. Speer's style—a blend of neoclassicism and a modernist impulse toward experiment—was also particularly suited to this. Looking back, he described how he was fascinated by the idea of 'creating, with the help of drawings, money, and construction firms, historical interpretations in stone and thus being able to anticipate the regime's claim that it would remain in power for a thousand years.'[21] Hitler himself enjoyed bending over drawings and models along with Speer and other architects. While respecting the professionals' expertise, he also introduced his own ideas, which were inspired by classical models and by imperial capitals such as Vienna and Paris, even if the Führer intended to trump them all with his plans for Berlin. As far as contemporary architecture was concerned, Hitler was impressed above all by the way Mussolini had dealt with Roman remains. The Fascists' remodelling of the Italian capital appropriated and extended them. Hitler's predilections were based on the idea that 'granite and marble' gave permanence to 'humanity's great cultural documents'. 'Thus our buildings should not be designed for 1940, not even for 2000', he explained in 1937, 'but, like the cathedrals of our past, they should project into the centuries to come.'[22]

Although 'Reich Capital Germania' got no further than the planning stage, those plans nevertheless had a tangible impact.

Trees were felled and streets widened. The Victory Column was moved from the square in front of the Reichstag to the Great Star and extended by seven metres. The necessary demolition work in the Moabit and Tempelhof districts began right away—at the expense of an already oppressed minority: Speer's agency terminated rental contracts and 'Aryanized' real estate in order to be able to offer replacement homes to the non-Jewish residents who had been forced out. Those buildings that could be wholly or partially completed already gave an indication of the aesthetic style of the city renewal project as a whole. The New Reich Chancellery was built under pressure before the outbreak of war. From the 'monumental forecourt', via the entrance hall and the 'marble gallery' to the Führer's grandiose, 400-square-metre office, this building was designed to overwhelm visitors. Speer used particularly expensive materials such as marble or rosewood. He also brought in well-known sculptors who were loyal to the regime. Josef Thorak, whom Hitler had long admired and who was a friend of Speer's, contributed bronze equine sculptures. Arno Breker dedicated a figure bearing a torch to the Party and one bearing a sword to the Wehrmacht. Thanks to Speer's backing, Breker finally became the Third Reich's representative sculptor, producing endless numbers of works for public buildings and charging huge honoraria for them.

The New Reich Chancellery was the showpiece exemplifying a genuinely Nazi architectural aesthetic intended to display the power of the Third Reich and anticipate its continued rise. Its starting point had been Nazism's mass rallies with their swastika flags and gigantic speakers' platforms as well as its locations for the performance of *völkisch* mythological and historical pageants. What began with hastily cobbled together stage sets soon ended in stone structures that were supposed to last forever.

These celebrations, 'infused with the spirit of the new national community', according to Wasmuth's architectural lexicon of 1937, had been of use in numerous different ways also in 'shaping buildings, squares, and streets from a spatial point of view'. The aim was to give 'millions of national comrades an appropriate architectural setting'.[23] Such statements reveal the leadership's latent fear that the emerging national community might turn out to be too transitory or too sluggish. Therefore it must have its eyes fixed more firmly on an imperial vision, not only at the Nuremberg Party Rally arena, an event attended above all by Party members, but also in urban centres. This project soon took a concrete form. On Königsplatz in Munich two 'temples of honour' and the 'Führer building' were put up. In Weimar a 'Gau forum' was created with Party buildings and a 'National Comrades' Hall'. More German cities were to be remodelled along the same lines.

From a stylistic point of view these buildings showed no trace of the *völkisch* taste for wood and gables. Instead, the dominant influence was neoclassical and inspired by Ancient Greek and Roman buildings with their straight lines, translated into the modern age with the use of up-to-date construction materials and methods. Other stylistic features were also used, as long as they could boost the imperial display. For the construction of the New Reich Chancellery Speer borrowed from baroque palace architecture. The planned remodelling of the port of Hamburg, on the other hand, was inspired by America. Here the architect Konstanty Gutschow was given the task of designing a 'Gau tower', a venue for events, and also a suspension bridge over the Elbe similar to the Golden Gate Bridge in San Francisco, which had opened in 1937. In building it, Hitler intended to demonstrate that the Third Reich was as modern as the United States but put this modernity much more purposefully to use to extend its power. The fact that, like many others, the Hamburg project was never realized, does not detract from the importance for the culture of the Third Reich of visionary plans for new and remodelled spaces. Moreover, these plans had a significant impact not only on Berlin but on other cities too. Existing residential areas were partially demolished, and Jewish residents in particular were driven out. In order to produce the necessary construction materials concentration camp inmates had to work in quarries or brickworks, the SS thereby making itself indispensable even to the public architecture of the Third Reich. The display of imperial power was inseparable from the regime's policy of persecution—a connection both Speer and Gutschow wisely kept quiet about later.

The construction and planning of monumental buildings was part of the preparation of the Germans for war and empire. The culture of the Third Reich glorified armed conflict and concealed its price. Along with the pacifists, pictures of disfigured faces and maimed bodies, distraught widows and impoverished orphans, had disappeared from the public sphere in Germany—unless they were presented as examples of 'degenerate art'. The heroic status given to soldiers, which was already becoming prominent in the final years of the Weimar Republic, had, since 1933, finally dominated commemoration of the First World War. In paintings such as *The Last Hand Grenade* by Elk Eber, whom Hitler appointed to a professorship, combatants in steel helmets contributed to the nation's great efforts. Films such as *Shock Troop* or *Operation Michael* suggested that individual self-sacrifice and comradely solidarity had been militarily decisive even in the trenches. Mechanized war on a mass scale was thus retrospectively humanized. At the same time, historical touring exhibitions made it visible in picture–text montages and even controllable like a model railway. Tin figures and miniature artillery could be set in motion and illuminated at the press of a button. An official German World War Museum was planned as part of the remodelled city centre of Berlin. Although this project never came to fruition, the glorification of the First World War was to be seen in the nearby Zeughaus, which provided pseudo-information about the history of the armed forces. It had a special section on the First World War that presented strategy and the nuts and bolts of military action as well as celebrating both Field Marshal Hindenburg and the 'simple corporal' Hitler. It was very popular with the public and was also used for reunions of veterans and commemoration ceremonies.

In order to make the Germans more willing to go to war and to legitimize their aim of creating a German empire, the Nazis tried to connect with various strands of commemoration. For this reason, the colonies that Germany had been obliged to cede in the Treaty of Versailles were an important point of reference. Although Hitler had little genuine desire to get back these territories, which lay primarily in Africa, he did hope that by making such demands he could prompt Britain to come to some arrangement with the Third Reich regarding world politics, while those with an interest in colonialism—the nostalgics, academics, and visionaries—were won over to Nazi aims. This kept them under control, while the Nazis also welcomed in principle their concern for ways in which Germany could exert influence on the world stage. The Reich Colonial Association had a million members and was tireless in producing propaganda in support of regaining the former German territories in Africa. Colonial exhibitions and celebrations were put on: 'Real live negroes, said to be former inhabitants of German colonies, demonstrated their craft-making skills', as a Social Democrat informant reported from the Cannstadt Fair in Stuttgart.[24] And the Nazi writer of teenage and young adult literature, P. C. Ettighofer, described with satisfaction how familiar 'campfire and battle songs' could still be heard in South West Africa. 'The young people are the same as the ones at home, only a bit more suntanned, and it looks to me as if these children's blond hair is even more dazzlingly blond.' Ettighofer concluded that the Germans were 'truly the master race in Africa'.[25]

To Hitler, such colonial–racist images of Africa were less important than the way colonies in Africa had anticipated a European empire, which was his main concern. Academic justifications were particularly significant. Long before 1933 'researchers of the West' and 'researchers of the East' had not simply fought for a revision of the Treaty of Versailles but had also latched onto the imperial experiences and visions of the First World War, when parts of Western and Eastern Europe had been occupied by Germany. These scholars were usually working at universities and institutes close to the borders and regarded themselves as intellectual outposts in the battle against external enemies. During the Third Reich they were promoted more strongly than ever before. They also benefited from an atmosphere that was positive towards *völkisch* and expansionist ideas. Thus historians gave legitimacy to Germany's future domination of Europe by, for example, reminding people of settlements and other German achievements on Dutch or Polish territory.

The leading representative of Rhineland area history was Franz Petri. In 1937 he traced the artificial separation of German and Dutch 'ethnicity', linking it to the 'ultimate questions of all development towards ethnic identity', and suggesting that the two might one day be reunited. A year later Werner Conze laid claim to the Baltic territory that had been ceded to the Poles in the Treaty of Versailles. 'The orderliness and living space [*Lebensraum*] enjoyed by Pomerelia were created and established by the work of Germans and above all by the German Order [of Teutonic Knights]. The period of Polish rule changed this only to bring destruction and downfall.'[26] Because of the rapprochement that had developed in the intervening time between Germany and Poland, Conze stopped short of demanding a revision of the border. Yet, like other 'researchers of the East', this future doyen of social historians in post-war West Germany constructed *völkisch* foundations for German dominance in East Central Europe.

While various geographers and historians in this way legitimized the imperial pretensions of the Third Reich, others played a role in preparing the Germans intellectually for a future war. During the Weimar Republic they had already become 'military scholars', on the one hand extending the thematic range of their individual disciplines and on the other focusing on military issues. For them the coming war was a comprehensive project that had to involve the whole of society in a more systematic way than had been the case between 1914 and 1918. However, it was the Nazi regime that enabled these 'military scholars' to give shape to this vision at special institutes and to extend their links to the political realm. The Department of War History at Heidelberg University described its mission thus: 'if total war penetrates every area of life, then it must be combated in every area of life and so be mastered. That can only be achieved, however, if there are people in every profession who are trained in the history of war and in the politics of defence.'[27]

Chemists and medical experts became involved in this development, albeit without also becoming military scholars, by devoting special lectures and seminars to chemical weapons and their physical effects. The fact that the experiments and technological applications linked to this subject were now quite openly contributing to preparations for military conflict did not trouble the researchers involved, because they were convinced nationalists. Their closeness to the political sphere brought them increased resources and made it easier for them in general to keep themselves at the cutting edge of science and technology. In the first years of the Third Reich there were even campaigns for a 'German physics'. The Nobel laureates Philipp Lenard and Johannes Stark had identified quantum mechanics and relativity theory as the products of Jewish influences and demanded that the discipline return to an experimental methodology. Such efforts to bring renewal on the back of *völkisch* ideas now became less and less important. For in the midst of preparations for war it no longer seemed opportune to reject scientific knowledge on ideological grounds. Insofar as theoretical physics had proved its relevance to military weaponry, its place in the Third Reich was secure.

Against this background the Kaiser Wilhelm Society for the Advancement of Science used skilful lobbying tactics. Its representatives exploited their personal connections with high-ranking officials in the Party, the state, and the armed forces. They built up networks with the army weapons office, which had existed since the early post-war years but now had its own research department, and with the Reich Research Council, established in 1937. And they exploited the fact that there was significant economic interest in militarily relevant research, which would thus bring in grants—for example the chemical industry's interest in chemical weapons research. In prestige buildings in Berlin, in the laboratories of numerous institutes, and in the army's quasi-secret test site at

Gottow in Brandenburg, scientists worked with representatives of the military and people from the political and economic spheres on projects of mutual benefit. In addition to grand displays, the imperial culture of the Third Reich thus also had a technical and functional dimension.[28]

Thus, as in the case of racial policy, the fact that by the end of the 1930s it was increasingly evident that the Nazi regime was making ready for war gave academics from a variety of disciplines new scope for research. But workers too benefited from the new political priorities. In the armaments industries they not only found well-paid jobs but also saw their manual skills and technical know-how acknowledged, for example planes built at the Junkers works carried the motto 'Junkers work — quality work'.[29] It was, nevertheless, proving difficult to win the majority of the population over to the idea of an imminent conflict. People who were benefiting from the new leisure opportunities and consumer goods, or at least hoped soon to benefit from them, did not wish to see these opportunities put in jeopardy for the sake of military operations. But in 1938/39 even unpolitical Germans began to recognize the seriousness of the situation. War propaganda now began to focus on concrete objectives rather than simply on pictures of military manoeuvres or battleships. The many newly created bunkers and the fortifications that had been springing up along the Reich's borders were unmistakably being built in preparation for the coming conflict.

Those reporting to the Social Democrats' exile organization from all parts of the Reich confirmed that the population's enthusiasm for conquering distant places was limited. Even Austria and the Sudetenland were of little interest to people outside the bordering states of Bavaria and Saxony. Yet zealous young people and Nazi activists were tireless propagandists and ensured that war was constantly talked about, so that no one could escape it. Even those who had no interest, for example, in the potential for alliances in the Balkans could not avoid becoming aware of these visions: 'In factory roll calls people are called on to support this development of large space politics as well as the colonial programme.' It was reported from north-west Germany that workers were feeling a mixture of anxiety and fatalism about an impending war. Though the public image of a united national community was misleading, it was not, the informant said, without effect: 'The superficial observer sees arms shooting up into the air and concludes from the uniformity of this movement that people are similarly aligned inwardly.' The many years of air-raid exercises had, he wrote, encouraged confidence that 'in the coming war Germany would for the most part be spared the terrors of air warfare', while the constant propaganda in favour of expansion coming from the government and the Party was in the long run making some impact even on people who tended to be unsympathetic to National Socialism: 'It is hard to resist the incredible pressure from influences all coming at you from one direction.'[30]

The German annexation of Austria in March and the Sudetenland in October 1938 aroused general concern that France and Britain might intervene and that a large-scale European war could again break out. To remove such concerns the Nazi leadership staged a confirmation of the Anschluss with Austria by means of a plebiscite, which was accompanied by a huge propaganda campaign. 'Three days before polling', as one report from Baden said, 'everyone who owned a car, motorbike or the like was given posters that they had to attach to their vehicles. Even the town street sweepers in some places had a sign on their carts reading, "Give the Führer a Yes".' Although the informant also commented that the ubiquitous propaganda 'got on everyone's nerves', at the same time he conceded that it was effective simply by being so overwhelming. In addition, the Social Democratic informants confirmed that there was widespread relief that war had, after all, been avoided and agreement all round on the crucial issue: 'Hitler has yet again enormously boosted his own power.' In Karlsruhe, it was reported, the convinced supporters of the regime had now more than ever become advocates of an impending imperialist war: 'The Nazis among the population have become deluded into thinking they have the right to do anything and that the whole world is frightened of them.' For a Silesian comrade the population's loyalty to the regime was, in spite of all misgivings, now beyond question: 'If Germany were to get involved in a war today, the whole nation would march. And it would probably take a long time before people actually thought hard about the war.'[31]

Once Austria came under German control it became a positive testing ground for Nazi cultural politics. In this there was a coincidence of Hitler's personal interest, the career ambitions of politicians from the 'Old Reich' (German territory defined by its pre-1938 borders), and the radicalism of home-grown Party activists. The influence of the Catholic Church was more openly opposed than before, and the Jewish minority marginalized with increased brutality. The pogrom that was to take place in November was already being anticipated in Austria. In cultural terms, the Nazis reduced Vienna to a centre for the production of historical costume dramas set in the nineteenth century (though positive allusions to the Habsburg Empire, which they hated, were forbidden), until from 1940 onwards the Reich Governor, Baldur von Schirach, again promoted opera and put on festivals. The Führer concentrated instead on Linz, where he had grown up. The city was now to outdo Budapest as the most beautiful on the Danube. The theatre there acquired an additional stage and generous subsidies. Although the new buildings Hitler planned for Linz, and which he supervised in many cases down to the smallest detail, were for the most part never completed, their construction was linked to wide-ranging, tangible alterations.

For Linz was to be the site of a comprehensive plan embracing the expropriated Cistercian monasteries in the surrounding coun-tryside, the nearby Mauthausen concentration camp, the Hermann Göring Reich Works, workers' homes in the outer suburbs, and the completely remodelled inner city. The Nibelungen Bridge was built at its heart, and equestrian statues of the legendary figures Siegfried, Kriemhild, Gunter, and Brunhild were commissioned for it. A Gau (district) complex with a parade ground and bell tower, and in the Arcades, an avenue with a new railway station, were to put all similar venues in the Reich in the shade. A cultural centre was to contain a library, an opera house, a concert hall, and a picture gallery. Works of art owned by Jews, from Austrian monasteries, and also, after the outbreak of war, from all over occupied Europe were seized for this gigantic Führer Museum as part of the Special Linz Initiative. Hitler's views on art were nowhere more plain to see than here. They combined *völkisch* ideas with nineteenth-century traditions and admiration for classical art of monumental proportions. However diffuse this mixture may appear, it nevertheless offered him an adequate basis for an increasing number of new large-scale projects, and the fact that buildings and communities already existing there mattered in Linz even less than elsewhere.

The Anschluss with Austria was, from a cultural point of view, also part of a more general development. In the last pre-war years Nazi cultural politics took on an increasingly imperialist style. State-sponsored reading tours took *völkisch* writers to the Netherlands, to Scandinavia, and to the Balkans. German books were marketed at reduced prices abroad—which benefited the sales of academic literature in particular—without the state subsidies behind them becoming known. The Third Reich made cultural treaties with Hungary, Spain, and Japan, and, after the outbreak of war, with Bulgaria, Slovakia, and Romania as well. These treaties promoted the exchange and translation of politically approved publications, in order to squeeze out the works of German émigrés in the countries in question. In south-eastern Europe in particular they boosted Germany's cultural prestige. For in that region there were authoritarian regimes, German minorities, and economies dependent on the Third Reich. Book fairs such as the one at the university library in Sofia in spring 1937, which presented around 2000 German titles, and later ones in Belgrade, Budapest, and Bucharest ensured that German influence in the Balkans increased at the expense of the traditionally strong French presence.

Cultural relations with powers that were in the process of forming the 'Axis' were more complicated, for both Italy and Japan set store by their political and cultural independence. Among orthodox Nazis, the Japanese were regarded as racially inferior. Moreover, Japan would not agree, when requested by the Third Reich, to exclude German émigrés from its own scientific and academic spheres. In view of the geographical separation, however, the Germans could get over both of these problems. From 1937 the Japanese empire was trying to extend into China and this served as a model for Germany's own imperial pretensions. Watching the cinema newsreels, Victor Klemperer was struck by how the latest Japanese conquests were celebrated, with the addition of pictures of Chinese refugee children being fed in Shanghai: 'The propaganda operates on the principle of the chivalric romance with the Japanese as hero and as benevolent helper and bringer of peace.'[32]

On the other hand, there had long been a rivalry between the Third Reich and Mussolini's Italy in foreign and cultural policy. The Nazis celebrated their own superiority, considering Italian fascism a half-baked compromise. In concrete terms, they disapproved of the fact that it placed insufficient emphasis on race and that modernist painters, architects, and writers continued to be prominent in Italian cultural life. It also annoyed them that the fascists still allowed the Catholic Church to exercise considerable influence over the population. Moreover, the Third Reich's representatives in Italy resented the presence of a number of active and influential German émigrés. The fascists in their turn were offended by the Nazis' claim to superiority. They were also displeased in 1935 when press commentaries and a documentary film presented a positive image of the Abyssinian empire, which Italy had just attacked.

Even though their rivalry could not be put aside entirely, the two regimes had increasingly close relations at the end of the 1930s, in respect of both foreign and cultural policy. They both intervened in the Spanish Civil War, which, in spite of all official denials, represented a show of fascist cooperation. At the same time, Mussolini rejected modernist art and gave preference to a monumental architectural style. And in 1938 he issued racial laws designed to reduce the alleged Jewish influence in Italy, in the universities, where they were no longer allowed to study, and in the Fascist party, from which they were excluded. In the Third Reich cultural relations between the two countries were promoted through the politically controlled German–Italian Society, which put on lectures and created its own research institute. Fascist films and Italian opera productions found their way into German cinemas and theatres. Accompanied by loud propaganda fanfares, Italy and the German Reich concluded a culture agreement, on the basis of which the exchange of books and translations was to be promoted and the works of émigrés proscribed, even if the Italians did not carry out the latter consistently. In addition, the Nazi regime put on a book fair in Rome whose visual appeal was boosted by photos of German authors and attractively designed posters. Goebbels even managed to arrange things so that the Film Biennale in Venice was enlisted to promote the 'Culture Axis' and gave awards to a number of German films, in particular Leni Riefenstahl's *Olympia*, her monumental depiction of the Berlin Olympics, which was chosen as best foreign film.

The decision to award the prize to Riefenstahl was so grotesque that the British and American members of the jury left the meeting and the Western press expressed outrage. This reaction was only one of many rejecting the Third Reich's imperial pretensions, for in the last years before the outbreak of war no-one could fail to see that Hitler's ambitions went beyond reshaping his own country. Admittedly, there were radical right-wing tendencies in many other European countries, which to some extent had narrowed the ideological gulf between them and Germany. Foreign observers had also followed with interest the cultural showpieces and social policy initiatives in Germany. Now that changed. Countries directly bordering Germany increasingly felt under threat, both militarily and culturally, and thus were keen to distance themselves. In the spirit of 'intellectual national defence' Switzerland styled itself a 'cultural community above races and languages'. There were even efforts to create a written language out of the various Swiss German dialects as a way of putting greater distance between the Swiss and their mighty neighbour.[33] Outside Europe too, the Third Reich was perceived as posing an increasing risk, even in regions where racism was not necessarily seen as problematic, such as in the southern states of America, in spite of the particularly intensive Nazi propaganda campaigns there.[34]

In the last years before the war, however, the leadership of the Third Reich was prepared to put up with these international defensive reactions. It aimed not to convince but to overwhelm. Their own claim to power was to be demonstrated at home as well to the wider world, from Speer's New Reich Chancellery, to the Nibelungen Bridge project in Linz, to the German book fairs in Rome or Sofia. This also meant that now the antisemitic policy of marginalizing the Jews was no longer held in check (unlike during the Berlin Olympics of 1936) by any concerns about image. The risk of incurring international censure was accepted, because internal 'purity' and external 'strength' were more important than any other considerations. For minorities in Germany, which for years had been marginalized and persecuted, the consequences of this were very serious, in particular for the German Jews, who endeavoured to stand their ground in increasingly desperate circumstances.

German Jews: Between Persecution and Self-Assertion

Only a few months after his arrival in Jerusalem, Martin Buber had got used to life there.[35] As he explained in a number of letters in the spring and summer of 1938, he and his wife had to some extent managed to set up a home. They had also, as far as elderly people were able to, adapted to the hot climate. As an academic in the field of Religious Studies, Buber could give lectures in Hebrew without difficulty, though he was aiming to be able to speak more fluently soon. Answering a friend who enquired about the effects of Arab terrorism, he wrote, 'You also asked if we are "safe". The fact is that people here are not safe. There are always bombs and in every part of the city (for example, there were two yesterday evening a few minutes away from us), but, strange to say, it's possible to live easily with this uncertainty. I'm sure you can understand this.'[36] The increasingly repressive and threatening climate for Jews in Nazi Germany had consequences for Buber even after his emigration. In the November pogrom the interior of his house was destroyed, along with the 3000 books still kept there. Moreover, the authorities demanded he pay the so-called Reich refugee tax. In order to get hold of this sum, the Finance Office responsible seized both Buber's house and his bank account, as well as money he was owed by Schocken, the publisher, which was being liquidated. At the same time, Jewish acquaintances in Germany wrote to him about the existential threat they were facing.

The escalation of Nazi antisemitism in the late 1930s prompted Buber to write an influential essay proclaiming the 'end of the German–Jewish symbiosis'. In it he reflected on the fundamental experience of the Jews throughout history of not being able to rely either on legal guarantees or on close relations with the majority population. For, as the most recent developments showed once again, they could be regarded 'as dispensable, even superfluous and burdensome from one day to the next'. The German–Jewish encounter, so fruitful for so long, was no exception to this

149

general rule, but instead had obscured it. Thanks to their German background, the new arrivals in Palestine were, however, equipped with 'abilities and values' that they could now employ to build up a new community. 'The contribution of German Jews', Buber concluded, 'must be particularly valuable and welcome. They bring us something of that German nobility of soul that has become an essential part of Jewishness and which their torturers deny and suppress.'[37] Buber's ideas shaped his life in his adopted country. In addition to university teaching he devoted himself in public lectures, articles, and books to the intellectual definition and substance of Judaism, at the same time keeping an edition of Goethe's complete works to hand next to his desk.

Immediately after the Nazi revolution, Buber could not have foreseen what he would experience and come to terms with intellectually in the late 1930s. Because of his international reputation as a scholar of religion and as one who had paved the way for Zionism, he could have emigrated at that point. He would have had reason enough. His home had, after all, been searched, and one of the deans at Frankfurt University had written to him in the spring of 1933 to ask him not to do any teaching. After initial doubts, however, Buber set about strengthening solidarity among German Jews under drastically more difficult conditions. Although, like many contemporaries, he at first underestimated Hitler, he quickly grasped that for the abruptly marginalized Jewish minority the Nazi revolution posed an existential threat. 'The children experience what is happening and say nothing', he wrote in May 1933, 'but at night they groan, awake from their dreams, and stare into the darkness: the world has become an unreliable place.' Schoolfriends, understanding teachers, their whole social world rejected them or was becoming inaccessible. Even their own parents could not help them make sense of it. The only meaningful way of dealing with this new situation was 'to reveal something unshakable in the child's world'. For Buber this fundamental stability could come only from a new understanding of Judaism. This new understanding was not to be based on an alternative 'völkisch concept of humanity' but on the specific character of Judaism, its sense of communality, as well as its immediacy. 'Teach your children Jewish things, seek to create a Jewish life for them—but that does not go far enough. You have to begin with yourselves. Judaism is more than form and content. It demands to be lived out as a reality in the whole of our individual, interpersonal, and communal lives.[38]

Buber did not merely call on others to work hard to educate, but recognized the implications for his own actions. Although originally something of a remote academic, he became one of the most important activists for Jewish education. He became the director of the Frankfurt Free Jewish Teaching Centre, which was based on the principle of intensive dialogue between tutors and students. In addition, he prompted the founding of more educational institutions in the Reich, which were open to adults as well as young people. The aim was to strengthen German Jews spiritually, intellectually, and socially, both for life in Nazi Germany and for the possibility of emigrating to Palestine. Courses in sociology and the history of Judaism were to supplement Hebrew lessons and biblical exegesis.

For Buber it was important that 'this education should be carried out in an environment infused with a Jewish mind-set, Jewish life, and Jewish goals.'[39] He contributed to this himself through his own lectures and seminars, which soon became nationally famous. He wrote for a broad readership and gave public lectures, even though they were banned at various times, and did not confine himself to matters of religion and education. Buber saw the fate of the Jews as an extreme instance of more general tensions of his era. His philosophy of individual responsibility and dialogue with others represented an alternative to people's uncritical surrender of themselves to the crowd or the group. As he put it in 1936, 'I consider the individual as neither the source nor the goal of human existence. But I consider the individual as the fixed and unchanging locus for the struggle between the world's motion away from God and its motion towards God.'[40]

Martin Buber's intellectual development, personal engagement, and popular impact are a prominent example of German Jews' attempts to assert themselves after 1933. Measures designed to marginalize the Jews—and these were constantly increasing in number and severity—were from the outset also directed against their cultural presence in Germany. Yet how far these would ultimately go was unclear until 1938/39. Opinion was divided on whether life was still possible for Jews in Germany, let alone desirable. For a number of years there was hope that their status as a minority facing discrimination might stabilize. Even Zionists, who advocated emigration to Palestine for religious or nationalist reasons, were unable to tell how much time there still was to get ready for such a step. In addition, individuals' prospects of finding a willing host country and of producing the necessary funds to emigrate were at best uncertain and at worst non-existent. The fact that many Jews were bound up with the German language and with German culture made the idea of life in a foreign country seem extremely difficult. Victor Klemperer repeatedly wrote to aid organizations and personal friends abroad, but he worried about his lack of active knowledge of foreign languages and wondered, 'But what good is all this activity? For one thing the prospect of a post is very small, since the German run has been under way for a good two years and is unpopular. For another and above all: What post could I take?'[41]

The events of spring 1933 had given the German Jews a deep shock. Left-wingers and modernists among them—the luckier ones at least—had been able to flee abroad to escape the concentration camps. But from then on they were robbed of any means of expression in Germany. In the first months of the Third Reich prominent figures such as the conductors Otto Klemperer and Bruno Walter and the theatre director Max Reinhardt were driven from Germany by threats of violence. Professors and junior academics had to quit the universities, just as pastors of Jewish extraction had to leave the Protestant Church. Soon after, the Reich Chamber of Culture was created, which systematically excluded Jewish musicians, actors, and writers. Jews were also increasingly excluded from leisure activities. As a result of pressure from local Nazis they were banned from public swimming pools or sports facilities. The island of Nordeney, hitherto a favourite of theirs, now turned as antisemitic as other North Sea resorts. At the entrance to Rothenburg ob der Tauber in Franconia, a sign informed visitors with pride that local antisemitism could be traced back to the Middle Ages.

Jews could respond to this extensive exclusion from German culture only by withdrawing to those possibilities still left to them by the regime, the Party, and the majority of the population. 'Holiday in Italy!', as the Berlin doctor Hertha Nathorff wrote in August 1936 in her diary, 'How lovely it was to spend four weeks without seeing signs saying "Jews not wanted", "Jews forbidden to bathe". Just to be a free human being again!'[42] The anonymity afforded by a big city environment permitted others to escape at least to some extent from the pressure of antisemitism and to enjoy what remained of the earlier liberal atmosphere. That was particularly true of Berlin, where the number of Jews in fact rose because many of them migrated to the capital from other parts of the Reich. Here they could still watch football matches or plays or listen to jazz bands and symphony orchestras without being harassed. As a young person Marcel Reich-Ranicki, later a literary critic, spent all his money on theatre and opera tickets, and could thus share in Berlin's cultural life, which, despite all restrictions, still maintained some continuity with the Weimar Republic: 'I had a passionate interest in everything. I positively soaked it all up. The theatre performances shaped my existence and left their mark on my everyday experience.'[43]

In July 1933 the Cultural Association of German Jews (*Kulturbund deutscher Juden*) was founded in Berlin. Its aim was to find opportunities for now unemployed musicians and actors to use their talents, to demonstrate the quality of their work, and to uphold humanist values. It quickly attracted 20,000 members. Its director was Kurt Singer, a qualified doctor and former deputy director of the Städtische Oper. Although Singer found it extremely painful to be excluded from German culture, he nevertheless tried to see the new situation as an opportunity and in doing so he was even prepared to work closely with the new authorities, for which he was later often criticized on the grounds that he had been too naïve and submissive. Dozens of other local and regional cultural associations were established based on the Berlin model and in 1935 were combined into the Reich Federation of Jewish Cultural Associations (*Reichsverband jüdischer Kulturbünde*). From then on their work was ultimately subject to control by the Propaganda

Ministry, which was determined to reverse the allegedly destructive mixing of 'German' and 'Jewish' culture. From the start, control of the Reich Federation was in the hands of Hans Hinkel, an SS officer and former activist in the Combat League for German Culture. Hinkel had already held a number of different posts, first in the Prussian Ministry of the Interior, then in the Reich Chamber of Culture and in the Propaganda Ministry. He justified the continued existence of the Cultural Associations, which was a contentious issue among Nazis, by claiming that it made it easier to monitor Jewish activities. In practice this meant that non-Jewish newspapers ignored the Cultural Associations' events and access to them was restricted to members and those given special permission to attend. The Associations were increasingly forbidden to perform plays written or music composed by (non-Jewish) Germans, a process that culminated in performances of Beethoven and Goethe being banned. On the other hand, the choice of specifically Jewish material was restricted and plays making indirect reference to the contemporary experience of persecution, or which gave a strong boost to the audience's self-confidence, were not permitted.

The activities of the Cultural Associations were therefore an attempt 'to keep the connection with the German *Heimat* [homeland] and to form at the same time a connecting link with our great Jewish past and with a future that is worth living for', as the director of a theatre in the Ruhr put it at the end of 1933.[44] Yet this attempt took place under conditions that were prescribed and defined by the Nazi regime. There could be no real autonomy. It was repeatedly brought home to heads of the Cultural Associations how arbitrary the censorship regulations and their interpretation in practice were. They also had to accept that Hinkel, an NS functionary, liked to attend the theatre in Kommandantenstrasse in Berlin along with his wife, chauffeur, and assorted friends, thus demonstrating his personal power over the Jews. And yet the Cultural Associations' theatre, concert, and opera performances, which were supported by contributions from 180,000 people from across the Reich, were important as a means of self-assertion. Here Jews could perform bourgeois culture, take part in it, and thus have the experience of being a community. The choice of permitted German authors and composers might be constantly shrinking, the search for suitable Jewish plays and compositions (which audiences did not necessarily want) might be difficult, but there were still many works (among them those of Verdi, Tchaikovsky, and Shakespeare) that could make up an ambitious programme.

On this basis a network developed stretching from Berlin to comparatively small towns. Even Jews from humble backgrounds who had never previously gone to the theatre or to concerts found the events offered by the local Cultural Association appealing. 'We gave performances in Cologne, Recklinghausen, in Duisburg, and throughout the Rhineland', as the actor Ruth Anselm-Herzog later recalled. 'We always had to have private digs as we were not allowed to go into hotels. And the performances always took place in some Jewish community centre.' The Cultural Association gave the ballet dancer Hannah Kroner-Segal her only opportunity to perform at all and so laid the foundation for her later career in the United States. Though she had trained with non-Jews, unlike them she could get no engagements afterwards. She was thus all the more grateful for these opportunities: 'During this period I did not have a sense of things being frightening or oppressive. Rather I felt immensely fortunate to have a stage at my disposal.' By contrast the singer Paula Lindberg-Salomon recalled the Cultural Association events above all as bringing consolation at a time when people had been 'brought together only by hardship'. 'The time came when we couldn't go to the theatre or a museum any more. People who were able or obliged to stay had to have some kind of stimulation.'[45]

Just as in the realms of theatre and music, in the world of books and publishing increasing numbers of antisemitic measures were introduced. For a time, admittedly, this restructuring stalled for economic reasons and as a result of political conflicts over jurisdiction. Thus publishing houses were only gradually transferred to Aryan ownership. At first Jews were excluded across the board from the book trade, only to be readmitted in many individual cases. The ban on non-Jews dealing in books by Jewish writers produced a number of grey areas in practice or was not fully implemented. By 1937, however, the plan was emerging clearly of allowing only a separate publishing and bookselling sector to provide a Jewish public with Jewish content. The businesses in question were subject, as far as content was concerned, to the Propaganda Ministry. The principle of a 'clean break' between German and Jewish culture had carried the day.

In publishing too, attempts were made to confront the increasing cultural ghettoization in a creative manner. Various publishers supported a renewal of Jewish culture, the most important among them being Salman Schocken. An assimilated Jew, he had owned a department store and been a philanthropist. As an autodidact he had developed an interest in Judaism before the First World War and in particular in Hebrew poetry and Yiddish folk literature. From being a benefactor who financed Jewish anthologies and manuscript collections he finally became an independent publisher, taking advice from Martin Buber. The Nazi revolution had produced a general rise in interest in Judaism among German Jews, and this prompted Schocken to extend production of popular titles offering intellectual and moral guidance. Although he himself emigrated to Palestine in 1934, his employees who remained behind in Germany continued the work until the Schocken Press was forced to shut down. Because its profile had been exclusively Jewish from the start, the press had to adjust less to the demands of the censor. Among its publications were almanacs, reading books for schools, and also the Schocken Library, which offered cheap editions. The press also held to its aspiration to be literary and academic: writings by Buber were reprinted and also a series of other theological, philosophical, and historical works as well as literary fiction and poetry. There was an edition of Franz Kafka's works, but it was soon banned and could only be sold abroad.

The Schocken Press's book production and the Cultural Association's theatre, opera, and concert performances represented both impressive achievements and difficult balancing acts. On the one hand, they had to get past the ever-present censorship, even at the price of close contact with power-hungry Nazis of the Hinkel type. On the other hand, they had to satisfy the expectations and demands of their Jewish audiences, most of whom were suffering from their marginalization in German culture. Zionist voices attempted to counteract this feeling and to encourage people to embrace more fully their Jewish identity. They also took initiatives in the education of children and young people, who, they argued, were not trapped in the old ways of thinking and saw it as an opportunity rather than as a loss of status to work towards building a new life in Palestine later on. By contrast, the adults' background as educated members of the bourgeoisie in the final analysis appeared to weigh them down and make them unable to adjust to the idea of life in exile, even if these very adults were now keen to have almanacs from the Schocken Press.

What was the point of the deep attachment middle-class Jews felt towards German culture under the conditions created by the Third Reich? For the religious Zionist Oskar Wolfsberg the answer lay in the 'personality', whose value could be preserved in drastically altered circumstances. This 'personality' could mediate between individuality and community and unite Goethe's thought with Jewish traditions: 'The physiognomy of our age and with it the countenance of our people have changed, and old values, particularly those from the age of emancipation, cannot be brought into the contemporary environment unless they are transformed. One such value is that of the personality.'[46] Unlike Zionists such as Wolfsberg, liberal Jews long clung to the hope that they had a future in Germany—until even they were forced to think about emigration. Although the time seemed to have come for Jews to focus on their specific history and religion and to be prepared to adapt culturally to distant countries, such as South Africa, Brazil, or the United States, to which they might emigrate, liberal Jews nevertheless still clung to the central notion in bourgeois culture of 'self-cultivation [*Bildung*] as the foundation of the personality'. Self-cultivation, they believed, provided a compass to help the individual cope with crisis and should not therefore be abandoned in favour of 'professional training as a passport to quit western European culture'.[47]

At the heart of these discussions was the tension between a renewal of Judaism on the one hand and the need to preserve core elements of familiar traditions of *Bildung*, on the other. They were destined soon to be theoretical, however, for, after the pogrom of the night of 9/10 November, German Jews were not merely marginalized and reduced to poverty but under an existential threat. Being physically assaulted and sent to concentration camps made people realize that they must emigrate, whatever the cost, but at the same time the prospects of finding a country willing to take them were bleaker than ever. The orchestrated burnings of synagogues were a visible sign to all that the legitimate presence of Jewish religious practice had now come to an end in Germany. Jews were now banned by law from attending theatres, concerts, dance performances, public lectures, film shows, and exhibitions. Even Cultural Association events could now take place only in Berlin and not in the rest of the Reich. While the theatre in Kommandantenstrasse remained in operation for the time being, Singer, its director, did not return from a trip to the Netherlands. Hinkel's control over the plays performed became even stricter, while the ranks of Jewish musicians, actors, and members rapidly dwindled. Salman Schocken's publishing house had to close down because printers refused to cooperate with it. At the end of 1938 the Propaganda Ministry announced its liquidation. After difficult negotiations it was possible to rescue only the stocks in the warehouse and over 200,000 books were shipped to Palestine.

Cultured Jews were especially hard hit by their final exclusion from German cultural life. Victor Klemperer described being totally banned from using the public library as 'the absolute end' and suffered as a result of 'this empty and breathless busyness, this absolute uncertainty'. At the end of 1938 he looked back with sadness to the time when he and his wife had still been able to go on outings in the car or occasionally to the cinema: 'It was a little bit of freedom and life after all—no matter how pitiable it may have been, no matter how it may have rightly appeared to us as imprisonment.'[48] What cultural activity remained under these conditions primarily served to express people's sense of threat and loss. Klemperer had no other option but to concentrate on his memoirs from the imperial era and the First World War. Hertha Nathorff, by contrast, managed to emigrate. In the train on the way to Bremerhaven, where she was about to embark with her husband on a ship to New York, she confided to her diary: 'I'm travelling for the last time at midnight through streets I know so well. The ceremonial archways are lit up. A nation must rejoice and honour its "Führer", while we leave, having lost our home country.'[49]

The distressing experiences that followed the November pogrom indicate what narrow limits were set to German Jews' cultural self-expression by Nazi antisemitism. Within a few years they had been completely excluded from the majority culture. They found themselves reliant on a specifically Jewish culture to which, even in the cities, they were increasingly confined. Many gradually adjusted to this marginalization by meeting at events arranged by the Cultural Associations or even regarded their turn towards Judaism as an opportunity. However, even this final protected area, which was already under hidden threat, was abruptly removed in autumn 1938. German Jews were reduced to hoping they would either be able to emigrate or survive in the Reich under drastically restricted conditions. How realistic such hopes were appeared extremely doubtful even before the outbreak of war.

Figure 5. France, 1941: Soldiers standing next to a mobile 'front-line bookshop'.

4

CULTURES AT WAR

Somewhere in France, 1941: Soldiers of varying ranks and branches of the armed forces are standing next to a mobile 'front-line bookshop'. They are all holding a book, which they are leafing through and reading. They look as if they are concentrating, almost immersed in their reading and oblivious to the index finger extended from the lorry. This posed photograph conveys a particular impression: the soldiers clearly have plenty of time to choose the titles they really want. For a moment they can disengage from other soldiers and leave behind their everyday role as occupiers. We cannot tell what books they are reading because the spines and titles are not decipherable, but we can assume those books are entertaining, perhaps crime novels or travelogues. There might be a German classic or a serious contemporary writer there too. That would reflect the priorities of the front-line bookshop, which by now is selling fewer war books than at the beginning of the conflict. Instead, the majority of its books fall into the category of popular fiction and, to a lesser extent, that of literary classics.

Leafing through books and weighing up their choices, the soldiers in the photo are acting just like customers at a station bookstall in peacetime. But, against the background of war and occupation, their apparently unremarkable behaviour has a different meaning. They are now part of an expanding culture designed to preserve the unity of the front and life at home and ensure Germany's dominance over Europe. This culture is promoted by propaganda-driven advertising, the exclusion of alternatives, and what for Germans is a very favourable rate of exchange. It is unlikely that the readers in the picture were buying French books, not only because of their lack of French language skills but also as a result of cultural arrogance. Soldiers and officers were for the most part convinced of their own superiority, even if they were not ardent Nazis. After the military successes of the Third Reich, they more than ever regarded it as being up to other nations to take an interest in German literature, music, and art, rather than the other way round. According to the description by a corporal of a bookshop set up for the occupation forces in Le Mans: 'The interior has clear and simple lines but also a certain cosiness, and, by comparison with French bookshops here, this is particularly striking, especially as the bookshop not only looks after the intellectual welfare of our armed forces, but beyond that also serves as wide-ranging promotion of our literature among the French, and this is culturally important to us.'[1]

The interested readers in the picture could probably not live up to such a claim to superiority because they were consumers of popular literature. Yet that too was very typical. While propaganda tended to emphasize the high cultural level of the Germans, both at the front and back home they were provided with plenty of entertainment. Thus 'troops' welfare' offered cabaret evenings and screened films. Although it promoted attendance at classical concerts, it tried not to overtax the audience. The typical mixture consisted of short and catchy pieces, such as Mozart or excerpts from operettas. A soldier stationed in the Netherlands summed up the general preferences in a poem: 'Behind the Atlantic Wall and in the distant east, where the ordinary soldiers are everywhere manning their posts on sentry duty, faces always light up when the artistes arrive and everyday routine seems lighter: "Are there pretty ladies too?" '[2] From Berlin, Propaganda Minister Goebbels banned both bourgeois and *völkisch* attempts to educate people: 'Keeping our nation in good spirits is important for the war effort too,' he wrote in February 1942. 'That is something we failed to do in the World War and paid for it with a ghastly catastrophe. We must avoid making the same mistake at all costs.'[3]

Goebbels's comment points to a basic problem in Nazi cultural activities after 1939. They were supposed to legitimize the war and compensate for it. The aim was to strengthen the Germans' will to fight, while also satisfying their desire for entertainment. For a time there was no contradiction in this. After defeating Poland the Third Reich conquered Denmark and Norway, the Benelux countries, and France in the first half of 1940. One year later parts of Yugoslavia and Greece were occupied. During the surprise invasion of the Soviet Union in summer 1941, even the Red Army seemed unable to resist the strength of the German assault. Against this background Germany's losses could be presented as limited and the campaigns in Western and Eastern Europe as examples of *Blitzkrieg*. Soldiers and members of the occupation administrations could regard themselves as belonging to an empire and have their need for relaxation met by orchestral musicians, popular singers, or mobile bookshops.

For about two years it seemed as though this enforced dominance by German culture could be long-lasting and the 'renewal' of Europe under the auspices of the Nazis might succeed. From autumn 1941 onwards, however, it became increasingly clear that the hegemony the Third Reich had only just achieved was extremely fragile. In the Soviet Union the Wehrmacht's advance had been halted and losses were mounting, with ever more troops being transferred from Western Europe to the eastern front. The British were threatening north German cities from the air and winning victories in North Africa. And by declaring war on the United States Hitler had finally made an enemy of a country whose economic power would soon reveal itself militarily. Although in 1942 Germany still controlled continental Europe, the tone adopted in its propaganda was becoming more existential, while at the same time entertainment was supposed to distract people from the seriousness of the situation.

Between spring 1940 and spring 1942, therefore, Germany's military situation deteriorated considerably. Yet from the start the Third Reich had been waging a war of cultures involving the national comrades, whether they were reading popular novels in France or watching comedies in the cinema at home. For Germany's elevation of its own cultural status was dependent on other cultures being devalued, however much several of them were strung along for a time for tactical reasons. There was much talk of a united Europe, but ultimately this rhetoric obscured the real aim. Violence and coercion lay behind the apparently conciliatory approach taken to Dutch artists and French intellectuals, no less than in the case of the wilful destruction of Poland or Russia's cultural heritage.

Combat and Entertainment:
Media and Propaganda

The singer played by Zarah Leander in the film *The Great Love Affair* is used to success: she has already given many admirers their marching orders before falling for the most confident and humorous of them. She is indignant at his periodic absences until he reveals to her that he is a fighter pilot. His dangerous work does not put her off. They become more involved and plan to marry during his next home leave. Their guests have already arrived, when he suddenly receives the order to report back for duty. The wedding has to be postponed indefinitely, and the relationship can continue only by letter and through longings expressed to third parties. The man who up to now has had an eye for all attractive women now wants to be happily married: 'I want to know who it is I'm coming back to. That someone is waiting just for me.' Though for a long time she valued her independence, the singer too is looking forward to their life together: 'We'll have a little house somewhere, not too far from Berlin. A proper home—not moving around, the way it's been up to now.'

On another leave they meet in Rome, but again the time is too short for them to get married. The pilot is needed and returns to the front, though this time voluntarily and without having been ordered back. The singer is beside herself, but sees things differently when she realizes the connection between his leaving and the war against the Soviet Union. 'I'm so ashamed,' she writes to him; 'while you are risking your life the whole time, I can't even manage to wait for you for a few weeks or a few months.' A ban on post to the front prevents the letter from reaching the pilot, and he breaks off the relationship in order to be able fly without a weight on his mind. But when he is wounded and sent to a sanatorium in the mountains she rushes to him and the two are reconciled: 'They made me fly three operations', he exclaims with his old optimism, 'just so we could finally have three weeks together.' The couple gaze into each other's eyes, but then look up to the sky as a squadron flies overhead. He will recover, but we do not know how long their life together will last.

The relationship between the singer and the pilot develops against the background of a national community increasingly geared to conflict. On the evening they meet, they have to go down to the air-raid shelter in the cellar. The atmosphere there is relaxed, however, and even cheerful; they play a boardgame with a young boy and offer all the residents 'real coffee'. But as Germany's situation becomes more serious, their love deepens along with it. While she is pining for him, she is making some guest appearances in Paris, where she sings for Wehrmacht soldiers. At first they just look at her with melancholy faces but then join in with what she is singing: 'The world will not come to an end, even if it sometimes looks grey. One day it will be brighter, one day there will be blue skies again.' And when the pilot renounces her in order to be able to devote himself entirely to his duty at the front, she sings: 'If I did not know in my heart that you will one day say to me "I love you", life would have no meaning. But I know something more: I know that one day a miracle will happen and then a thousand dreams will come true. I know that a love that is so great and wonderful cannot fade so soon'. The greatness of their love matches the greatness of the nation, and as the war grows more challenging, so their relationship deepens. Their love is an existential matter because its fulfilment is uncertain. The singer and the pilot may manage to marry, but their relationship may be brought to an irreversible end at any time if his plane is shot down.

This is the message conveyed by the Third Reich's most commercially successful film, seen by 28 million people. It marked the high point of Zarah Leander's career.[4] The Swedish singer and actor had first found fame in Vienna in 1936. She became the

German equivalent of Greta Garbo (there had been a lengthy search for such a figure) and a replacement for Marlene Dietrich, who was now working in Hollywood. She managed to combine seemingly contradictory qualities: glamour and authenticity, sensuality and purity, independence and self-sacrifice. As a result she was able to give a human face to Nazi gender stereotypes. 'In films and on the stage I only ever played one role,' as she later wrote, 'in all kinds of costumes and changing settings: the role of Zarah Leander.' But in saying this she failed to see how well that role fitted into the culture of the Third Reich. As a result of her special position Leander was highly paid and provided with a villa in Berlin. In return she was expected 'to appear at a variety of evening events to lend them prestige'; she was seen at the annual press ball or at Göring's banquets and she was also successful in raising donations for the Nazi Winter Aid programme. In retrospect she conceded that her mentor, Goebbels, 'was not without a certain intellectual charm' and made 'intelligent comments about films'.[5] During the war Leander sang for the Wehrmacht's radio request programme and appeared as part of German Culture Week in occupied Paris. Her greatest contribution to the war, however, was her role in one of the few films set in a recognizably Nazi present. It engaged with widespread experiences and fears but they were overcome in a plot with emotional depth that expressed the sense of individual commitment to the national cause: it was the war that made this great love affair possible.

The Great Love Affair brought together two central aspects of Nazi war culture: the determination to fight and the desire for entertainment. That was evident in the way that not only the homeland but also the front was presented. At the start of the film the air war is depicted as still being something of an adventure, almost a game. The pilot climbs laughing from his plane, after surviving enemy fire and landing the plane by executing a skilful manoeuvre. Only later do the squadrons assume a more threatening aspect. It becomes clear that the fate of the individual depends only to a very limited extent on his own combination of boldness and technical expertise. The Nazi representation of war focused on this tension. It propounded an existential seriousness, for the individual was risking his life. At the same time, it suggested that the national community led by Hitler was on top of the conflict. According to its own propaganda, the Third Reich was successful in more than just military terms. It overcame dualisms that had previously defined war in the twentieth century. It neither one-sidedly promoted traditional heroism, which had shown itself to be an anachronism in the trenches of Verdun, nor did it emphasize mechanized mass warfare to the extent of making masculine virtues recede into the background. For that reason individual role models, such as the pilot in *The Great Love Affair*, were so important.

This overcoming of the tension between technology and heroism shaped the images of mobile warfare in the media far beyond the realm of popular film. This type of warfare was presented in magazines, radio programmes, and cinema newsreels as a total work of art, in which individual effort and community cohesion, human activity and technological resources, astute planning and dynamic execution complemented each other perfectly. Radio lectures by members of the Wehrmacht, stirring 'reports from the front', and compilations of the noises of battle suggested the German forces were forging unstoppably onwards. Newsreels gave a vividly sensuous impression of war and drew even the rural population, previously not particularly interested in film, into the cinema. By using mobile cameras they gave the audience the impression of being eye witnesses, determined their responses by choosing accompanying music that perfectly captured the mood, and, by incorporating Wehrmacht reports, suggested that the military information they offered was objective.

In documentaries such as *The Campaign in Poland* (1940) or *Victory in the West* (1941) individual clips from the fighting were combined in a highly effective way into a montage. Animated maps were designed to demonstrate the injustice of the Treaty of Versailles and the encirclement of Germany by the Western powers and their allies in eastern Central Europe. There were pictures emphasizing the alleged suffering of 'ethnic Germans' in Poland or demonstrating that France did not shrink from deploying Senegalese troops and thus undermined the superiority of the white race. Preparation for war was thus legitimized in retrospect and elevated to the level of an unavoidable necessity to secure the continued existence of the nation. The battles themselves were presented as a harmonious and efficient cooperation between the various branches of the armed forces: tanks rolled on unstoppably, while aircraft cleared the path for them by bombing enemy positions.

These documentaries never created an impression, however, that military effectiveness had been left to machines. All through there was emphasis on the crucial contributions of men, the much lauded pilots or paratroopers as well as the sappers with their 'death-defying commitment' to repairing damaged bridges and the simple infantrymen with their phenomenal 'ability to keep marching' on hostile terrain. The films and accompanying commentaries repeatedly homed in on small groups overcoming seemingly insuperable obstacles. 'A few German soldiers risked death to force a breach in the concrete and steel of the defensive wall.' The most towering individual achievement in the films was Hitler's. The Führer was shown not only as a strategist of genius surrounded by his loyal supporters and surveying maps. With his mobile Führer headquarters he also took part personally in mobile warfare and gave German soldiers a welcome 'surprise' by appearing unexpectedly to take a parade.

Such presentations created the image of a war that, while demanding courage, was always unquestionably going to turn out well, thus obscuring the fact that a military leadership that depended strongly on Hitler's intuitions and accepted that it would consume scarce resources rapidly would sooner or later encounter problems. But that did not detract from the cultural potency of these pictures. *Blitzkrieg* seemed to be an anticipatory defence against the threat of enemy invasion, a defence planned by an artistically inspired genius and executed by units of resolute men who were cooperating efficiently. Thus *The Campaign in Poland* aroused particular fascination in places where the newest film and military technology were genuine novelties, namely 'in rural areas, which it reached by means of mobile film units'. As the SS Security Service reported: 'The performances there, particularly the afternoon ones, were positively packed out.'[6]

This idealized image of war was presented so skilfully and reinforced so strongly through repetition that to many contemporaries it seemed beyond doubt, even if on occasions it was contradicted by the experiences of individual soldiers at the front. The principles of the Führer cult and national solidarity had been confirmed because, so the argument ran, they had saved the Germans from an existential threat and brought about undreamt-of military achievements. According to this view, the war was simultaneously unavoidable and positively capable of being determined as the Germans saw fit. 'Nazi propaganda', as a Social Democrat informant reported in February 1940 from Berlin, 'has taught the nation that this war must be won by Germany at all costs.' And two months later the news from the capital was that 'a mood of relative optimism' had developed with regard to the outcome of the war: 'The thought that Germany might lose this war never even occurs to most people.'[7]

Ultimately the successful campaigns of 1939 and 1940, as, for example, the *Völkischer Beobachter* repeatedly emphasized, were based on cultural superiority. Thanks to the Third Reich's policies the Germans had rediscovered their ethnic roots and values. Now they could confront 'the West's wheeler-dealers and profiteers' not only with an 'unbeatable military power', but also with 'a new mind-set conscious of its revolutionary power'. In France the ideals of 1789, formerly so powerful, had long since faded because, it was said, they had degenerated into a licence for egoism. 'The West has reached its end internally. "Personal gratification" has sucked the marrow out of it and made it sterile.' French rationalism had also proved inadequate, for the precisely calculated fortifications of the Maginot line had been unable to withstand the Germans' ability to take control of unexpected circumstances and engage with unconditional commitment. It was not technology that had been victorious 'but living human beings, *German fighters*'. The conquest of Poland, on the other hand, was justified on the grounds that from the outset Poland was not part of Europe. There might be European elements there, but these were the product of foreign, in particular German, influences and thus gave the impression of being 'grafted on, learnt or copied'. 'Every Gothic cathedral in this country was constructed by a German master builder; every place of worship or grand building from the Renaissance period bears the mark of German and Italian craftsmen.'[8]

The narrative of legitimate war spread by propaganda was not only accepted by national comrades but also produced by them. In their letters home and accounts of their experiences during the Polish campaign soldiers described a nation that had long been hostile to Germany, while also being inferior to it in every respect. Racial prejudices associated the Poles and, in particular, Polish Jews with decline, dirt, and malice. What the 'researchers of the East' had expressed in inflated academic language was here stated directly. While such views showed a continuity with nationalist traditions, the radicalization brought about by the Third Reich was evident. Added to this was pride in having decisively ended an existential threat to Germany and to the German minority in Poland. The two combined provided the basis for a far more aggressive project, that of Germany's mission of renewal in Europe. 'We soldiers are true to our Führer/We are creating through you a new East!' as one corporal wrote in rhyming German: 'A word from you and we are ready to storm the West at any time'.[9]

In view of Poland's military defeat, resistance there was treated as completely unjustified. Therefore, not only were 'partisans' ruthlessly pursued, but reprisals were carried out on the civilian population. Quite a number of soldiers included such operations in their own personal war narratives and in so doing contributed to the dehumanization of the Jewish population in particular. They took photos, for example, of Germans taking the residents of a building in Czestochowa (Tschenstochau) from which shots had been fired to the nearby marketplace and then executing them in a park. Another sequence of photos shows how Jews in Konskie were forced to dig a grave for dead German soldiers. When an officer ordered them to stop and the prisoners attempted to move off, a lieutenant of the reserve opened fire. Chaos then broke out and twenty-two people were shot. This escalation can be seen only indirectly in the pictures—in the shocked and tearful face of Leni Riefenstahl. The director was making a film there that was never completed. Some of its footage was, however, used in *The Campaign in Poland*.[10]

Leni Riefenstahl's horror provides an example of how being prepared to fight did not necessarily mean swallowing whole the Nazis' ideas about Jews and Slavs being 'subhuman'. When the documentary *Baptism of Fire*, about the role of the Luftwaffe in Poland, was premiered, some members of the audience appeared shocked at the terrible effects of bombing. Women even expressed pity for the victims of the destruction of Warsaw. The Nazi leaders responded to such reservations by accelerating the process of making German society more clearly racist. National comrades were to be more sharply defined as distinct from external enemies and internal 'opponents'. The Wehrmacht high command was also involved in this, its propaganda department deliberately focusing on 'sharp racial contrasts'. Although on the western front the French themselves did not provide grounds for emphasizing racial differences, 'German soldiers of particularly fine physique' could be contrasted with 'particularly brutish-looking Senegalese negroes and other coloured prisoners'.[11]

Most of all, the political leadership of the Third Reich intensified antisemitic propaganda. Pictures of impoverished and ragged Jews in Polish ghettos were published in newspapers and magazines. In 1940 three films that had been given much publicity appeared in cinemas. *The Eternal Jew* compared Jewish influence in Europe with a plague of rats and culminated in the bloody kosher butchering of a cow. It was well received only by convinced Nazis, however. *The Rothschilds* showed the rise, allegedly by deception, of the cosmopolitan banking family in nineteenth-century England. After only two months the film, which had already been seen by 8.5 million people, was withdrawn for reasons that are still unclear. *Jew Süss* was seen by over 20 million Germans. Veit Harlan's film was based on a true story from the eighteenth century, though it was given an antisemitic spin: a powerful Jew divides a morally righteous nation and manipulates its ruler.

Greed and lust for power lead Joseph Süss Oppenheimer to attempt to gain the confidence of the spendthrift and impressionable Duke of Württemberg. Because he lends the Duke considerable sums, the latter permits him to extort road tolls from the Swabians and to fleece them in other ways. Süss also provokes the increasingly tyrannical Duke to resist the Estates, who are opposing him. The conflict becomes personal when Süss asks one of his opponents for his daughter's hand in marriage. The girl's father is unwilling, however, and instead marries her to her fiancé. Thereupon Süss has the father and bridegroom arrested, while he rapes the daughter. The young woman (acted by Kristina Söderbaum, who was known as the 'Reich drowned corpse' because of the numerous suicides she played) drowns herself. Adopting the battle cry of 'The Jew must go', the people finally rise against Süss. A court condemns him to death for his shady dealings and in particular for having sexual relations with a Christian woman. Pleading for his life, he is finally hanged, a change to the source material that Goebbels personally insisted upon. Cinemagoers reacted to this emotionally charged plot in part by calling for the Jews to be expelled once and for all, but in part with sympathy for the main character, who, as played by Ferdinand Marian, exuded a certain erotic power.

Although the success and impact of antisemitic films could not be guaranteed, the propaganda in them aimed at excluding Jews was massive and unmistakable and was part of their complete marginalization. They were not permitted to share in bourgeois or consumer culture in any way. In his diary Victor Klemperer described how he had to suffer his home being searched so that 'cultural treasures' could be confiscated. When he was forced to move to a so-called 'Jews' house' almost all his books and notes were 'put in storage, probably never to be seen again'. He was also banned from using commercial lending libraries. Not only the consumption of culture was becoming a problem for Jews. Consumer goods such as clothing were almost unobtainable, which is why Klemperer took the view that, even before the introduction of the yellow star in September 1941, he was identifiable as a Jew to those around him. He had no choice but to keep on wearing 'the unfashionably tight black trousers of a suit from about 1922'. It also became apparent to him that restaurants were now equipped with signs saying 'No Jews allowed' rather than the customary 'Jews not welcome'.[12]

As the wife of a Jew, the Hamburg teacher Luise Solmitz, who had felt positive towards the Nazi revolution, was also affected by the antisemitic policies. As she experienced the British bombing of Hamburg, she took a critical view of the war as well. Now she kept the bourgeois culture she loved separate from the present, rather than, as in 1933, hoping it would be revitalized in the new era. On the anniversary of the death of the late-nineteenth-century novelist and poet Theodor Fontane she thought back to the 'free and happy era of middle-class ascendancy, when people could converse at their ease'. Popular culture had never suited her. She found it 'embarrassing and painful' to follow the war in the newsreels. The hit song 'That can't upset a sailor', which cheered up many Germans, made her 'want to vomit'. At the beginning of 1941 her view of the Third Reich was sounding negative and resigned: 'By rigidly refusing to compromise they will turn any-one with idiosyncrasies, a life of their own, personality, and indi-viduality into an enemy of the state, and will regard human beings only as tools of the state.'[13]

The complete exclusion of the Jewish minority from German society was, according to Nazi logic, vital for strengthening the national community in the critical situation created by the war. The same principle justified many additional measures aimed at international influences and supposed inner weak spots. The works of French or British dramatists and composers were hardly ever performed and Hollywood films were banned. 'Asocials' and homosexuals were persecuted even more severely than before and dragged off to the SS-run concentration camps. In addition, the Nazi leadership now gave instructions for the mass murder of the mentally sick and disabled. Whereas there had been public calls to support the sterilization programme before the war, the 'euthana-sia' programme was carried out in the strictest secrecy. Rumours about the killings nevertheless soon began to circulate and caused serious concern. In response to the population's scepticism with regard to euthanasia, work began on a feature film that, as Goebbels put it, would instruct people 'without the targets of the instruction even noticing they are being instructed'.[14]

At the centre of the plot of the planned film was a medical consultant who advocates active assisted dying, finally practises it, and must justify himself in court as a result. Various scenarios in which the doctor ends the suffering of seriously wounded or incurably sick people by ending their lives were discussed. The distinction between 'euthanasia' and death at the dying person's request was to be intentionally blurred, to allow moral issues to be raised at most on an individual level. Juridical restrictions would necessarily appear outdated. The film achieved this by portraying a pathology professor, whose wife is suffering from multiple sclerosis and has lost the will to live. Having failed in spite of intensive research to improve her prospects of a cure, he gives her a lethal substance. For this loving and compassionate action he is prosecuted. In the course of the legal proceedings the jury discuss the pros and cons of the matter, while the doctor attacks 'those who act in accordance with outmoded views and antiquated laws'. In this way the film legitimized Nazi plans to make euthanasia legal.

While filming was in progress, there was growing criticism from the Catholic Church, in particular from Clemens August von Galen, the Archbishop of Münster, about the killings in the specially equipped institutions. The final version of the film attempted to take these Christian misgivings into account, and before it reached cinemas in August 1941 under the title *I Accuse* explicit Nazi and anti-religious references were cut. The tragic life of the doctor's wife was given more emphasis and it was left open whether he was in fact acquitted or not. Because the film was classified as being 'of particular artistic merit' and therefore not liable for entertainment tax, it was shown even in remote areas. Though many people went to see it, responses were divided. In spite of all the attempts to make the message more muted, it was absolutely clear that the film was designed to justify the regime's euthanasia policy and Christians responded critically. The Bishop of Berlin,

Count Konrad von Preysing, preached a sermon against the film on the grounds that it propounded a purely materialistic view of life and was trying to boost support for the killing of human beings. Other Catholic bishops took up this line of criticism, among them Simon Konrad Langersdorfer in Passau. Langersdorfer even issued a pastoral message in which he argued that it was not only the Christian prohibition of killing that was being undermined but also 'one of the most fundamental moral laws of human coexistence'. And together with the priests in his diocese he mounted a campaign targeting euthanasia policy in general. Langersdorfer's intervention had such widespread repercussions that I Accuse disappeared from cinema programmes in that region of the country.[15]

This controversy brought a long-standing conflict to a head. Nazi cultural policy had shown itself to have anti-Catholic tendencies even before the war, but the Church and its milieu could count on some protection through the Reich Concordat that had been agreed with the Vatican in 1933. In addition, many Catholics took a positive view of the forcible exclusion of Communists in the wake of the Nazi take-over of power. The Catholic milieu remained numerically strong and active enough to be mobilized to resist any overstepping of the boundaries. Although ethnic nationalist and pagan activists in the NSDAP repeatedly had anti-clerical plays performed in order to demonstrate their power over Catholic believers and to usher in the new age, they were met with vehement protests, which in some cases led to the productions being removed from the programme. In spite of this defence of their milieu, more serious measures were soon on the horizon. The Nazis increasingly restricted Church influence over schools and the press. Their suspicion of popular Catholic culture increased as the outbreak of war drew closer. They moved against amateur theatre groups by confining their performances to religious venues and insisting they were led by someone loyal to the regime, thus excluding priests. Local Party officials banned plays on occasion without any legal basis. Even the famous Oberammergau Passion Play did not take place from 1940 onwards, in spite of its antisemitic content. As, in addition, Catholic kindergartens were being closed, journals banned, and monasteries dissolved, the more critical bishops such as Galen, Preysing, and Langersdorfer regarded their Church as under threat from the regime. This also prompted them to speak out publicly against the justification of euthanasia in *I Accuse*.

Protests of this kind, however, remained the exception. Nor did they jeopardize Catholics' commitment to the war, which from the summer of 1941 onwards was also being fought against 'godless Bolshevism'. And yet they indicate that the total gearing of German culture to Nazi values did not occur without a hitch. There was a strong minority of predominantly young people who were completely convinced of these values. Other Germans took a basically positive view of them because of their nationalist attitudes. There were sections of the population, however, that most definitely had reservations, with the result that consent for the war overall was dependent on success and thus had a latent instability. For many the fulfilment of pre-war promises of consumer opportunities were more important than territorial gains. Hence cinemagoers, for example, were annoyed by advertising for substitute products. On the one hand, *Das Schwarze Korps* boasted that Germans needed 'no stimulants, no spirits to give them courage, and no tranquillizers to combat frayed nerves'. On the other hand, the SS grew heated about the fact that young women looked for husbands 'in secure positions' or that 'bourgeois sightseers' were more concerned about their summer holidays than about the war and even then were constantly whingeing.[16]

This biting criticism was designed to legitimize the SS's elitism and claim to power by contrast with the more pragmatic attitude of the Propaganda Ministry in particular, whose aim was to keep the population's spirits up. Germans still demanded relaxation and recuperation, especially because other consumer goods were in short supply. Even during the war they attended football matches. They went on holiday to the Black Forest or Garmisch-Partenkirchen, even though dogmatic Nazis considered this super-fluous and the regime restricted holiday advertising to regional destinations in order to limit civilian rail traffic. After an initial dip caused by the outbreak of war, nightlife began to boom again, as the American Vice-Consul in Hamburg reported in November 1939: 'Today customers again stand on the tables and sing in the taverns along the Reeperbahn, the cabarets where the German version of American swing is played are packed with civilians and soldiers, and the operas and theatres are well-patronized.'[17] Three months later a Social Democrat informant wrote from Berlin: 'All places of entertainment are doing excellent business, supported by the authorities and in spite of the strict black-out. That's in fact what drives people into the bars. Crowded together there with other people in the same boat they can cope better with their everyday problems.'[18]

For pragmatic Nazis such as Goebbels, culture was to strengthen people's resolve in wartime precisely by satisfying their need for entertainment. For that reason the emphasis quickly shifted again from saturation propaganda to more popular formats. Interest in the newsreels was waning and so, from 1941 onwards, the cinemas again showed more musical spectaculars, crime films, and melodramas. After a drop in attendance at the beginning of the war, the theatre world could expand again thanks to special shows for soldiers or munitions workers. Farces, comedies, and operettas were put on. While classical plays were still performed in order to satisfy middle-class audiences and to continue to legitimize the Nazi leadership as promoters of high culture, here too their entertainment value became more important and there was a preference for Kleist's or Shakespeare's comedies over their serious dramas. The radio stations made efforts to create a varied and attractive programme. A Reich Light Music Orchestra was even created, which integrated elements of jazz into the trivial and lively pieces it played.

Every Sunday afternoon there was a programme of musical requests, a format that had existed since 1936 as the 'Radio Requests for Winter Aid'. Now its function was to maintain the link between the front and those back home. Supervised by Goebbels, who took care of every detail, individual preferences were put together to form a larger whole. Whether these preferences were high-brow or popular, within the request programme no distinction was made between them: hits and waltzes were played just as much as choral music, excerpts from chamber music, and movements from Mozart serenades. Soldiers could send in requests to the radio station and at the same time represent a national community in miniature: 'Now radio station, listen carefully: "Room 9" in the field hospital. That's where we met. Five mates from the front, with limbs in plaster. Well-known throughout the hospital. We're known as the "plaster squadron".' There were even requests for specific sounds, for example from members of the Africa Corps ('It's very hot in the desert here, so let's hear the fizzing of a bottle of beer.') It fitted the generally humorous tone of the requests that sketches by well-known performers were interspersed between the pieces of music. The presenters announced not only the pieces played but also the names of new-born babies, including those whose fathers were serving and had been killed.[19]

The fact that the request programme was broadcast for the last time at the end of May 1941 indicates the growing difficulty in reconciling the determination to fight with the wish for entertainment. With the intensifying British bombing raids and the invasion of the Soviet Union, that was the year in which the war became an existential matter. It was hard to produce a counterbalance to this realization or to give it a positive spin with success stories. Combining ethically motivated willingness to die and romantic devotion in the manner of *The Great Love Affair* was becoming increasingly challenging. At the same time, however, Germany's dominance over vast stretches of Europe extended the Third Reich's influence and opened up new areas of activity. In both 'the West' and 'the East', the Germans were now in a position to gather experiences of empire.

Experiences of Empire: Occupation and Looting Art

Ernst Jünger enjoyed the years he spent in Paris. As a captain in the army, he saw the sights and visited the museums of the French capital, strolled through its narrow streets, and observed life in its squares. Beyond that, Jünger had a genuine interest in French culture. He bought second-hand books, sat and read in the Bibliothèque Nationale, and went to the theatre. He benefited from his good knowledge of the language when talking to

French intellectuals. As a literary man and commentator on the contemporary scene, this world city inspired him. A prominent representative of 'soldierly nationalism', he had contributed to the intellectual weakening of the Weimar Republic, but after 1933 had increasingly distanced himself from the Third Reich. For him Paris was 'still the capital, symbol, and bulwark of the patrimonial high culture and unifying ideas, in which nations now are singularly lacking'. Jünger regarded culture as something specifically German or French but at the same time as transcending national differences, and as a result positioned himself as something of an outsider in the Third Reich. 'In such large graveyards', he pondered after visiting Père Lachaise cemetery, 'the unity of culture becomes apparent in the power it exerts, which remains beyond any conflict'.[20]

In addition to his intellectual curiosity and his European perspective, Jünger enjoyed the sensuous side of French culture. He ate in expensive restaurants or hotels and occasionally went to a club: 'There was a revue with naked women appearing before rows of officers and officials from the army of occupation and a volley of popping champagne corks. They are well built except for their feet, which have been ruined by their footwear.' It would have been possible to enjoy such evenings as a tourist in Paris before the war, but now they were part of an experience of empire. As a result of the occupation many German men were in the French capital, where they had plenty of leisure time and, because of an exchange rate kept artificially favourable, plenty of money at their disposal. In spite of his decidedly distanced and cosmopolitan perspective this was the case with Jünger too. The sexually frank performance in the club was in his view 'geared to the mechanics of desire' and confirmed at the same time a national stereotype:

The revue, in his opinion, 'clearly showed the coquettishness of the Gallic race'. [21]

In his role as an observer Jünger could take advantage of the privileges accorded to occupation officers, which extended even to that of strolling: 'In the evening a wander through the empty streets of the city. Because of assassination attempts the population are not allowed to leave their homes from the early evening.' As a press censor who maintained lively contact with French artists and intellectuals, he helped to shape German cultural policy in France. The fact that he was also perceived as the representative of a hostile army of occupation seems something Jünger was hardly conscious of. When he bought a notebook in a stationer's shop he was taken aback to see that the shop assistant looked at him 'with surprising hatred... with the kind of ecstasy with which the scorpion perhaps drives its sting into its prey'. Although he wrote with sympathy about the marginalization and deportation of the French Jews, in his reflections he engaged less with Nazi policy than with modernity as a whole: 'I often see human beings now as suffering souls who are forced through the teeth and cogs of a machine that shatters them rib by rib, limb by limb, even though they cannot be destroyed as human beings and perhaps even gain something from it.'[22]

Jünger not only formulated general observations but was also a precise chronicler of his time in Paris. On the orders of the commanding officer, he documented how members of the Communist resistance took action against the German occupiers. They shot soldiers and officers on the way home, often from the theatre or cinema. They used explosives to destroy a German bookshop, a Wehrmacht officers' mess, and a nightclub. As a reprisal the occupiers excluded the native population from evening leisure activities and executed hostages.[23] The tone of his memorandum was sober but he supplemented it with the farewell letters of the hostages, which he translated into German, even if he did so first and foremost to reassure himself. 'Reading them gave me strength', he wrote in his diary: 'At the moment they are told they will die, human beings seem to free themselves from the blind dominance of the will and to understand that the deepest of all connections is love.'[24]

Jünger's experiences, his observations, and his reflections indicate the imperial character of Third Reich culture in wartime. Even before 1939 this culture stretched beyond Reich territory through international propaganda as well as through Germany's annexations of Austria and the Sudetenland. After the occupation of extensive parts of Europe it could be found as readily in Paris, Amsterdam, or Krakow as in Munich or Berlin. The Nazi leadership was aiming to demonstrate its own cultural superiority to an international public. This coincided with many Germans' longing for new experiences. Thus the occupation of the French capital also involved showcasing German cultural dominance and encompassed weighty symbolic gestures as well as apparently banal ones. German troops marched through the Arc de Triomphe, paused beneath the Eiffel Tower, chatted up local women outside the Sacré Coeur, or poked about in the bouquinistes' displays along the Seine. Theatre and musical life in the capital quickly recovered from the war and the French defeat, but the Paris opera was now draped in swastika flags and performed more works by Beethoven, Mozart, and Wagner than before. The Berlin Philharmonic, which gave several concerts only three weeks after the Germans had marched in, was followed by orchestras from Cologne, Dresden, and Munich, which played in the Palais de

Chaillot or the Théâtre des Champs-Elysées. Herbert von Karajan conducted the Aachener Stadttheater ensemble and the orchestra of the Berliner Staatsoper. Busch's Circus performed, as did many military bands, the Regensburger Domchor, and, in the hope of finding an audience that could understand German, the Schillertheater from Berlin, which brought a production of Schiller's *Intrigue and Love*.[25]

German cultural policy in occupied Western Europe was not confined to symbolic appropriations and attractive offerings. It also aimed if not to cripple then at least to control indigenous cultural activities in line with Nazi principles. In Paris this control was exercised on Hitler's instructions by Joachim von Ribbentrop's Foreign Ministry. The ambassador Otto Betz pursued a comparatively pragmatic policy, even though it brought him repeatedly into conflict with the propaganda department of the Wehrmacht and the SS. Cultural life in Paris was in many ways left untouched, at least while it seemed not to pose a political threat. The occupiers at first pursued a policy of restraint with regard to films, which allowed French productions to flourish. Only *Jew Süss* out of the many German propaganda films was shown in many cinemas—and received an enthusiastic reception from the native population. Theatre in Paris also positively flourished under German occupation, with premieres of plays by Jean-Paul Sartre and other important writers. This restraint on the part of the Germans in cultural matters was aimed at reassuring the population and convincing them of the advantages of occupation.

Pressure tended to be exerted covertly. The German occupying powers threatened newspapers with having their vital access to paper withdrawn if they published critical articles. On their orders the French police searched editorial offices and looked for

CULTURES AT WAR

proscribed publications in bookshops and publishing houses. Many school textbooks were banned or compulsorily adapted, and university academics known for their political views were closely watched, as were Catholic youth organizations. The occupying authorities aimed above all to ensure antisemitism permeated cultural life. The mere suspicion of being Jewish could put an actor's or director's career at risk. The managers of theatres and cinemas had to make a written declaration that they would not employ any Jewish staff. If they gave any false information they risked being denounced by rivals. This process of 'Aryanization' opened up an opportunity for Germans to acquire cinemas cheaply. As, in addition, older French films were censored if they featured Jewish actors or technical staff, German productions gradually dominated the French film market. For all the apparent moderation, the Third Reich's cultural hegemony was still the overriding aim in occupied Paris.

In the Netherlands the approach was at first similarly restrained. From the Nazis' perspective the population was 'racially related' to the German one and should be encouraged to collaborate. Although the press was censored, the aim was above all to work with docile editorial teams on newspapers and radio stations. People remained unconvinced, however, being shocked by the Germans' behaviour and influenced by the counter-propaganda put out from London by the Dutch government in exile. In addition, Party and SS representatives within the occupation administration pushed for a hard line to be taken, to the point of Germanizing the country. Soon repression gained the upper hand over appeals for cooperation. Germany's cultural assimilation of the Netherlands was to be achieved by force. A Dutch Chamber of Culture with various subsections on the German model was established, and writers, painters, and musicians were forced to join. Jews, being excluded, followed the pattern of the Cultural Association, familiar from pre-war Germany. Its former Berlin general secretary, Walter Levie, who had earlier emigrated to Amsterdam, took the initiative. At the Joodse Schouwburg, as the theatre was renamed, works by Gustav Mahler or Felix Mendelssohn were now performed under the supervision of the occupiers, though musicians and concertgoers were obliged to wear the yellow star, until the Cultural Association was finally dissolved in July 1942.

The Germans who had the task of implementing cultural policy in the occupied countries of Western Europe were for the most part uncritical, to the point of being positive, in their attitude to the Nazi project. The same was true of women who were sent by the Wehrmacht to France or the Netherlands as telephonists or telex operators. These quasi-military activities were presented euphemistically as genuinely feminine 'assistance'. Paris in particular was enormously attractive to Wehrmacht auxiliaries of this kind, who often came from the German provinces. One of them remembered getting to know Paris: 'Yes, you could walk about in Paris without being frightened or anything'. There was also the pleasure of living a life of luxury. A Wehrmacht auxiliary later told of her life in an Amsterdam villa that had 'previously belonged to a Jew': 'and on the walls all silk wallpaper and the bathrooms — this was the first floor, because I lived on the first floor — they were marble.'[26]

Even those whose values were different and who viewed the regime more critically could find things to enjoy about their new experiences in a foreign country. As a soldier in the Wehrmacht, Heinrich Böll found his periods in France and Belgium provided him with welcome changes from the, to him, deadening routine of barracks life. The future novelist enjoyed seeing 'the fine city of Antwerp in the afternoon sunshine' and having the prospect of viewing 'the Breughels and the narrow old streets'. Even he was influenced by Nazi prejudices, however: his perception of France was shaped both by cultural fascination and by preconceived ideas and defensiveness. In Le Mans Böll wandered through empty streets, past small, old houses, until he caught sight of the cathedral, 'which has an elevated position and looks so strange with its Moorish elements, but it's splendid and complex and it's hard to believe that it was built by this nation, these repulsive men who loll about like women.' As a Catholic believer he was easily influenced by stereotypes of French immorality and saw 'nowhere even a trace of chastity, which is the mother of all strength'. Then again, after taking a walk through a village he expressed respect for what he assumed were national characteristics: 'Oh, I somehow really love these hedges. They give everything a kind of cosiness, a special quality. These French are truly individualists.' Böll envied the men's ability to be 'politically completely unfree' and yet to behave like 'young gods' and for that very reason he was confirmed in his belief that the Germans could 'endure and sacrifice so much in a tough and relentlessly undemonstrative way'.[27]

In this way, the occupation of France, Belgium, and the Netherlands offered the Germans ample opportunity for collective ego-boosting. Countries with an important cultural heritage were now subject to German control. Although their contemporary culture was certainly interesting, they appeared to have nothing capable of resisting German dynamism. To that extent other cultures were not regarded by the occupiers as a challenge but rather perceived as a range of consumer options, in particular in Paris, where good restaurants, sunny pavement cafés, sexually liberal revues, and cheap records beckoned. Only German culture seemed capable not only of maintaining its own traditions but of revitalizing and renewing them, and that was why it could successfully assert its claim to lead Europe. The interaction of the German experience of empire and a sense of cultural superiority became even more evident in Eastern Europe. There, next to nothing was found worthy of acknowledgement as indigenous heritage. The only attraction was the prospect of continuing the historic German influence in the region and being able to build something up from scratch.

Standing bored outside a barracks in Wesseling in the Rhineland in June 1941, Böll was thinking of settlements on the North American plains. Responding to news from the eastern front he thought it would be 'marvellous to press forward into the infinite vastness of Russia'. 'Soldiering' and 'settling, this power to cast off all culture and civilization and begin absolutely from scratch' seemed to him to be similar in essence and equally attractive.[28] Unlike Böll, Ernst Jünger was, in fact, transferred from France to Russia and could find nothing positive about the change. On his walks through the city of Rostov 'the images of disenchantment kept coming back'. Although he paid tribute to what he took to be the naïve lack of affectation in the population, he felt the absence of the 'higher levels of human life', in particular 'the generous, benevolent power of the arts'.[29] Another German soldier expressed himself much more negatively: 'No trace of culture, no trace of paradise', he wrote shortly after the German invasion; 'the primitiveness, the dirt, the type of people show us that we shall have a huge task in colonizing this territory.' And a year later a Wehrmacht captain considered any plan to colonize hopeless. The problem with the Russians was 'not the wretched hovels and roads' but the fact that they were 'on such a low level intellectually. And no amount of education can change that. It's simply a fact.'[30]

Such perceptions and assumptions were as much the consequence of Nazi policy as the condition for it. The Third Reich deliberately destroyed the cultural foundations of the occupied regions of Eastern Europe in order to ensure its own lasting claim to power and to legitimize that claim. People who were allowed to practise their traditional religion in only a restricted way, who were shown poor-quality films, and who would, in future, receive only minimal education would, it was calculated, lack the resources to put up any resistance to the occupiers. The more dilapidated the buildings, the more impoverished and uneducated the native population appeared to be, the more impressive German culture must seem by contrast. Even the most routine theatre or music performance confirmed this sense of superiority. As Arthur Greiser put it in 1942, 'The Pole has a quite different attitude to everyday things and to culture in Europe.' The Gauleiter of the Warthegau (the territories in western Poland that had been incorporated into the Reich) sketched a picture of a population that was as pious as it was gluttonous. Precisely because of their lack of culture, he claimed, the majority felt 'completely at ease' under German domination. Stirrings of renewal came only from Germans from the Reich or from the Baltic region, who were coming in droves to the Warthegau in response to the regime's policy of annexation and Germanization. In Posen (Poznań), according to Greiser, 'cultural life could not have developed the breadth or the high level it has in fact attained without migration from the Baltic area. The fine Gau theatres the Führer has had built would not have anything to perform, the symphony concerts—one a week—would not be possible if settlers were not there who support culture and are themselves on a high cultural level.'[31]

Since putting on such frequent events required a large number of personnel and performances by Germans were regarded as being of higher quality, there was high demand for artists from the Reich. Concerts and cabaret evenings for the Wehrmacht as part of the 'troops' support programme' provided well-paid work for tens of thousands of members of the Reich Chamber of Culture. It also exempted them from military service. From Paris, via Prague, to Krakow there was an abundance of festivals and guest performances, new German-speaking theatre companies were founded and exhibitions opened. Even artists who in other ways found it difficult to negotiate the maze of Nazi cultural organizations were given a boost. Hans Pfitzner, for example, had never been short of right-wing radical ideas, but he had not become the leading composer of the Third Reich—not least as a result of his notoriously difficult personality, which had already aroused Hitler's displeasure during the Weimar Republic. In the Warthegau, however, he enjoyed the support of Greiser, whose wife was a pianist and performed a concerto by Pfitzner. In addition, he was made director of the 'Posen Music Week', giving him the opportunity to show off his talents and be awarded a lucrative prize. He even had a street named after him. Hans Frank was also a music lover and admired the ambitious composer. As head of the Generalgouvernement, the occupied parts of Poland, Frank was keen for the Krakow Symphony Orchestra, which he had founded, to play Pfitzner's works and even for Pfitzner to conduct them. For his journey to Krakow, Frank gave Pfitzner the choice between his official limousine and his private railway carriage.

As the examples of Greiser, Frank, and Pfitzner show, cultural politics in the annexed or occupied territories in Eastern Europe were as much a means for individuals to create a public image as an expression of Nazi propaganda. Arthur Greiser's plans for a Gau forum in Posen included an assembly hall with standing room for no fewer than 40,000 and an art gallery along with imposing administrative buildings. In consultation with Hitler, and by using forced labour, the Gauleiter renovated the palace built for Kaiser Wilhelm II in 1910. The result was a residence he could make available to his Führer that at the same time provided luxurious offices and private accommodation for himself. Greiser also founded the Reich University of Posen, which as well as researching the 'German East' boosted his own prestige. In addition, the Reichsgautheater, as the reopened city theatre was called, staged drama, opera, and operettas, while touring theatre companies, newly established cinemas, and lorries with film projectors carried German culture to even the smallest communities. The Kaiser Friedrich Museum celebrated the ethnic art and identity of the region. In the first year of its existence it was visited by 50,000 Germans; the Polish population, on the other hand, was not allowed in.[32]

The German administration of the Warthegau aimed to banish Polish influence of any kind from the regional culture. It removed street signs and religious statues from public spaces. It also confiscated numerous works of art and more than a million books in Polish, which were either put into storage or sold.

Greiser himself secured a Flemish painting for his offices that had previously belonged to an aristocratic Polish family, as well as valuable furniture from the Posen Palace.[33] Like him, many high-ranking Nazis were involved in stealing art in occupied Europe and, as they did before the war, they were doing so to compete for status, power, and Hitler's favour. Thus Hermann Göring had 31 drawings by Albrecht Dürer removed from a museum in Lemberg (present-day Lviv in the Ukraine) in order to present them in homage to his Führer. In Poland Göring, Himmler, and Frank secured control over culturally valuable objects at the very start of the occupation. To do so they had the resources of their own organizations and agents at their disposal. Numerous art historians and pre-historians had official responsibility for preserving and restoring monuments, but in fact they spent all their time systematically stealing art from churches, art galleries, and private collections.

Although the official guideline was only to release works of lesser quality to individuals to enable them to demonstrate their rank and importance, the Nazi elite's obsession with prestige meant that that rule was soon discarded. Göring frequently visited the Jeu de Paume in Paris, where artworks confiscated from Jewish owners were stored. On these visits he chose some 600 works for his own collection without ever paying for them. Frank adorned his four residences in the Generalgouvernment with confiscated paintings, among them Rembrandts and Leonardos. The boundaries between theft and acquisition were fluid and there was no distinction between public and private funds. Owners could be pressurized and confiscated collections were put up for sale. Thus Goebbels and Speer made careful inspections in Paris, both in person and via agents, and ordered crateloads of artworks. Hitler instructed that large numbers of paintings and sculptures should be acquired for his Führer Museum in Linz, above all from France, the Netherlands, and Italy. At the same time, he took direct advantage of German territorial conquests to have tapestries in Prague Castle seized, as well as works by Raphael, Rembrandt, and Leonardo on show in Poland.

In occupied France a conflict flared up over who had the authority to register art of German provenance, to seize it, and to bring it back to the Reich. At first Goebbels was responsible for 'reclaiming cultural artefacts from enemy states'. His rivals were not idle, however. Göring maintained his own network of art agents and was now an enthusiastic admirer of French eighteenth-century art. Heinrich Himmler's Ancestral Heritage (*Ahnenerbe*) had its eye on pre-historic monuments and the medieval Bayeux Tapestry, depicting the conquest of England by the Normans. The foreign minister Joachim von Ribbentrop gave the 'Künsberg Special Unit' the task of seizing government files and artworks from museums and private homes. Goebbels, who only rarely got to Paris and received no support in this matter from Hitler, lost ground.

The person who profited most from the occupation of France was Alfred Rosenberg, the *völkisch* ideologue. He and his Combat League for German Culture had suffered a significant loss of influence at the end of the 1930s, but he now enjoyed new and extensive powers as the organizer of the theft of cultural artefacts. His 'task force' began by confiscating books, manuscripts, and musical instruments, even before Hitler gave him authority to secure 'ownerless' artworks (in other words artworks previously owned by Jews) for the Reich. As he noted in his diary, Rosenberg could report proudly to the Führer that among the items discovered in the Rothschild family collection were a 'trapdoor and concealed cellar with 63 crates of manuscripts, books and the like, including a box containing porcelain buttons belonging to Frederick the Great'.[34] He benefited from an alliance with Göring, who had the task of exploiting the occupied territories economically and the powers that went with it. Thus Rosenberg's task force could transport the artefacts they had stolen by train, have them guarded, and in many cases remove them from their Jewish owners' safe deposit boxes. This assistance naturally called for some kind of reciprocation. The Reich Marshal used this means to gain unlimited personal access to paintings that appealed to his taste or could be bartered.

Rosenberg was also active on the eastern front, authorized by a Führer order and in spite of the competing activities of Ancestral Heritage and the Foreign Ministry. Even before the invasion of the Soviet Union he, a Baltic German, had succeeded in impressing on Hitler his views about 'the racial and historical situation in the Baltic provinces, the Ukraine's struggle with Moscow, and the necessary economic link with the Caucasus'. Equipped with the authority of a 'Reich Minister for the Occupied Eastern Territories' he could make use of the German civil administration and communicate to its members 'that we have a certain amount of elbow room here, that we are in a space that positively cries out for German rule'.[35] Acting on this motto, his task force gained possession of valuable paintings, archaeological objects, religious icons, and historical documents. Tens of thousands of objects were carried off in freight cars, among them the dismantled amber room, which was a gift from the Prussian King Friedrich Wilhelm I to Tsar Peter the Great. Since the boundaries between cultural theft and the war of annihilation were fluid, confiscation and destruction went hand in hand. In some instances this was done intentionally to rob Russians, Balts, and Jews of their cultural foundations; in others it happened in rather a random fashion— as when a Wehrmacht unit turned the Tchaikovsky museum in Klin into a garage and heated it with priceless scores.

This behaviour was imperial in character because only the German occupiers had the right to decide what would happen to the cultural artefacts gained by conquest. Whether they destroyed, suppressed, stole, or partially consumed the indigenous culture, their basic assumption was always that their own culture was of higher value. The power relationship underlying this quickly became so taken for granted that even soldiers like Heinrich Böll and Ernst Jünger, who were sceptical towards Nazism, no longer perceived it as such. In France and the Netherlands, in Poland and the Soviet Union it seemed that a dream had come true. German cultural superiority, a belief widely held from as far back as the later nineteenth century, could now, so the occupiers assumed, be imposed on the whole of Europe and made secure for the long term. That was the ultimate aim of Alfred Rosenberg's or Arthur Greiser's activities and the summation of the experiences of Wehrmacht soldiers on the streets of Paris or in the villages of Russia. As long as the Third Reich was successful militarily, it could determine the cultural renewal of Europe.

The Renewal of Europe? Limits of Cultural Collaboration

At the beginning of July 1940 Willem Mengelberg, the renowned, sixty-nine-year-old conductor of the Amsterdam Concertgebouw Orchestra, gave an interview to the *Völkischer Beobachter*.

He expressed his passion for German culture, recounting how he had experienced the capitulation of his country less than two months before while on a concert tour in the Reich: 'When the armistice was concluded, we stayed up the whole night. It was in Bad Gastein!' he enthused. 'I've been there ten times already to take the cure, so we sat down with all our friends, ordered champagne, and celebrated this tremendous moment together. It is truly a tremendous moment and world history will confirm it. Europe is set on a new course.' The fact that the Netherlands' ties to 'the West' were now severed was something he considered 'really not so bad', particularly as cultural life would not be adversely affected. 'We've always had a particularly close connection with Germany's intellectual life. And if the West recedes, Germany will come even more markedly to the fore.'[36]

Mengelberg's comments, which were published in Dutch translation in *De Telegraaf* a few days later, sparked controversy. At this point press censorship meant that there could be no more public debate, but various music-lovers expressed their outrage in anonymous letters to the Concertgebouw Orchestra. 'The champagne you drank in Bad Gastein has cost you the sympathy of our nation as well!!!' as one of them exclaimed to Mengelberg. The management recommended that the conductor should wait for six months before returning from abroad. Mengelberg himself took the view that the *Völkischer Beobachter* had misrepresented him, for he had not drunk the champagne to celebrate the Dutch capitulation. He nevertheless continued to insist on his admiration for Germany and its musical culture, having cultivated it over decades. He simply could not grasp the fact that the Third Reich and its expansion would have an impact on that. Although this distinguished him from the country's minority of convinced pro-Nazis, he nevertheless welcomed Hitler's victory as an opportunity for the cultural symbiosis between Germany and the Netherlands that he had long yearned for.[37]

In 1940 this hope of Mengelberg's was shared by others. Before the war there had been close contacts between Dutch and German culture. The Dutch operetta singer Johannes Heesters had been successful in the Reich and praised for it by the press in his home country. Now the new German rule would bring consolidation and support for cultural life and this appeared an altogether attractive prospect. Because of his prominence and his public statement, however, Mengelberg became an unwilling symbol of collaboration, even when his initial enthusiasm had long made way for a much more sober appraisal. Like him, many artists who were at first well-disposed to Germany were alienated by the occupiers' blatant and yet also unpredictable hegemonic policies. Jews were ruthlessly marginalized; the unpopular Dutch National Socialists were given free rein. Mengelberg himself intervened in various ways to help Jewish musicians in the Concertgebouw Orchestra and was unhappy that he could no longer perform the works of Gustav Mahler, whom he admired. He could not make up his mind to commit himself to any of the cultural organizations, which were dominated by the occupiers. But he continued to conduct orchestras from Berlin to Bucharest, and this made him an important figure in the Third Reich's European cultural policy. Mengelberg could be integrated into the Nazis' art rhetoric, for example when in July 1940 Goebbels's culture journal *Das Reich* praised the fact that 'straddling two cultures through his birth and his musical activities he strongly inclines towards the German side' and interprets his role as conductor accordingly. 'He has a strong character and knows how to achieve his aims, a master of orchestral discipline, and at the same time an impulsive artist who responds intuitively to each moment.'[38]

Among Europe's cultural elite Willem Mengelberg was not the only person who manifested a sympathetic attitude towards Germany. The rapid military victories of the Third Reich seemed to have decided a conflict that was already central to the First

World War, namely that between 'Western', in particular French, and German culture. Britain, which in any case had less cultural appeal, was an isolated island country whose colonial empire had, moreover, shrunk as a result of Japanese conquests. In the eyes of many observers this was a reality people had to come to terms with, but it also offered an opportunity. For Germany was considered worldwide as the land of music, literature, and science. Even if people did not already feel connected to Germany culturally, as many educated Dutch or Finns did, there was much to be said, for example in Romania or Bulgaria, for a reorientation away from the hitherto dominant country, France. The fact that the Third Reich had banned modernist, left-wing, and Jewish influences from Germany and was now attempting to do the same in the occupied parts of Europe troubled only a minority of people. Right-wing attitudes had been prevalent among European intellectuals long before 1939. From this perspective, 'purging' the country of Communists and Jews, and also of American influences, offered nations an opportunity to preserve, renew, and even extend their own cultures. Only gradually did it become apparent that nationalist ideals were very hard to reconcile with German dominance, though even this realization did not necessarily deter people from intellectual collaboration.

Such debates went on even in France, which was particularly under threat from the Third Reich's imperialist exercise of power. Hitler and Goebbels were, after all, explicit in their aim of imposing the pre-eminence of German culture over French culture throughout Europe.[39] People could easily let this threat slip their minds, however. In Paris the ambassador Otto Abetz, his diplomats, and Wehrmacht officers as well expressed their admiration for the culture of the defeated country. If a Parisian artist or intellectual sought contact, they would be invited to interesting discussions, events at the German Institute, which was set up in 1940 by the cultural wing of the German embassy, or receptions—not to be sniffed at at a time of economic hardship. For all their appearance of moderation, however, the occupiers set the rules and it was in people's interests to fit in. After all, German controls did not seem likely to end soon, in particular because the authoritarian Vichy regime in the south, which was allied to Hitler, offered no hope of relief. Anyone in Paris who wanted to put on a play or produce a film had to pass the German censor. That meant not only avoiding anti-German statements but also allusions to or the involvement of Jews. Thus, even the writer and philosopher Albert Camus, who later joined the resistance, removed references to the works of Franz Kafka from his reflections on the *Myth of Sisyphus*. Sometimes more than compromises were involved. Just as in the Reich, it was possible to profit personally from the exclusion of Jewish owners of publishing houses, university teachers, or librarians.

For some intellectuals, eliminating the contributions of Jews to French culture and accepting German dominance for the foreseeable future was not a case of acquiescing in what had to be; in fact they were gaining their heart's desire. These collaborators belonged to an extreme right-wing milieu that since the turn of the century had had nothing but contempt for republican values. They hated Jews; they also hated Freemasons, who were linked to republicanism and were frequently considered responsible for the alleged decadence of the country. These intellectual collaborators saw France's defeat as a confirmation of their ideas as well as the opportunity for a thorough-going renewal. They wanted to go further down this road than the conservative nationalist government in Vichy with its rhetoric of 'Work, Family, Country'.

They admired Third Reich culture, which seemed to them in equal measure traditional, creative, and dynamically masculine and thus contrasted favourably both with Americanism and Bolshevism. People tried to convince themselves that Germany was both the model and basis for a transformed European culture, in which France also would play a significant role.

Thus, for example, Jacques Chardonne, author of novels about life in provincial France, informed his readers how much he admired the new Germans: 'The intellectual freedom of these young leaders took me by surprise,' he reported after a visit to the Reich, 'as did their naturalness, modesty, elegance, signs of true superiority. These warriors have much grace.' The dominance of these 'leaders' and 'warriors' was not only deserved, he said, but benefited other nations, to the extent that one might wonder 'if it is Germany's victory or Europe's'. France, which under the Republic was sluggish, inwardly weakened, and only free in a sterile way, might gain from this.[40] Lucien Rebatet saw France's defeat as an opportunity for renewal in a much more radical form. In his widely read recollections of the war recently lost against the German Reich, this antisemitic journalist advocated 'liquidating the past completely'. He intended, he said, to ensure 'that no common ground remains between the Jewish, democratic France—vulgar, dumb, grotesque in its flashiness, pathetic in its panic—and the chastened but purified France of the armistice'. Only a 'French National Socialism' could point the way to the future.[41]

The motives behind cooperation with the Third Reich therefore ranged between pragmatic accommodation, attempts to maintain continuity, and collaboration based on conviction. Artists and intellectuals did not differ in this from ordinary French people. That is shown by the staged encounters between the cultures of the two countries. The semi-official exhibition of the work of the Nazi sculptor Arno Breker in the Paris Orangerie was a great success. It was unclear, however, if the visitors' admiration was directed at Breker's monumental sculptures of male bodies, his political stance, or his close connection with France, where he had lived for several years during the Weimar Republic. Invitations to visit Germany were given to French artists; some found pretexts not to go, whereas others accepted. Literary people went to two European writers' congresses in Weimar, while eight film stars paid a visit to the Ufa studios at Babelsberg and to Goebbels himself. At the various receptions linked to the visit, the *völkisch* writer and Nazi functionary, Hanns Johst, for example, expressed the view that 'nowadays Germans are not pursuing any imperialist goals' and said he felt 'genuine and deep respect for France'.[42] However, the group of travellers included not only collaborators such as Chardonne, but also artists who were naïve and simply curious about Germany and a number who attempted to intervene on behalf of their countrymen who were prisoners of war.

The ambivalent perception of the Third Reich in France did not perturb the German rulers. Their aim was not to convince French cultural elites of the principles of National Socialism (which, they liked to stress, were not designed for export), but rather to present the superiority of German culture and the second-rate character of the French equivalent as immutable facts. This was the line taken in the Reich as well, where visits by foreign writers, musicians, and film actors were highlighted in numerous newspaper articles and newsreels as indicators of international recognition. The prominent figures in the Third Reich were, in any case, concerned most of all to boost their own egos. They repeatedly gave themselves credit for any successes and attributed any scepticism abroad to a lack of understanding. 'As far as the French are concerned, cultural propaganda is still the best propaganda,' Goebbels dictated. 'I will therefore drive it home even harder than hitherto'.[43] And Rosenberg appeared gratified by the success of his speech in Paris in February 1941, as 'the applause was noticeably prolonged'. 'It was the number one topic among the French', he declared, for whom it had marked 'a new intellectual direction'.[44]

In occupied Eastern Europe the German authorities aimed much more clearly than in France to Germanize countries at the expense of their indigenous cultures. In Poland no opportunity was given for intellectual collaboration, let alone to preserve native traditions under foreign rule. By arresting professors, students, and priests, imprisoning them or deporting them to Sachsenhausen concentration camp, the Nazis aimed to eliminate those who sustained Polish culture. Ukrainians with a nationalist outlook were, by contrast, in a more favourable position at first. They had reason to assume the German occupation would give them more scope for cultural development than they had had under Polish dominance or Soviet oppression. In the south-eastern part of the Polish Generalgouvernement, where they were an ethnic minority, and later in Kiev their cultural institutions were promoted. Theatre, opera, and film blossomed, and the Ukrainian variety of Orthodox Christianity could be practised. This impression that Ukrainian culture was being encouraged, combined with traditional antisemitism, served to legitimize Ukrainian participation in the Nazis' extermination of the Jews. Before long, however, it became increasingly clear that Ukrainian independence was not part of the Third Reich's plan. Instead, exploitation and repression were dominant, and under German control there was only very limited scope for a national culture.

In the satellite states dependent on Germany the situation was different. Even without the immediate pressure of occupation, people had to make certain adjustments and tolerate the introduction of Nazi foreign propaganda. These circumstances did not, however, conflict with the project of national renewal in the various states. In Romania the cultural climate had been dominated even before the outbreak of war by the radical right, with the result that neither the political alliance with the Third Reich nor participation in the Holocaust was regarded as a significant break with the past. In this way the territories ceded in 1940 to the Soviet Union could be regained and even Transnistria and its capital, the Black Sea port of Odessa, annexed—to the great disappointment of the Ukrainian nationalist movement. To be open to German culture appeared more of an option than a necessity. The Romanians were at liberty to prefer popular films or political ideas from fascist Italy to German ones or to focus on their own traditions. Nevertheless, in many respects the Third Reich was felt to be positively attractive. To the intellectual Nichifor Crainic, German influence seemed 'productive', by contrast with French: 'French culture enslaves, German culture liberates. French culture annihilates personality; German culture reveals the deep essence of the individual.'[45]

In Europe in the early 1940s there was thus an abundance of projects for cultural renewal that seemed compatible with the expansion of the Third Reich or that hoped to take advantage of it. Among them were the Romanian, Hungarian, and Slovakian variants of nationalism. This was particularly true of the fascist visions of violent purges and rebirth in the Croatian Ustasha state and, in spite of a certain rivalry with Nazi Germany, in Mussolini's Italy. Even in the absence of a project for renewal, specific considerations might encourage openness to German culture. Finland responded with relief to the German invasion of the Soviet Union, with which it had also been waging war. There was hope that Ribbentrop's special unit, which was engaged in stealing cultural artefacts, would secure Finnish documents and works of art, though this hope proved vain, as the archives and museums in Moscow and Leningrad remained beyond the Wehrmacht's reach. In Norway there were radio staff who saw the changes that ensued after the German occupation as an opportunity to develop more popular programmes that would be less stuffy and educational. And educated Greeks at first hoped that the Germans, with their prestigious culture, would treat them more respectfully than the Italians who had been occupying parts of their country.

From the German perspective, these developments were not restricted to the national context in question but were part of a renewal of Europe as a whole. Thus the representatives of the Third Reich could go on giving themselves credit for things that went beyond the secure establishment of their own overlordship. Germany, it was claimed in *Das Reich*, was 'the very heart and powerhouse of the European continent', the driving force behind a 'revolution through which not only have state structures been changed but new forces and methods have been developed in the nations' struggle for survival'. To that extent it was fundamentally different from Britain, which was materialistic and purely concerned with its own interests. 'That is what they are like', wrote Goebbels indignantly in one of his numerous articles (for which he was handsomely paid). 'Do not take the trouble of trying to understand them properly. They will always remain a mystery to us Europeans.' Finally, as he wrote in a further article, 'Europe's hour' had come, because the Germans, together with the Italians, were making sure 'that the Western world cannot be abused again as if it were only the hinterland to the British Empire'.[46]

According to *Das Reich*, this combination of European renewal and German dominance brought varied and satisfying experiences, both individually and collectively. In Vienna people were able to make use of their proximity to the culture of the Balkan countries and thereby 'again become an important centre of European life'; in Bruges it was possible to admire the architectural glories of the Germanic Middles Ages; backward Bulgaria gave people the opportunity to enjoy the country's 'devotion and loyalty' to Germany. In Alsace and Lorraine the Germans removed from public spaces the French influences that had been artificially grafted on, including the 'garish posters for Byrrh, Pernod, Dubonnet, or whatever all these apéritifs are called'. It was also possible to live as a member of the German avant-garde in the Warthegau and because of the modest circumstances there enjoy the weekly film show, even if it was somewhat out of date and of poor quality: 'Even so, everyone who is German and those who have newly arrived meet there, officials and young lads, soldiers and labour service girls, military police and estate managers, and the blonde, strapping BdM leaders from the Reich'[47] (the Bund deutscher Mädel [League of German Girls] was the girls' equivalent of the Hitler Youth).

From June 1941 onwards, however, it became clear that the sacrifices required for this German but equally European project would not be confined to waiting for the next film showing in a remote little town. After the invasion of the Soviet Union the war was finally presented as a war between cultures demanding an existential commitment. As Goebbels ranted, the British and Americans had made it their business 'to crush Germany between the millstones of Bolshevism'. 'What do the two of them care about Europe or culture or civilization or humanity! They only talk about them if they see it as in their interests.' *Das Reich* presented the struggle on the eastern front as the defence of Europe against a system that was based in purely materialist terms on the support of the proletariat. Bolshevism, it claimed, threatened the 'vital force of nations, pure and simple' along with the 'historical and intellectual past'—everything 'that has elevated Europe from a geographical term to something of world-historical importance'. When, during November 1941, it became increasingly likely that war would be declared on the United States there was talk of a 'shared pride in Europe' in order to justify it. Far beyond Germany's borders, it was claimed, people were convinced 'that a state that has not a single city overflowing with beauty and history like Würzburg, Berne, or Palermo is certainly not destined to rule Europe, and that it would be better to fight on for another thousand years than to have to settle for the spirit of American skyscrapers'.[48]

The Third Reich attempted to communicate an attractive message to the benevolently neutral, allied, and occupied countries (with the exceptions of the directly oppressed Poles, Czechs, Serbs, and Russians) that German dominance was not only compatible with their individual national concerns, but it was also in the interests of Europe as a whole. Goebbels's Propaganda Ministry was promoting a focused European cultural policy that for a short time was attractive and engaging, for French world dominance in cultural life before 1939 had had its disadvantages for smaller countries. It had meant that writers, for example, could only gain international recognition if they were read in Paris and endorsed the Enlightenment values held there. In contrast to this, the new

German dominance held promise of a resurgence of the Romantic idea that literature should have close ties to the nation and help to form national identities. From Finland to the Balkans this was, in principle, a welcome development, in particular because the exclusion of modernists, left-wingers, and Jews was also agreeable to these countries. In autumn 1941 this new direction was adopted at a 'Writers' Conference', with 37 representatives from 15 countries, most of them authors of nationalist novels with a rural setting. The idyllic venue for the conference was Weimar, around 1800 the intellectual home of Goethe, Schiller, and the theorist of Romantic nationalism, Johann Gottfried Herder, and thus ideally suited as a contrast to Paris and to metropolitan civilization in general. A round of champagne receptions and formal banquets accompanied the founding of the European Writers' Union, which had the appearance of being a promising, forward-looking project.[49]

The renewal of Europe under German leadership was not, however, the exclusive province of the cultural elites, but also had a popular aspect. The Third Reich tried hard to gain international audiences for its own films and newsreels, above all at the expense of film production in the United States. New marketing and even production companies were established and cinemas requisitioned. At the same time, there was hope of building on the popularity of dramas featuring Zarah Leander, costume dramas with Marika Rökk, and comedies with Heinz Rühmann. German productions filled the screens and film magazines in fascist Croatia; they increased their market share in nationalist Hungary too as well as in neutral Sweden. *The Great Love Affair* was particularly appealing to audiences, both in German-speaking Switzerland and in occupied Belgium, though there the restrictions on local production and control of distribution meant that there were few alternatives. The International Chamber of Film, which had come into being back in 1935 but had in the meantime been dissolved, was re-founded to coordinate film-making throughout Europe. It ensured German dominance by regulating the market and threatening sanctions, in particular blocking European producers from acquiring the necessary film stock, which was produced in Germany. It was accompanied by a rhetoric celebrating European cinema as substantial in content and rooted in the various nations and thus a contrast to the alleged materialism and superficiality of Hollywood cinema.

Signal, a magazine produced jointly by the propaganda departments of the Wehrmacht and the Foreign Office, also focused on the renewal of Europe. Innovative advertisers, journalists, and photographers tried to reach an international readership through editions in various languages. In this they were very successful, for the magazine was bought in Axis-allied countries such as Hungary, Romania, and Bulgaria, as well as in occupied Belgium and France, neutral European countries such as Portugal and Sweden, and as far away as Persia and Japan. In spring 1942 the total print run came to over two million copies. Attractively designed and lavishly illustrated, *Signal* communicated an impression of the unstoppable spread of German dominance. Handsome Wehrmacht soldiers were shown everywhere hoisting swastika flags, bathing naked in Thermopylae, or settling into life in the North African desert. They were welcomed enthusiastically by the people of Bosnia and fought alongside French volunteers; they were seen with Finnish infantrymen and Slovakian fighter pilots. Pictures of Danish girls, an Italian aircraft engineer on home leave, and Spanish Red Cross nurses attending the Salzburg Festival emphasized the European character of this German dominance.

The coverage given to Japan's military successes and Muslim guests in Berlin, from the Grand Mufti of Jerusalem down to students and scholars, gave the magazine a global perspective too.

In addition to the numerous illustrated reports from the new Europe, *Signal* published articles asserting that German and European interests were identical. Whereas Britain despised the continental nations and had neglected them in favour of its empire, Germany, it was claimed, because of its central position was dependent on the unimpeded exchange of cultural and economic goods. In the face of the threat from Britain and the Soviet Union, Europe had no choice but to form a coalition 'that is fortunate in having a powerful advocate, namely Germany, which is one with it in life and in death.' Having mobilized fears of Communism, the magazine used the topos of the existential decision and extended it to cover the whole of Europe: 'Victory or defeat will decide whether Europe will finally be of one mind, will be able to keep itself secure from external interventions, and will also have a voice in the world. Europe will either rise again in a new form or it will be eliminated.' 'European living space' was the future vision that beckoned, mobilizing and uniting 'the interests of all European nations' in a 'world consisting of autonomous spheres'.[50]

Such soaring rhetoric clashed with reality, however, in particular in places where the Third Reich was the occupying power. Its violent domination was admittedly often veiled by those who were tasked with German cultural policy on the ground. In Western Europe especially, diplomats and military leaders were careful not to make explicitly Nazi comments. Instead they expressed their admiration for the national cultural heritage in question and made offers of cooperation to sections of the native cultural elites. But this did not alter the fact that, at the same time, the Party and the SS were exploiting their power with complete ruthlessness, that censorship was practised and art stolen.

Germany's cultural and scholarly achievements may have been widely recognized, but when the occupiers hoisted an enormous swastika flag over the Acropolis, confiscated hundreds of thousands of radio sets in Norway, and in the Netherlands made their policy of Germanization ever clearer, the willingness to collaborate, which had certainly been there at the beginning, quickly evaporated.

Even astute contemporaries failed, however, to see this problem clearly. By repeatedly emphasizing the spread and the prestige of German culture, Nazi propaganda spoke to the values of the educated middle classes. The resulting pride made people blind to the link between the 'renewal' of Europe and imperialist expansion. Thus in September 1941 Werner Heisenberg bemoaned to his wife the fact that Copenhagen colleagues had boycotted his guest lecture for political reasons: 'It is strange that, although the Danes can lead totally normal lives and are doing well, so much hatred and fear has been created that even communication in the cultural sphere, which used to be a given, has now become almost impossible.'[51] What the famous physicist euphemistically referred to as 'communication in the cultural sphere' was, in the final analysis, based on military force and for that very reason fragile.

Figure 6. Audience members returning home from a concert in Berlin, winter 1943/44.

5

CULTURE OF DESTRUCTION

A snow-covered street in Berlin early in 1944: With the exception of one man in uniform, the passers-by with their hats, coats, and sturdy shoes look middle-class. They have been to a concert. The programme was made up exclusively of works by non-Jewish German composers, for French, English, and Russian music has not been played for years. The ruined building in the background vividly evokes the changed living conditions in the Reich capital as a result of the air war. The concert has taken place in the daytime so that people can return home before it gets dark. Many events are now timed so that at the end audiences or spectators can reach their homes and air-raid cellars in good time to be protected from the nightly raids. Music offers some relief from concentrating on the daily struggle for survival and is a now rare opportunity to enjoy bourgeois culture. But these brief intervals of recreation can be kept apart less and less from the political consequences of Nazism.

The picture was taken by Hanns Hubmann, who was a photographer for the *Berliner Illustrierte Zeitung* and *Signal* and contributed to many reports glorifying war. By contrast, his photo of the concertgoers is ambivalent because it can be interpreted both as evidence of the catastrophic situation in Berlin and as proof of its residents' determination to endure. We do not know when precisely it was taken and which concert the Berliners were leaving. It could have been a performance by the Berlin Philharmonic; they continued to play regularly in the city during the winter of 1943/44.

The Propaganda Minister Joseph Goebbels aimed to 'give the population some opportunity for relaxation'. As the Gauleiter of Berlin he wanted to avoid 'the Reich capital being slowly suffo-cated by enemy air raids' as this, he feared, would make the rival cultural metropolis of Vienna seem more attractive. In his customary manner Goebbels intervened personally to support bombed-out artists, maintain film production at Babelsberg, and patch up theatre buildings. He spoke enthusiastically of a concert given by the Philharmonic in Berlin Cathedral rather than in their concert hall in Kreuzberg, which had just been destroyed by bombing: 'The cathedral is full to the brim with people who have suffered through the bombing and has a festive appearance. Unfortunately the acoustics are not particularly good, but Furtwängler inspires the orchestra to incomparable achievements.'[1] Goebbels was aware of the symbolic value accorded the perform-ances of the 'Reich Orchestra'. To prevent Allied bombs causing gaps in the ensemble, in May 1944 his ministry decreed that in the event of air raids the musicians 'should go to the nearest bunker with their families'.[2]

The members of the Philharmonic thus had one more privilege over other people in that they had access to air-raid bunkers rather than having to rely on the less effective cellars in their homes. But the destruction of their traditional venue and the removal of instruments for storage outside Berlin showed them that even their work was being affected by the war. They were not sticking voluntarily to the number of concerts planned for the season, but rather doing it under pressure from Goebbels. During the early years of the war the orchestra enjoyed great success and was often invited to play in other German and European cities. Although such possibilities were now limited, the Philharmonic was due to perform in spring 1944 in France, Portugal, and Spain. While there, they would also be involved in making a feature film, a romance in which, at the time of the 1933 revolution, a violinist wins the heart of a member of the orchestral board's daughter and progresses from playing popular music to being a member of the orchestra. *The Philharmonic* reached cinema screens in December 1944, at a time when other orchestras had already been disbanded, but the showpiece German orchestra was still performing.

The example of concert life in Berlin demonstrates that, during the second half of the war, destruction was having an increasing impact on culture in the Third Reich. That culture consisted on the one hand in the attempt to hold on to established forms of expression and habits of cultural consumption, both in German towns and cities and, though under much more extreme conditions, in the Jewish ghettos. On the other hand, culture was not only subject to violence, but was used to legitimize and motivate it. In the guise of antisemitic fantasies and racist visions of social order, it had, since the summer of 1941, underpinned the systematic murder of European Jews. At the same time, the destruction perpetrated by the Third Reich was starting to rebound on Germany. Air raids were intensifying. Soviet, British, and American troops later advanced from Russia, Italy, and finally France towards the borders of the Reich. The Allies as well as the various European resistance movements had to mobilize culturally too for their huge efforts and in the process drew virtually no distinction between 'National Socialist' and 'German'. While the war entered its final phase, culture continued to represent a contrast to the ubiquitous devastation, offering distraction and consolation for a few brief moments. But, at the same time, it was providing inspiration for the Third Reich's life and death struggle.

In the Shadow of Extermination: Culture and the Holocaust

In July 1942 Philipp Manes, a First World War veteran, was deported to the ghetto in Theresienstadt. Years earlier Nazi policy towards the Jews had already had a serious impact on his livelihood. As a result of Aryanization he had lost his fur business and, since the outbreak of war, had been forced by the regime to work in a factory. As a sideline, he had published articles. This had been his passion until in 1935 the Reich Chamber of Literature forbade him to publish any longer. Like all Berlin Jews, Manes found himself also excluded from theatres, opera houses, and concert halls. Deportation deprived him and his wife of almost everything, including their books and sheet music. And yet, despite the grim circumstances, Manes, now 67, tried to make a new start. Although in the 'show ghetto' of Theresienstadt, to which international visitors were regularly taken in an attempt to deceive them, conditions were significantly better than in the extermination camps, they were nevertheless life-threatening. Even so, a varied cultural life had developed there, to which he was able to contribute.

Manes organized an increasingly successful series of events that he himself inaugurated by giving lectures on Berlin during the imperial period. 'Word had quickly gotten around Theresienstadt that a kind of cultural community had developed in Room 38', as he noted with pride; 'every month new listeners came, wanting tickets to specific lectures, and unfortunately, I often had to say no.' Manes also started a poetry competition, promoted the development of drawings based on Theresienstadt, and organized theatre evenings. He could not manage to put on whole plays, but he had people read the various parts, thereby giving actors living in the ghetto the opportunity to perform. To supplement the frequently presented comedies aimed at a Czech audience, he delved into the classical canon of German high culture: 'Was there any doubt about what should be presented?', he asked rhetorically. 'Goethe, of course. And if him, then only *Faust*.'[3]

Engaging with German literature and music did not at all mean excluding Jewish culture. Martin Buber's Hassidic stories were part of the shared reading. The famous Berlin rabbi Leo Baeck and other scholars spoke on religious, philosophical, and historical subjects. Manes was convinced that 'many who were half-hearted, uncertain, or aloof from Judaism were reclaimed as convinced adherents'. By engaging with German and Jewish culture and enabling other ghetto residents to do the same, Manes was able to supply a counterweight to people's desperate need to concentrate on their daily survival. This interest also helped him to separate himself off from those Jews in Theresienstadt whom, for a variety of reasons, he disapproved of: Viennese, whose ill temper made him lose his 'affection for the imperial city on the Blue Danube'; materialists, who could not 'live without trade' and managed to get better food for themselves by dubious means; and informers, 'who betray[ed] their co-religionists for the most appalling reasons'.[4]

Philipp Manes's activities in Theresienstadt were extraordinarily extensive, but they were not untypical. Jews throughout Europe attempted in any way possible to maintain cultural activities, whether in the ghettos and camps, in underground movements, or in 'Jewish Houses' (where Jews in 'mixed marriages' continued to live within Reich territory). As with Manes, this was their way of finding something to set against their existential helplessness in the face of Nazi Germany: autonomy, the preservation of tradition, and an orientation towards the future. Differences of opinion were nevertheless evident. Attitudes to German culture, which before the war had been important to educated Jews throughout Europe, were particularly contentious. Should one remain loyal to it and so resist antisemitic attempts to marginalize and exclude Jews from this culture? Or should one strike out in a new direction, based on other national identities, the Jewish heritage, or a Zionist faith in the future? Whatever people decided, Germany remained an important point of reference, whether positive or negative. 'According to one elevated gentleman, I am too emphatically "German". To another, I am not Jewish enough for the ghetto', Manes complained. He justified himself on the grounds that he had not become familiar with 'the past and the great intellectual and spiritual development of Judaism' until he came to Theresienstadt and as a result had made efforts to choose lecture topics reflecting this.[5]

The debate about the cultural orientation appropriate to the situation was conducted against the backdrop of the threat of extermination. Although Manes retained his optimism and energy for a long time, even he sounded increasingly fearful for his life. 'I love to take refuge in Schubert when my soul is in turmoil', he noted in September 1944, 'when tormenting concerns press too intensely, when thoughts turn to yearnings for what is far away and cannot be reached because everything seems so terribly uncertain and reason finds no anchor.' One reason why diaries, chronicles, even sociological studies were written in such quantities in the ghettos and concentration camps and so carefully hidden was because their authors did not expect to survive. The importance of such texts was considered to go beyond documenting personal experience; they were to provide evidence of the fate of the Jews for posterity. That was true of Manes's 'factual account', which breaks off suddenly in October 1944 because its author was deported to Auschwitz and immediately murdered there.[6]

Extermination hung even more heavily over life in the ghettos of occupied Poland, in Warsaw or Lódz (soon to be renamed Litzmannstadt) than over Theresienstadt. Hygiene was a severe problem and food was extremely scarce.[7] Yet there too it was still unclear at the beginning how things would develop. The Polish and German Jews deported to the ghettos from autumn 1941 onwards hoped to do more than survive physically; they also wanted to derive psychological strength from holding on to their cultural values and to find something with which to combat the daily struggle with hunger. In addition, it was important for them to pass on cultural education to children and young people and so make them guarantors of Jewish continuity, however improvised the schooling in the ghettos might be. Culture could maintain a sense of continuity with the past, as well as an appearance of normality in the present, and hope for a better future. As a reaction to the complete marginalization caused by antisemitism, in the ghettos cultural emphases on the one hand shifted towards Jewish religious traditions, literature or music, and the use of the Yiddish and Hebrew languages. On the other hand, the cultural influences of the pre-war years were still important, precisely because since then the world had changed beyond all recognition. Identification with German culture belonged to that vanished world, and many Jews continued to hold on to it.

Thus professional directors and actors, as well as enthusiastic amateurs invested huge energy in the theatre, put on regular performances of plays, and created sets and costumes. In addition to familiar dramas, new comedies making fun of ghetto life were staged. In specially set-up concert halls and even in soup kitchens soloists sang operatic arias and entire symphony orchestras played classical music. 'You heard surprising things then', Marcel Reich-Ranicki recalled of his time in the Warsaw ghetto. 'In one courtyard Beethoven's violin concerto, in the next Mozart's clarinet concerto, both, admittedly, unaccompanied.'[8] Popular songs could be heard in revues, in cafés, and in the street. 'Songs from the revues quickly became popular and were heard everywhere in the ghetto', as a literary and theatre critic later described the situation in Litzmannstadt. 'Audiences consisted mainly of working-class people who sought and found relaxation in the theatre.'[9] Other cultural activities went on in the private sphere: reading and discussion circles met in homes, amateur drama groups rehearsed in attics and cellars. Observant Jews prayed together, discussed matters of faith, and kept the Jewish festivals, even though it became increasingly difficult to keep to the ritual laws. There was also a positive literature boom, though the products were accessible to few readers because of the difficulty of publishing.

Since various ghetto orchestras repeatedly breached the ban on performing music by German composers, as well as by the Polish composer Frédéric Chopin, symphony concerts were for a time forbidden in the spring of 1942. Life in the ghetto was increasingly at risk from the murderous arbitrariness of the German rulers. Any musician, literary figure, or theatre-lover could be the victim of a shooting, hostage-taking, or deportation to an extermination camp. Adam Czerniaków, the chair of the Jewish Council in the

Warsaw ghetto, took his own life in order not to be forced to take part in compiling deportation lists. Shortly before his suicide he noted, 'I am reminded of a film: a ship is sinking and the captain, to raise the spirits of the passengers, orders the orchestra to play a jazz piece. I have made up my mind to emulate the captain.'[10] Marcel Reich-Ranicki recalled how in September 1942 tens of thousands of Jews were taken to Treblinka, some of whom took their instruments with them. 'The Germans just love music', they explained. 'Perhaps they won't send someone to the gas chamber who plays for them.'[11]

In the face of their impending murder, music, literature, and religion acquired even greater significance for the Jews than previously. One activity had been part of ghetto culture from the outset, namely the documentation of conditions for posterity, and this gained increasing importance. In Litzmannstadt and Warsaw historians, social scientists, and journalists gathered material about social life in extreme circumstances. While they themselves were struggling with hunger, disease, and cold, they recorded events and wrote encyclopaedic articles. Going beyond their official work as chroniclers, they developed new initiatives, writing about aspects of the economy, daily life, and religion or conducting interviews. But life in the ghetto was documented also by people with no professional skills, in photos, drawings, or texts, always in the hope that these testimonies would be preserved for posterity. They were by no means deceiving themselves about the limitations of these efforts. 'And even if I could steal their muse from Homer, Shakespeare, Goethe, and Dante,' a young resident of the Litzmannstadt ghetto wondered in June 1944, 'would I then be capable of describing what we are suffering, what we are feeling and experiencing in this life? Is that even remotely possible?'[12]

A minority of Jews in the Reich and in occupied Europe could for a time escape deportation to the ghettos and extermination camps, either because they were married to an Aryan or by going underground. In this situation cultural expression absolutely had to be individual and discreet. Chamber music, choral singing, and play rehearsals were out of the question, whether in Jewish Houses or secretly in attics or community garden shelters. If anyone in hiding went to an opera house or cinema, he or she risked being recognized and denounced. Even so, as in the ghettos, not only food, hygiene, and clothing, but also cultural activities remained important. It was precisely because opportunities were so limited and people's own futures were so much in doubt that they pondered, wrote, and sketched. Another reason was to reassure themselves about the fragile 'boundary between civilization and culture'. That was how Victor Klemperer, who thanks to his non-Jewish wife Eva was living at this time in a Dresden Jewish House, put it. He was made to do forced labour, while fearing that he might still be deported. His hopes that the Allies would soon be victorious were repeatedly disappointed. He wondered with apprehension whether being deprived of things he took for granted such as toilet paper, toothpaste, or new clothing did not make people 'spiritually shabby and *unfree*'.[13]

To confront this danger Klemperer worked, as far as his strength allowed, on an analysis of the language and mindset of the Third Reich. By turns hoping to survive and fearing death he took refuge repeatedly 'by turning to what is now my work, these notes, my reading'. He really wanted to be 'the chronicler of the cultural history of the present catastrophe', 'risk continuing with the diary', and 'bear witness to the very end'.[14] Even this was difficult because his house was repeatedly searched by the Gestapo, who might have found his notes. For Klemperer, National Socialism placed a question mark over the foundations of his own thinking as a German. He studied Zionism intensively. He had always been opposed to it and even under drastically changed circumstances he held to this view: 'I'm German, the others are un-German; I must not forget this: mind and spirit are decisive, not blood.' A short time after, however, he had partially revised his view, no longer regarding the Third Reich as a foreign body in his own nation. 'I can no longer believe that National Socialism is completely un-German,' Klemperer noted. 'It is home-grown, a carcinoma made of *German* flesh, a strain of cancer, just as there is a *Spanish* flu.'[15]

At the same time as Victor Klemperer, Anne Frank was also keeping a diary. Her relationship with German culture was completely different. As she had arrived in the Netherlands in 1933, aged only four, she wrote in the language of her adoptive country, showing herself to be an intellectually engaged, imaginative, and fluent writer. She read German classical writers more to please her father than out of personal interest, but she did so cheerfully. 'Daddy has brought the plays of Goethe and Schiller from the big bookcase. He is going to read to me every evening', she noted. 'We've started with *Don Carlos*.' Though she had a love of learning and books, she distanced herself from the culture from which her family had been excluded and whose representatives were now threatening her with deportation. A short time later Frank drafted a fictional advertising brochure for the rear part of the tenement building in central Amsterdam that sheltered her and other Jews. In it she turned the regime imposed by the occupying force on its head. She ruled that 'German stations are only listened to in special cases, such as classical music', that 'no

German books may be read, with the exception of scientific and classical works', and that 'all civilized languages' were permitted, 'therefore no German!' Her dreams for her future life in freedom were focused on studying art history in Paris and London, but above all on being an accepted member of society. 'I love the Dutch, I love this country, I love the language and want to work here', as she summed up her attitude in the spring of 1944. 'And if I have to write to the queen myself, I will not give up until I have reached my goal!'[16]

Anne Frank was betrayed along with her family and deported to Auschwitz-Birkenau. Later she was moved to Bergen-Belsen and died there in March 1945 of typhus. At the end, although she was already very weak, she told stories to the children in the camp.[17] As she faced being murdered, she found it meant a lot to be able to recall poems from memory or to speak to other camp inmates. Even for those who managed to survive for a time in the extermination camps, keeping a diary, writing, or drawing were mostly impossible. The effort and the pain were too great, the struggle for daily bread was too bitter, the materials needed too scarce. One of the few exceptions was Ana Novac, who was sent at the age of fourteen from Transylvania to Auschwitz-Birkenau. 'Fortunately, the hut is never completely dark and I can write,' she said of her diary, 'The main thing is that I can shake off the load of unbearable thoughts. Get rid of them.' She found it helped to characterize the camp, its guards, and its inmates with precision and at times with black humour, for example the Hungarian Jewess who complained about the conditions in Auschwitz: 'German culture! What a disappointment for someone who spent her holidays in Baden-Baden and had read *Faust*! How could a nation so obsessed with hygiene build such appalling latrines!'[18]

Although songs were sung and concerts put on in secret in Auschwitz-Birkenau, any more extensive cultural activities required the permission of the German guards. Even so, several orchestras were formed, whose performances were harnessed to the policy of oppression in the camp. They had to play military marches when the inmates left the camp to perform hard physical labour and returned in the evening. When new prisoners arrived, popular music gave them a false impression of the realities of the camp. There was no escape from such music if they were lying in the 'prisoners' sick bay' or were being 'selected' for the gas chambers. The camp's orchestras and jazz groups were also used to entertain and divert the SS functionaries. Their achievements were impressive, for example when Alma Rosé, Gustav Mahler's niece, was conducting and was brave enough to ask for quiet at the Sunday concerts of her 'Auschwitz Girls' Orchestra'. At the same time, these achievements were appropriated by a system in which the SS demonstrated its power over life and death on a daily basis. Anyone who could not march in time with the orchestra was beaten or judged no longer fit for work and murdered. The musicians were in no way guaranteed survival, but were subject to the same conditions as other prisoners. Alma Rosé herself died in April 1944 from poisoning. The cause has never been explained.[19]

The experiences of the prisoners in Auschwitz and other extermination camps resulted from a Nazi policy that between summer 1941 and spring 1942, through a complex decision-making process, developed into the systematic murder of all European Jews. Why were the Nazis unwilling to allow the Jewish minority to exist even in the most reduced circumstances in ghettos and labour battalions? Behind the intensified persecution lay the old antisemitic fantasy that people could find redemption by banning the Jews from their society. Hitler's *Mein Kampf* (My Struggle), as well as numerous other Nazi writings of the early 1920s, had been shot through with this fantasy. Since the takeover of power it had been given increasingly concrete expression in official measures and legislation, until it peaked in the public shows of staged violence of November 1938. The antisemitic goal of extermination became increasingly radical during the course of the war, while at the same time the number of Jews living under German rule grew enormously. After invading the Soviet Union and declaring war on the United States, the Third Reich saw itself as caught up in an apocalyptic struggle against Bolshevism and capitalism—two systems whose roots it traced back to the influence of Judaism. Since the Nazis assumed there was a race that was spread throughout the world and acted in a coordinated manner, they considered even completely defenceless inhabitants of Eastern European villages or ghettos a threat. On 26 April 1942 Hitler explained his reading of the war at the last meeting of the Greater German Reichstag: according to the Führer, the Jews were hostile to any characteristic features of European peoples and aimed to 'remove all those cultural foundations that, having accrued a thousand years of genetic heritage, might give these peoples intrinsic value, or serve as warnings for the future. What remains is no more than the animal part of human beings and a Jewish stratum, which, once it becomes dominant, is a parasite that ultimately destroys the soil that nourishes it.'[20]

If, given their immutable racial characteristics, the Jews were regarded as destroyers of humanity and culture, it seemed vital to rob them of their cultural and physical existence. This, in turn, prompted fear of their revenge if the extermination were not carried out thoroughly. This circular logic kept emerging from Nazi speeches, from magazine articles, and from the copies of *Der*

Stürmer on display in showcases in the street, even if the concrete methods of extermination were kept quiet. Though the majority of Germans did not welcome the move to systematic murder, they accepted it or put up with it. The regime's propaganda was also effective to the extent that it contributed to the extermination of the Jews in Eastern European countries, whether occupied or still engaged in fighting. This was evident in particular in relation to the Wehrmacht's involvement. Many soldiers not only absorbed the regime's propaganda but helped produce it. They took photos of massacres or justified them in their own words. What was at stake in this war, as a German lieutenant wrote from the Soviet Union, was 'the world-wide influence of the Jews, who resist our solution to the Jewish question by trying to annihilate the German nation'. Both sides were thus engaged in a 'war of religion which can end only in complete extermination'. Another soldier wrote a letter to *Der Stürmer* in which he argued that Jews should be viewed when stripped of all their possessions: 'Anyone who claims to know the Jew without having seen him in his place of origin, the East, is mistaken! The Jew can only really be known if he is studied in a place where, without the effects of culture, he can carry on his grubby activities.'[21]

Such statements created a dichotomy between authentic German culture and (hitherto craftily hidden) Jewish lack of culture. The implication is that, if all forms of disguise are removed, the essential nature of this racial enemy will be revealed. The Nazis conceived of this removal of a culture that was, in fact, merely a facade as a symbolic process to be enacted on the Jews step by step on their way to genocide. Consequently, no German or even Polish composers could be played in the ghettos and, in the end, the last remaining outlets for 'Jewish' culture, such as the Mahler concerts of the Amsterdam Cultural Association, were terminated. By the same logic members of the SS exposed prisoners in concentration and extermination camps to humiliating hygiene conditions. Subjecting Jews to Aryan power also involved capturing their poverty and distress in photos and using the pictures as antisemitic propaganda. Moreover, it meant designating this minority as belonging to the past, as an obstacle that could finally be overcome on the road to a new age. This was the ultimate purpose served by the work done by 'researchers into Jewishness', by the theft of millions of books and archival sources by Reichsleiter Rosenberg's task force, and by the Jewish Central Museum in Prague, where the SS had the collection curated by Jewish staff— though this did not, in the end, save the latter from deportation.

This idea that the Jewish presence had already become history was also fundamental to the plans for German domination of Eastern Central Europe. The extermination of the Jews and the simultaneous suppression, deportation, and partial murder of the Slav population appeared to make possible a rapid racial and social transformation. 'Researchers into the East' and SS leaders invented a mission for national comrades from both the Reich itself and the German minorities in other European countries: dispersal over a geographically wide area combined with concentration in ethnically 'pure' territories. In these newly settled areas they were supposed to develop an ideal society that went beyond what was possible in the *Altreich* (Germany as defined by its borders before 1938), whose structures were only partially adaptable. As Heinrich Himmler dictated in January 1942, 'Only a healthy link between town and country can raise political, economic, and cultural life to the level of Teutonic–German culture.'[22] In his speech in Posen (Poznań) on 4 October 1943 he stated explicitly who was obliged to pay the price. He justified both the murder of the Jews and the exploitation of Poles and Russians: 'Whether other nations are prosperous or die of hunger only interests me in so far as we need them as slaves for our culture; otherwise it doesn't interest me.'[23]

From the summer of 1941 on, the Nazis translated their murderous antisemitism into action more systematically than before. Their aim was to be rid of any Jewish heritage and to move forward into a new age. That involved first robbing the persecuted Jews of their culture, initially by ghettoizing them and reducing them to survival level and then by annihilating them physically. At the same time, this procedure was designed to demonstrate that the specific character of the Germans as an ethnic group had to be rescued from an existential threat emanating from a minority that remained unalterably alien. The European Jews tried with all means still at their disposal to defend themselves against this logic, and Germany remained an important point of reference for their intensive cultural activities, in both positive and negative respects. Yet, while more and more Jews were falling victim to the Nazis' destructive urges, the war situation was changing. Increasingly, the opponents of the Third Reich were gaining both military and propaganda successes—and they were becoming increasingly reluctant to differentiate between Nazi and German culture.

Against German Culture? The View from Abroad

During the course of 1942 the famous German novelist Thomas Mann's mood slowly lifted. Together with his daughter Erika, he had at first bemoaned the Allies' 'ineffectual, feeble-minded conduct of the war', while a range of military setbacks caused him to expect a lengthy conflict. Then, however, positive news reached him about the situation on the eastern front, even though it did not lead him to hope that that would have a significant impact on Germany: 'All the reports suggest growing hopelessness, though it will not lead to a revolution, or not for a long time.'[24] Parallel to this, in his view, cultural mobilization in the United States seemed to be getting more effective, as was indicated for example by Alfred Hitchcock's thriller *Saboteur*: 'Excellent Nazi characters. The whole thing instructive to the uninformed.' From autumn 1942 onwards Mann foresaw 'that in spite of force and effort this dreadful madness will end in a bloodbath'. But people in the United States continued to be uncertain 'whether they do really want to destroy fascism or not' and hence could not show 'Europe any dignity, clarity, or inner strength'.[25]

When he noted these observations in his diary Mann was living in California. He was part of a German–European exile community that met regularly to exchange ideas and enjoy music and whose members he supported as much as he could, notwithstanding numerous personal tensions. Culturally, he was still very bound to his country of origin, but at the same time he distanced himself from it: 'I shudder at the thought of setting foot in Germany again', he wrote to an American patroness; 'I make no secret of the fact that I've had enough of my nation.' Mann even claimed that he had 'always been something of a foreigner mentally', while keeping very quiet about the nationalistic statements he had made during the First World War. In line with his basic attitude, he engaged with the everyday life and culture of the United States, more so than other exiled intellectuals, though it must be said that they were less comfortably situated than he. He settled with his family in a modernist home in Pacific Palisades near Los Angeles and described an evening with American intellectuals that, in spite of his imperfect English, he 'positively enjoyed'.[26]

Thomas Mann not only provided comment on the Allied struggle with the Third Reich but took part in it himself. As an internationally renowned writer he had for years been giving public lectures advocating concerted action on the part of the United States to oppose Nazi Germany, at a time when large sections of the American public wanted to stay out of the war. Under the title *Listen Germany!* he gave radio talks that were broadcast by the BBC to his former homeland. In them he described the murderous effects of the policy of annihilation, compared Nazi promises with reality, and explained the Allies' war aims. At first he presented himself as a national author cut off from his traditional audience, 'banned as a writer and an individual by your leaders; my books, even when they deal with the most German things, Goethe for example, can speak only to foreign, free nations in their own language.' Yet Mann's talks increasingly betrayed his disappointment that the Germans were still not prepared to abandon their Führer and were therefore deservedly feeling the effects of his policies and would be held responsible for the crimes of the Third Reich. 'If there is such a thing as Germany; if there is such a thing as the nation as a historical figure, a collective person with a character and a destiny,' Mann said in January 1945, 'then National Socialism is no more or less than the form that a nation, the German nation, adopted twelve years ago.' In saying this, Mann, who for decades had regarded himself as the leading representative of the nation of culture (*Kulturnation*), had become committed to the idea of cosmopolitanism as a civilizing influence.[27]

Mann's public addresses and private comments engaged with universal cultural issues that confronted the opponents of the Third Reich from Hollywood to Moscow. The first task was to convince the populations of the various countries involved of the fundamental threat posed by National Socialism. In the United States in particular this task was far from simple. The Third Reich seemed far away and, before the outbreak of war, it had hardly been perceived as a threat. Now it was directing its destructive policies against nations and minorities that many Americans felt indifferent towards. While people were aware in the occupied parts of Europe of the inhumanity of Nazi policies, they were also conscious of the risks involved in any kind of rebellion, which is why resistance was limited and people had to be persuaded to join it or even to regard it positively. In Britain and Russia, countries that had not been defeated but were under immediate threat, the population had to be mobilized for a war whose end appeared far off. Everywhere propaganda, in the form of pamphlets, pictures, and films, was aimed at strengthening the nations' own cultures and defining them through opposition to the Third Reich. To what extent that opposition extended to *German* culture in general was at first unclear. This uncertainty also had an impact on German artists and intellectuals in exile. Their involvement in propaganda against the Third Reich was partly welcomed but in part also viewed with suspicion or even blocked. And their potentially most important contribution, namely in reaching the Germans, was hard to achieve because the latter were to a great extent isolated from foreign influences. That was the experience even of a writer as prominent and with as strong a media presence as Thomas Mann.

Once the United States was no longer simply supporting Britain with arms but had in December 1941 officially entered the war on its side, its self-perception changed. The image presented was of a nation that made political decisions by consensus and upheld the values of democracy and the rule of law. That was how, it was implied, America had succeeded in uniting various ethnic groups and achieving the highest living standards in the world. The Third Reich offered the perfect negative foil. A cartoon contrasted the 'Hitler way', where a worker was driven with whips wielded by steel-helmeted state henchmen, with the 'American way', where employers and employees sat at a table under the protection of Uncle Sam to negotiate a compromise. Numerous firms combined advertising for their own products, from Pepsi-Cola to Chesterfield cigarettes to Wrigley's chewing gum, with advertising for the military, work in the armaments industry, or the purchase of war bonds, the implied message being that there was a fundamental distinction between American consumer opportunities and the general shortage of goods in Nazi Germany. Film directors and movie moguls also played a key role in this cultural mobilization of the Americans, even though, until then, the opponents of fascism among them had been in a minority.

Was National Socialism primarily a regime based on ideology or the product of a particular country and its culture? There were various answers to this question. Many people in the United States felt close to the Germans, in contrast to the Japanese, whose public image was strongly influenced by racial prejudice. That these Germans were now the enemy, while Russian Communists were now allies, was a message that had first to be made plausible. In view of the prevalence of antisemitic prejudices among Americans, great care was taken to avoid giving the impression that the war was being fought 'for the Jews'. One possibility was to present Nazis as the embodiment of a deplorable anti-democratic mentality that was not limited to members of one nation. Thus the 'Nazi types' that Thomas Mann admired in Hitchcock's *Saboteur* were not Germans, but rich American traitors. However, levelling anti-fascist criticism at upper-class Americans carried with it the danger of highlighting the glaring inequalities in American society and thus of threatening internal cohesion.

Other expressions of popular wartime culture in the United States were certainly not free of ethnic stereotypes designed to provoke a sense that its enemies were foreign and to cement national unity. The animated film *The Ducktators*, which promoted war bonds, presented Hitler, Mussolini, and General Hideki Tojo in ways that perpetuated national clichés. They appeared as grotesque ducks that gain power over naïve and submissive poultry. One hen speaks out at first for peace and mutual understanding, until she finally faces the fact that the ducks representing the Axis powers must be stopped by force. Even a radio broadcast about the adventures of Superman resorted to familiar ethnic prejudices regarding America's enemies. The programme-maker rejected criticism by arguing that his job was to fire up childish hatred and in doing so could not distinguish 'between the individual and the state whose ideology he defends': 'A German is a Nazi and a Jap is the little yellow man who knifed us in the back at Pearl Harbor.'[28]

One of the serious Hollywood films featuring Nazis was Hitchcock's *The Lifeboat*. After a sea battle in the North Atlantic an ethnically and socially diverse group of Americans is brought together in a lifeboat. The shipwrecked travellers pull a German out of the water and treat him as a prisoner of war. The man makes a friendly impression and enjoys singing. He cunningly gains their trust and increasingly divides the group. Because of his nautical experience and skill at the wheel and the rudder he has an air of authority. He begins to issue orders, which causes one of the group to exclaim, 'What do you know? We got a Führer!' He almost succeeds in steering them towards a German warship. The Americans finally see their mistake, overpower the enemy, and throw him into the water. In view of the peril emanating from Germany Hitchcock wanted his film to be a call to internal unity. It was, however, criticized for presenting the enemy as intelligent and determined, while the allies were naïve and quarrelsome. One of the passengers complains: 'What's the matter with us? We not only let the Nazi do our rowing for us but our thinking'. Whereas propaganda officials accused many Hollywood films of underestimating the Germans and presenting them as incompetent or critical of the regime, Hitchcock had to defend himself against the opposite charge.

Fritz Lang, on the other hand, a native of Vienna who had emigrated in 1933 from Berlin to Hollywood, could not have been accused of unintentionally depicting German superiority. His thriller *Hangmen Also Die!*, for which Bertolt Brecht wrote the screenplay and Hanns Eisler the music, gives a fictional account of the events following the assassination of Reinhard Heydrich in Prague in May 1942. The film's message was that, with the aid of cunning and self-sacrifice, gains can be made, even against overwhelmingly powerful occupiers. The Czechs, who hold seminars in private homes because of the closure of the Charles University, applaud a famous passage from Bedřich Smetana's symphonic poem *The Moldau*, do their best to resist the occupying power, and speak faultless American—as Lang intended in order to help the audience to identify with them. By contrast, the Gestapo men, played mostly by Jewish exiles, bark their orders in a strong accent. In the role of Heydrich, Hans Heinrich von Twardowski, who had emigrated in 1933 on account of his homosexuality and had been specializing in Nazi roles for some time in Hollywood, shouted in his mother tongue, 'I demand that in Czechoslovakia German be spoken. Do you understand?! German! German! German! German!'

The perception in the United States of the distinction between Germans and Nazis became increasingly hazy as the war went on and news arrived of the crimes perpetrated by the Third Reich. And this did not happen only in animations or thrillers. Frank Capra's propaganda film series *Why We Fight* (1942) explained to American soldiers why their country was involved in the conflict. Shots from *The Campaign in Poland* and *Victory in the West* were used to illustrate how the Nazis waged war. The series blamed Hitler's rise on 'certain distinctive German characteristics': an 'inborn love of regimentation and harsh discipline' had made what was once the land of 'poets and philosophers' into an empire of suppression and expansion and turned its inhabitants into mindless and insensate weapons. By contrast, the propaganda experts in the Office of War Propaganda, who were focusing on psychological warfare against the Third Reich as well as on internal mobilization, wanted a sharper distinction to be drawn between German culture and its perversion by the Nazis. 'Nazi ideology', as a memorandum from January 1943 stated, '*contradicts* the decisive tendencies and achievements of German culture (German classicism, humanitarianism, and idealism)'.[29]

How German culture and the Third Reich were related therefore remained a controversial issue within the American debate. Intellectual commentators on the Third Reich also engaged with it, among them many exiles who themselves felt very close to German culture. Although even these intellectuals attributed characteristics such as a willingness to subordinate themselves and reverence for authority to the Germans, unlike film directors or poster designers they felt an obligation to explain them. Time was pressing, insofar as it was necessary to develop some idea about how the German population should be treated after the hoped-for military victory. And because virtually no information was coming directly from the Reich, they were dependent on long-distance diagnoses of a population that was unwilling to rise up against the Nazi dictatorship even when the fortunes of war had long since turned.

Was the catastrophe the result of the Protestant–Prussian tradition of loyalty to the state going back to Martin Luther and Frederick the Great? Or was the nineteenth century, when the military put down the 1848/49 Revolution and Bismarck created national unity with blood and iron, crucial in determining the course of events? Such analyses of the historical roots of National Socialism did not condemn German culture as a whole, though they did point the finger at a number of its aspects as they related to political developments. Rival attempts at explanation combined psychological insights with Marxist analysis of class, giving less weight to cultural aspects. Thus Erich Fromm saw the explanation for Hitler's success in the appeal of his sadomasochistic personality 'with its inferiority feeling, hatred against life, asceticism, and envy of those who enjoy life'. These impulses had resonated with lower-middle-class Germans, who, in the wake of 1918, had lost their economic, social, and family security.[30] Whatever weight was given to long-term and short-term, intellectual, political, or socio–psychological factors, one thing was certain: more was needed than just liberating the Germans from Hitler's rule and disarming them. In view of the burden of guilt they had heaped on themselves, a mixture of supervision and re-education, the details of which were as yet unclear, appeared necessary.

In Britain the same view was taken. There the threat from the Third Reich had been felt for longer and much more directly. Although there had been intensive discussion about how to interpret the Nazi regime, on the whole there was even less willingness than in the United States to differentiate between Nazis and Germans (whom the Prime Minister Winston Churchill was fond of calling 'Huns'). The British also came to view themselves differently in the course of the war. There were new hopes of overcoming class divisions in society and of developing a culture no longer exclusively defined within the triangle formed by Oxford and Cambridge with their universities and London with its institutions and literary circles. Good-humoured endurance, tolerance towards other members of society, and pragmatic common sense were now seen as shared British values. Germany, associated as it was with militarism, subservience to authority, and a propensity for dangerous fantasies, provided the negative counterpart. It had its own sound: British films and radio programmes were full of voices barking out commands, soldiers' boots pounding to the beat of military music, and machine-gun fire accompanied by Wagner melodies. This signified an unmistakable contrast not only to the British but also to continental Europeans with their patriotic songs and resistance to German oppression.[31]

In the occupied countries native cultures increasingly asserted themselves against German rule. The at first widespread belief that the expansion of the Third Reich might boost national renewal in the countries concerned faded in the second half of the war. Exploitation and repression became more intense. In addition, the Germans now found themselves established on the territory of former allies such as Italy and Hungary and in the southern half of France, hitherto ruled from Vichy. There they had support only from the extreme right and diehard collaborators. Given that the military balance was at the same time clearly shifting in favour of the Allies, resistance movements throughout Europe were gaining support among the local population. From the Peloponnese to Emilia Romagna to the Massif Central in France partisans were active, appealing, for example in the still familiar song 'Bella Ciao', to a romanticized folk culture and identifying this with their nations. At the same time the ideological base of the resistance movement broadened out and as a result various political and religious groups could join it. Pressure was put on the native populations of the various countries to make no distinction between Nazism and German culture. The seemingly unpolitical Ufa feature films, popular precisely because of the lack of American alternatives, deserved by this measure to be boycotted. This also accounted for posters advertising the fantasy film *Münchhausen* (1943) being daubed with swastikas in Paris and Amsterdam, although its screenplay had been written by Erich Kästner, who was discreetly critical of the regime.

Even where cultural self-assertion and the struggle against the occupying power coincided, there were still a few people who held to the view that good Germans existed. But the degree of violence used by the SS and the Wehrmacht against the civilian population increasingly undermined that conviction. The Dutch resistance paper *Vrij Nederland* argued that the German 'nation as a whole' had never lost its 'barbaric characteristics', in spite of having produced European cultural figures such as Goethe, Bach, and Frederick the Great. It had, therefore, remained a 'foreign body in western Europe' and, as a result of the Nazi revolution, had become a 'deadly threat' to other countries. A 'different Germany' existed only under cover.[32] When, after the liberation of Paris in August 1944, the bodies of victims of torture and murder were discovered, Albert Camus expressed his shock in a resistance journal about perpetrators 'whose faces were formed like ours'. The French writer and philosopher took the view that in 1933 'an entire nation had become involved in the destruction of souls'. The good manners of those who had 'offered their seats in the Métro' could not hide that fact, nor could 'Himmler, who made torture a science and a profession, but who, when he came home at night, used the back door so as not to wake his favourite canary'.[33]

The situation in Russia was fundamentally different from that in France, the Netherlands, or even the Ukraine. For the German conduct of the war and occupation were violent to such a degree that there was at first no scope for attempts at collaboration and there were no grey areas with regard to the population's behaviour. Contrary to expectations raised by a Marxist world view, the German working classes showed no signs of refusing to fight Communists. The Russians came to see only too clearly that the Wehrmacht was waging a war of annihilation based on racist ideology. The Germans' belief in their cultural superiority found expression in the mass murder and untrammelled plundering of the civilian population. A Stalingrad kitchen maid reported her experiences with the occupiers before the battle: 'Back when they first took Stalingrad, they could get what they wanted. They needed clothes, good shoes, gold, watches, and they got everything.' It was possible to leave the city, but only in exchange for 'gold watches, good boots, men's suits or coats, good carpets', which she and her family did not possess. Whereas German war rhetoric emphasized determined fighters acting on their own initiative, the Russian perception was completely different. One captain was struck by the 'strength of the Germans' mechanical discipline'; 'the general mass of soldiers followed their officers' commands without question', even if those same soldiers as individuals had said they were sick of fighting.[34]

Such experiences and intense Soviet war propaganda increasingly turned the Germans as an entire ethnic group into the enemy. Members of the Russian intelligentsia, admittedly, still had great respect for the culture that had produced Goethe and Beethoven. In addition, exiled Germans were involved in Soviet propaganda and post-war planning (provided they were Communists particularly faithful to the party line). These were exceptions, however, and seemed to have no connection with the SS men and Wehrmacht soldiers of the present time. Communist ideology and Greater Russian nationalism blended in the existential struggle against the Third Reich. The regime also made important concessions to the Orthodox Church and to those who wished to commemorate the rule of the Tsars because military success demanded that sections of the population with conservative views be mobilized. Hatred of the Germans, combined with suspicion of the non-Russian populations in the Soviet Union, provided the glue that held this heterogeneous culture together during wartime. The writer Ilya Ehrenburg, whose Jewish background put him even more at risk than other Russians, wrote: 'If you have killed one German, kill another. Nothing gives us so much joy as the sight of German corpses.' Another writer, Lew Kopelew, later recalled trying, as a political officer, to prevent his soldiers from committing acts of violence against the civilian population when they marched into Germany. His superiors accused him of undermining soldiers' morale and spreading the 'propaganda of bourgeois humanism'.[35]

The increasing tendency among the Allies and in the occupied countries to see Germans and Nazis as one and the same was the direct result of Third Reich's entire approach to the war—an approach from which it benefited in the short term, as it made it easy, internally, to claim that Hitler's rule was the only option. The implied message was that the German people could not abandon National Socialism because in the eyes of the Allies they were now bound up with it, come what may. The British and American bombing raids could be used as evidence of this claim; they did in fact target not only armaments production but also the civilian population, in order to destroy its morale. Goebbels spoke repeatedly of the Allies' war against the Germans and everything they held dear, including historic buildings and museums, which, because of their historical inferiority complex, the Allies were determined to destroy: 'When English and American *terror bombers* appear today over centres of German and Italian art and reduce cultural treasures that were the product of centuries of work and creativity to dust and ashes in just an hour', the Propaganda Minister declared at the opening of the German Art Exhibition in late June 1943, 'then it is a violation of sound common sense to accord cultural significance, of all things, to such an egregious crime.'[36]

Thomas Mann had only contempt for such complaints: 'Threats of retaliation with poison gas for the inhumane phosphorus bombs,' he noted after reading comment in the German press about the air raids, 'the word "inhumane", the word "culture", the word "humanity".' However, what Mann referred to as 'the Nazis' culture lamentation'[37] was shared by many Germans who lived in the towns and cities affected by the bombing or who hoped to return there from the front. In addition to concern over their own survival, people experienced damage to churches and the destruction of historical old towns as attacks on their own identity. They provided evidence of the threat posed by the Allies to things that people knew and valued over and above the ebb and flow of politics, things that linked the present to the past. The Propaganda Ministry had the destruction of buildings documented in drawings and photos, thereby also making it easier to keep quiet about the numbers of killed and injured. The 'desecration of Cologne Cathedral' thus provided Nazi propaganda with welcome arguments to support its message that Germans must fight to preserve everything that German and European life consisted in. 'Out of a whole series of base and criminal acts, this is the most brutal slap in the face to all who are culturally aware that the Anglo-Saxons have had the temerity to perpetrate.'[38]

The Allied air raids, the dogged struggle of the Red Army, and the growing resistance in the various European countries resulted from the Third Reich's methods of waging war and its imperialist rule. But they needed the ideological justification and mobilization through propaganda that accompanied the renewal of national cultures from Russia to the United States. These national cultures defined themselves by contrast with their opponent. The hope that even 'in the present shameful era the true Germany that we so admired is still alive in secret and waits with us for the hour of liberation', as a Greek educated in Berlin put it,[39] was expressed less and less. For years the Third Reich itself had promoted the idea that Nazi and German culture were identical and had met with broad agreement from national comrades. Now this equivalence was turned back on Germany, in propaganda films and resistance pamphlets as well as in the form of bombs falling on historic buildings and old city centres.

There were, admittedly, efforts on the part of oppositional groups in the Third Reich itself to counteract this identification. Resistance, whether from Christian or secular, conservative or social democrat motives, made a distinction between German and National Socialist values. But, even if it had been successful, it would have come too late to regain the international trust that had been lost long before. To the writer's own great disappointment, Thomas Mann's radio talks, which people could only listen to by taking a considerable risk, did not bring about any uprising against Hitler's regime. As Allied troops finally advanced to Germany's borders the cultural alternatives became increasingly clear. People either created a narrative in which they were innocent or they experienced the end of the Third Reich as their own personal downfall.

Innocence and Downfall:
The End of Hitler's Culture

At the turn of the year 1942/43, along with the change in the military situation came a change in the position of Adolf Hitler. The meteoric rise and extensive powers of the Führer had rested on his successes. For many contemporaries Hitler's victories over internal and external enemies became a self-fulfilling prophecy and justified his claim to be a genius. Now that bombing raids were on the increase and Allied forces were advancing, it became very difficult to maintain this image. Hitler responded by prophesying the annihilation that the German nation must expect from the Jewish-controlled Allies, if they put up only half-hearted resistance. Were the Germans to be defeated, as he said in a radio address in January 1944, the 'fate of the German nation' would be to be 'totally annihilated by Bolshevism'. Precisely because they had suffered serious losses of men and materiel they must fight on in order to preserve the core of the nation, including its cultural capital, which could not be affected by the destruction of external things. Hitler regarded the destruction of German cities as an opportunity. Although, as he said, he mourned the 'irretrievable loss of historic works of art', his optimism regarding culture was unchanged: 'Glorious new cities will blossom from the ruins.'[40]

Hitler had always seen himself as an artist whose thoughts and intuitions were inextricably bound up with the fate of the German nation. He clung to this vision of himself even when defeat began to loom on the horizon. That was why he was so preoccupied in the Führer Headquarters with architecture and spoke at such length about cultural matters. There was 'no better way of preparing for defence than by inspiring people with enthusiasm for their cultural heritage,' he pronounced in one of his monologues there. 'The destruction of valuable cultural artefacts has a more powerful impact on people than when one of our factories is destroyed.' For Hitler, the more fragile the military situation of his Reich became, the more culture shored up the German claim to superiority. It had a value that was independent of recent successes or failures. The Germans had produced the 'greatest artistic achievements of the nineteenth century', he claimed. 'The English, French, and Americans' had 'absolutely nothing as significant to set beside their thinkers'. Romanticism was particularly important to Hitler, and he regarded it not only as an epoch in literature, music, and art history but also as the foundation of German identity. Expatiating on the subject in June 1943, he said: 'Our nation simply has a very highly pronounced feeling for Romanticism that is a completely closed book to the Americans, who can never see beyond the concrete jungle of their skyscrapers.'[41]

What the Führer was really thinking is hard to discern. He avoided putting anything in writing, most especially things of a personal nature. What he said to third parties was always tactically motivated and for him there had, in any case, never been a clear boundary between authenticity and his public profile. There is, however, evidence to suggest that Hitler was fully aware of the increasing hopelessness of the situation and would not admit it primarily because he wished to retain his authority as Führer and sustain the Germans' willingness to fight on.[42] It was less a case of his losing touch with reality and more one of his determination to control the staging of the inevitable downfall—his own and that of large sections of the German nation. Adopting the manner of the artist of genius, he bent over maps of the various theatres of war and over architectural plans for Berlin and Linz. In the second half of the war he made few public appearances. Instead, he drew plans of fortifications and bunkers for the 'East Wall', a defensive line intended to run from the Baltic to the Black Sea. He also invented names for new models of tanks. For him the most important task was to finish murdering the European Jews and to be remembered by posterity as a great historical figure. To have subordinated himself, even if only in part, to the professional expertise of the military or to have put out feelers for a separate peace would have been totally incompatible with this objective.

Hitler was especially fascinated by a particular strand of German Romanticism. At the time of the Wars of Liberation against Napoleon, poets had assigned mythic grandeur to those willing to die a sacrificial death for their own nation. Later Richard Wagner derived accounts, simultaneously memorable and complex, of the pain and beauty of heroic downfall from Teutonic sagas and medieval legends. The notion that true heroism finds its fulfilment in death was a cultural commonplace of the German bourgeoisie. A glorious end was an emotionally appealing fantasy that generally had no impact on people's real lives, although in the First World War Romantic ideas had been deployed to glorify death on the battlefield. They had even been used as an argument—not adopted at that time—for fighting on in 1918 regardless of the prospects of victory, rather than capitulating 'without honour'.[43]

Within the radical right-wing movements of the Weimar Republic these topoi were reshaped into a vision of the intellectual and spiritual transformation of the nation by a chosen elite. Thus, Hitler's rise too had acquired quasi-religious legitimation. Now, in the last phase of the war, the Führer again took up the topos of self-sacrifice and adapted it to justify his politics of catastrophe. He linked it with an aesthetic of death and destruction, from the 'scorched earth' policy that was his legacy in the Soviet Union to the Battle of the Bulge against the Americans in the Ardennes. From his youth Hitler had identified with Wagner's heroes—outsiders who rebel against the established order and thus find glory and fulfilment. His favourite opera was the composer's musically still immature early work *Rienzi* in which a people's tribune in the later Middle Ages mobilizes them to rebel against the Roman elites. Rienzi is finally destroyed by intrigues and incomprehension, but this sombre finale does not shake his faith in his divine mission.

In orchestrating a catastrophic end, the Führer was close to solving a fundamental cultural problem that, to all appearances, he himself felt to be such. On the one hand, it had always been his ambition to create an authentically National Socialist culture, and this is why he periodically bemoaned the inadequacies of paintings and films that aimed to do this. On the other hand, the Third Reich had appropriated popular and bourgeois culture, both as a pragmatic move in its power politics and as a reflection of the tastes of its leaders. In so doing, while it had gained support among the population, it had lost definition. It was therefore no accident that, when Hitler wished to point to German cultural achievements, he came back again and again to the nineteenth century, rather than referring to recent examples. Buildings and architectural projects were the exception to this rule in the Third Reich. They also strengthened Hitler's claim to be a genius and a visionary. Because he was concerned about his image among future generations, the Führer occupied himself tirelessly with plans for new buildings. He simultaneously situated these plans in a wider context, that of an empire that could only come into its own by destroying the existing world.

The suspicion that Hitler was deliberately charting a course towards his own and his nation's destruction was already in circulation. It was cited by top military leaders looking for support within the Wehrmacht for a coup and by those who, after being captured, addressed the German population from Moscow. In one of his radio talks Thomas Mann told the Germans that their 'so-called heroism' amounted to a crime not only against other nations but 'against Germany itself, against the German nation and its culture'.[44] Since the defeat at Stalingrad Nazi propaganda had been tasked with counteracting this suspicion. It aimed to invest the sacrifice of individual lives with higher meaning, at the same time as suggesting that, after the 'final victory', attractive prospects would open up for survivors. Joseph Goebbels, who during the first half of the war had found himself on the back foot in the rivalries over cultural policy within the leadership, now gained new and extended powers. His rivals Rosenberg and Ribbentrop, as well as Göring and Himmler, had been more influential in the occupied territories in Europe. But now power in the Reich itself was what mattered once more, and Goebbels still had extensive control over the press, film, and theatre. He thus assumed a central role in the cultural 'final show-down', though other prominent figures in the regime were also active.

The radical version of Nazi propaganda consisted in developing or adopting philosophical and pseudo-historical justifications for militarily pointless sacrifices. While the fighting at Stalingrad was still in progress Göring made a speech on 30 January 1943 to members of the Wehrmacht. The Reich Marshal was a particularly appropriate person for this task because, as a former fighter pilot, he had military credentials. He referred to the heroic struggle of the Burgundians against the superior numbers of Huns in the *Nibelungenlied*. He also alluded to the Battle of Thermopylae in 480 BC, in which a small group of Spartans had resisted the advancing Persians and all been killed. Such endurance was 'hopeless but not insignificant', Göring said. He emphasized this by adapting the famous lines by Friedrich Schiller: 'The day will come when people will say, "If you should go to Germany, tell how you saw us lying at Stalingrad, as the law, the law ensuring the security of our nation, ordained".'[45] A few weeks later, in the Berlin Sportpalast, Goebbels declared 'total war' and, to the acclaim of his audience, asked ten questions regarding the Germans' willingness to fight. In the months that followed he invented ever new formulations by which to argue that the present setbacks and losses were ultimately unimportant. The military crisis was producing substantive gains because it was revealing the 'fundamental strength of our nationhood'.[46]

In addition to such appeals to ethnically based moral sentiment, Goebbels counted on the impact of shocking descriptions of British bombing raids and bleak scenarios resulting from a Soviet invasion. These reinforced the Germans' self-image as innocent victims and also suggested new ways in which the civilian population could participate in the war. In addition to featuring in speeches and articles, they now became the subject matter for films. In the family drama The Degenhardts (1944) Heinrich George played a family patriarch and civil service administrator in Lübeck. Having been pensioned off, Degenhardt questions his purpose in life, keeps the humiliation from his family, and wanders aimlessly through the streets of the town. But after the bombing of Lübeck he is needed once more and can face new challenges using the expertise gained in his former profession. The war provides not only Degenhardt's children but also their father with an opportunity to fulfil themselves through patriotic activities, even though the latter's professional life is over.

In addition to being valued at home, soldiers serving at the front also provided opportunities for positive identification. The message being conveyed here was that the determination of the Germans and the genius of their Führer made them able to overcome even numerically and materially stronger enemies. Newspapers and magazines were full of portraits of courageous and decisive 'lone fighters' such as fighter pilots, mountain infantrymen, or tank commanders who swept their comrades along with them and defeated Russians or Americans. They were intended to prove that the intellectual and moral superiority of the Germans still translated into military successes, and also that leadership was not a matter of rank but arose from the actual situation if people had the correct mental attitude. The *Deutsche Allgemeine Zeitung*, which reflected the opinion of the educated middle classes, proclaimed: 'The outstanding mental capacity of German troops in close combat will always be victorious over rigid and insensible Bolshevist robots.'[47] The *Berliner Lokal-Anzeiger* published the story of a young NCO with the typical Berlin surname of Klabunde. Known as a 'fearless daredevil', he had once taken over command after several of his superiors had been eliminated. On another occasion Klabunde had volunteered for a reconnaissance patrol and had 'smoked out' one of the Soviet bases: 'In intense close combat using hand grenades and among densely packed reeds the young NCO led his men *forwards amid the storm of battle*.'[48]

The idea that 'mind' and 'will' were crucial to victory could also be conveyed through mythically enhanced evocations of the Wars of Liberation against Napoleon, which were used more and more often in the second half of the war. In Veit Harlan's film *Kolberg*, an extraordinarily costly production, the population of a Pomeranian fortress town refuses to surrender to French forces in 1807. Led by a representative of the citizens, Joachim Nettelbeck (played by Heinrich George), and Major Gneisenau, the people of Kolberg mount a heroic defence, risking their lives and the buildings of their town 'without hesitation'. Despite all apparently sensible misgivings and adverse circumstances, they inflict such heavy losses on the French that the latter finally cease fire and retreat. As Nettelbeck says at the end, 'Truly great things can only ever be born in pain.' When six years later Gneisenau, now a Prussian Field Marshal, refers to this example to support the idea of a national army, King Friedrich Wilhelm III opposes him by saying, 'You are a visionary, a poet, a German dreamer. Reality is not like that, Gneisenau.' Gneisenau responds, 'I know reality, Your Majesty, I stared it in the face back then at Kolberg.' The Field Marshal finally succeeds in convincing the monarch. Goebbels personally commissioned the film and, with Hitler's support, intervened repeatedly in filming. He aimed to promote the complete identification of the nation with the war, which he considered more valuable than professional military expertise or economic calculations. Between planning and premiere, however, Germany's military situation had deteriorated even further, resulting in fears that the film might undermine the audience's morale. Goebbels therefore instructed that a number of particularly graphic combat scenes be cut. Although *Kolberg* did in fact reach cinemas early in 1945, there was no longer an audience for morale-boosting films.

Goebbels had no illusions that all Germans would be impressed by tales of heroic self-sacrifice, even if they made use of elements of German cultural tradition. Even before 1939 his success as Propaganda Minister had been linked to his finely tuned sense of what people needed in the way of popular entertainment. Later too he had done his best to provide distractions from the ugly realities of war. Since the turn in the war, however, this had become a great deal more difficult. Goebbels responded by emphasizing that people could not just slink away from the national community. This would not only be contemptible but also pointless, because Germany's enemies would in any case not accept it—an allusion to the murder, already at an advanced stage, of the European Jews, whose co-religionists, according to Nazi ideology, were behind the governments in Washington, London, and Moscow. At the same time, he continued to give those who survived the crisis with honour the hope of a happy future. And he continued to work on the principle that he could compensate for personal hardship, anxieties, and losses by providing opportunities for recreation.

What were these opportunities for recreation during the last two years of the war? Radio and cinema programmes were still dominated by hit songs and feature films, even though Goebbels often thought them substandard. The tendency to escape a present that was increasingly hard to project in a positive light into fantasy worlds became more pronounced than before—and this made it easier for members of the audience to affirm their own innocence. In *Münchhausen* (1943), one of the first German films in colour, Hans Albers plays the eighteenth-century baron, an inveterate liar, who is sent to Russia, given the gift of eternal youth there, and has a series of adventures. *The Punch Bowl* (1944) shows Heinz Rühmann as the Berlin writer Dr Pfeiffer, who travels incognito to a small town at the turn of the twentieth century in order to relive his lost school years. After various comic episodes he wins the heart of his headmaster's daughter and breaks off his engagement to his fiancée in the city. At the end of the film he confesses to having invented the story as well as himself: 'Only the memories we carry with us are true, the dreams we weave, and the longings that motivate us; we'll content ourselves with those.'

In spite of all appeals to dreams and longings the cultural synthesis of National Socialism was falling apart. It had been based on the idea that *völkisch* renewal, bourgeois taste, and popular entertainment were reconcilable. During the first half of the war the Germans' opportunities to display their culture, practise it, and consume it had been extended, at the expense of other Europeans. But now this development was blocked and even reversed. In towns and cities bombs were destroying theatre buildings and concert halls. Football matches were frequently having to be cancelled. More and more newspapers and journals were halting publication because of a shortage of paper and the regime's deliberate policy of merging titles. The effects on film were less acute. In spite of bombing raids many cinemas remained intact and Goebbels exempted production staff and actors from bans or conscription. New locations for showings could be quickly created, some in the open air. Evacuated city-dwellers could see films in smaller towns, though there they were in competition with the locals for the few seats available. In addition, there was outrage because Western European 'foreign workers', whose labour was to be harnessed for the anti-Bolshevist war, were allowed to go to the cinema. Germans had got used to being at the front of the queue, and this situation cast doubt on their having priority. Finally, even radio entertainment was not without its problems. Many listeners demanded it, whereas others considered it out of place in view of the situation. The sense of something's being inappropriate could arise suddenly, as when, shortly after an air raid on Essen, the hit song 'I'm dancing to heaven with you' was inadvertently broadcast, provoking indignation among regional listeners.

Germans, therefore, certainly had legitimate alternatives to stories about willing self-sacrifice that diverted them from war experiences and expressed hopes of survival. Even so, there were unmistakable signs of people wanting to dissociate themselves from the culture of the Third Reich. Austrian patriotism experienced a surge of support. Before the Burg Theatre in Vienna was closed in summer 1944, the audience applauded whenever there was a mention of the Habsburg Empire in any of the plays performed. People also started looking abroad. Zarah Leander, for example, travelled to her native Sweden in 1943 and stayed there until the end of the war. German lovers of swing who were unwilling to content themselves with the jazz adaptations of the German Radio Orchestra had other options too.

During the early years of the war, a group called Hamburg Swing Youth had gone some way towards establishing a jazz-oriented counterculture. They combined their musical taste with a decidedly casual style of dress, dancing, and behaviour, and with occasional shows of disrespect towards Nazi bigwigs and expressions of doubt about the war. In this way they challenged the Hitler Youth, the Gestapo, and ultimately Himmler himself, evidencing the regime's difficulties in maintaining effective repression. But in the autumn of 1942 they were crushed. Dozens of swing fans were sent to concentration camps and subjected to violent treatment. Nevertheless, people copied them in other parts of the Reich, most of them more circumspectly, although a number took the serious risk of distributing circulars about American jazz. By 1943/44, however, the Allies were broadcasting from Italy and, after the Normandy landings, from France, so that soldiers could listen to Benny Goodman, Glenn Miller, and other American musicians. This was also possible in southern Germany, while in northern Germany people could receive the BBC Home Service or the Danish stations.

It was nevertheless rare for Germans to take a decisive stand against the Nazi war. The widespread view was that civilian life could only begin again properly after a victorious end to the military conflict; in fact it was often seen as the actual purpose of the conflict. The *Deutsche Allgemeine Zeitung* summed up this vision: 'The consumer will again be given freedom for this is the *essence of any culture*. Among the many millions that make up a nation there are as many desires, needs, and ideals and these will be fulfilled in one way or another.' Individualistic expectations such as these were accompanied by interpretations of the war experience itself that gave it a higher meaning. The paper discerned in Berlin, already partially destroyed and still under bombardment, a 'purposeful straightforwardness' that matched not only the challenges of the day but also the character of the population. That included interests that went beyond securing one's own immediate survival, such as theatre, music, and art, as well as film comedies: 'The new film *The Punch Bowl* was particularly popular, proof that an injection of humour and an hour of boisterous fun are particularly necessary in difficult times and will never fail.'[49]

The image of the individualistic consumer of the future and the uncomplicated and good-humoured city dweller of the present overlapped with that of the German who was willing to make sacrifices and might lose his or her life at any moment at the front or through bombing at home. The *Deutsche Allgemeine Zeitung* saw no call in this for emotional rhetoric, for 'as the sacrifices required of the individual have become greater, the desire to elevate them to heroic status has receded'. This 'great era' was producing extraordinary deeds, but they should 'be understood simply as people doing their duty'. While this modesty might appear self-evident, it still had to be given meaning: 'Everything in this war will be seen to have had its purpose.' The very fact that the Germans had made such sacrifices absolved them of any guilt. The claim to cultural superiority that had informed all the rhetoric of war was now brought in to reassure people of their moral purity. A front line reporter claimed that German soldiers were kind to women, children, and butterflies. They read Goethe instead of enjoying nude photos like the Americans: 'There is infinite delicacy at the front. It is cheerful and yet serious. It has nothing to do with rank or age, or with profession and education.'[50]

Wehrmacht soldiers rarely described their lives in such poetic formulae, yet even they saw themselves overwhelmingly as taking part in a legitimate defensive war. In his letters home Corporal Günther Krenzin, in civilian life a toolmaker in Berlin, expressed no inclination to sacrifice himself. He longed for an end to the conflict because he 'was sick to death of army life' and was therefore pinning his hopes on the miracle weapons' (V1s and V2s). Being a consumer of culture was part of his hope for a peaceful future in which he could 'go to the cinema' again with his wife. At the same time, he held on to his memory of a world not shaped by war. While at the front he saw a romance that had been shot before the first heavy bombing raids on the capital: 'Yesterday I went to the cinema, saw *City Melody* and our dear old Berlin again as it once was. It made me so sad to think of how it looks now and afterwards the longing to be home again came back and was really strong.'[51]

Hans-Joachim S., a businessman in civilian life and also a Berliner, was much more heavily involved in the Nazi project than Günther Krenzin. In Russia he had tried 'to show the local population something of German cleanliness and hard work', but soon made disillusioned comments about the 'underhandedness' there and 'lack of culture'.[52] He was 'not 100% edified' by Göring's speech during the Battle of Stalingrad, because he was fully aware that, like any soldier, he had to be 'prepared from the word go to sacrifice his life'. For him too any ideas of a good life in the future involved being a consumer. 'When we have another nice little Opel', he wrote to his wife, 'we'll also get a portable radio and lots of other things that will help us enjoy life.' Thoughts like these kept his spirits up, along with his belief that 'Hitler's cause' was just, 'or at least better than the Bolshevists' and plutocrats' and Jews'.' Hans-Joachim S. underwent officer training. He grew 'increasingly used to military ways of thinking' and created his own 'little idealistic world view', which on the one hand 'made life significantly easier' for him and on the other helped him to maintain a sense of personal commitment to National Socialism.[53] He could see no alternative. In his eyes it was better to 'help fight for the final victory than to be enslaved to foreign nations'. Only if the soldiers kept fighting 'to the last man' would his wife and children have the prospect of a 'better future'.[54]

Few Wehrmacht soldiers felt inclined to interpret their fate in the light of Spartans, Nibelungs, or the people of Kolberg from the time of the Napoleonic Wars. Instead, the experience of war induced feelings of being defenceless and unheroically resigned to die in the face of an increasingly desperate situation. In letters home the language was more direct and the point of view more pragmatic than in Goebbels's propaganda slogans. The notion of 'culture' was associated more with a longing for basic personal hygiene or relaxing music than with imposing German rule over others. A Berlin soldier, Lutz Raumer, wrote to his parents from a field hospital: 'Someone has set up a radio one floor below us, so at least we get a bit of culture.'[55] But the term continued to carry an assertion of superiority, expressed as moral self-justification, even if it was much less confident than a few years before. According to Major Wolfgang Panzer, a Heidelberg academic and member of the NSDAP, the Germans could not 'simply abandon everything to the enemy, if only because they disregard any agreement and cultural heritage means nothing.'[56] For many soldiers, and for officers in particular, Nazi attitudes and turns of phrase remained convincing almost to the end of the war, as the use of terms such as 'world view' and 'final victory' in Hans-Joachim S.'s letters indicates.

On the home front the incessant bombing raids increasingly determined public life. Fire storms, rubble, and the chaotic movements of people fleeing from the city to the country completed the panorama of destruction. The Norwegian journalist Theo Findahl described the 'strangely oppressive *end-of-the-world* atmosphere' in the lobby of the Hotel Adlon in the centre of Berlin and drew on historical analogies: 'Here a world city is truly going under before our very eyes. Memories of scenes from novels about Carthage and the fall of Rome, and of the catastrophic destruction of Pompeii race through one's mind.'[57] In these circumstances there was precious little scope for showy National Socialist public events. Talk about retribution using new-fangled weapons and the allure of occasional hints that a radical new beginning might arise out of the ruins were not able to make up for this. Instead, Church voices now sounded more convincing. Bishops and pastors, both Catholic and Protestant, interpreted the bombing raids as a punishment, an opportunity for repentance, and a precondition for future redemption. Although they were thereby distancing themselves from the Nazi rhetoric of retribution, at the same time they mediated the idea of a war for which the Germans bore no concrete responsibility and which they were being forced to go on enduring.

Under current conditions it was difficult to hold masses and church services at all. The same was true of cultural events, which grew increasingly rare towards the end of the war. For a time Goebbels tried to keep theatre and musical life going in spite of the growing number of theatres and concert halls that were destroyed. He found it increasingly difficult, however, to reconcile this with the demands of 'total war', of the kind he tirelessly promoted. He complained that the staff of the Berlin Metropoltheater had 'simply done a bunk after the last air raids' and that the many Strength through Joy events were giving scope for a 'bit of cultural war profiteering'. Goebbels decreed that from 1 September 1944 theatres would be closed across the Reich and that concerts would be restricted, which resulted in a reduction in the number of performers released from war service on the grounds of being 'indispensable'. As far as cultural politics were concerned, Goebbels, who was increasingly involved in the conduct of the war, concentrated either on morale-boosting propaganda in the manner of *Kolberg* or on plans for the post-war period. He, who at one time had so loved to make a grand entrance in the opera house or concert hall, now, like many other Germans, used music for private reflection. After listening to the radio one evening, he noted: 'Beethoven's music was just made for these times.'[58]

This combination of improvisation and vision that we can observe in Hitler and Goebbels also left its mark on the area of culture most directly affected by the bombing war, namely architecture and town planning. In the interim the Führer had forbidden the development of plans for the post-war period. But then he gave in to the argument that it was not only possible to make good the destruction temporarily but also necessary to take timely steps to prepare for reconstruction. In this area Albert Speer was in competition with Robert Ley, the Reich Housing Commissar and Head of the German Labour Front. Ley and other radical National Socialists wished to promote the nation's health by building towns with a large number of individual, single-family dwellings with a garden. Speer and his colleagues, by contrast, preferred more technocratic solutions: they were glad that the bombing had eliminated large amounts of the nineteenth-century housing stock. There was now little talk of monumental buildings and geometric axes, however. According to Speer in November 1943, the aim was not 'to create a new city centre inspired by high art', but to build quickly and thus avoid future traffic jams: 'Somehow or other we must, as far as possible, stick to the existing layout of roads and try to widen them.'[59]

Thus, architects and town planners on the one hand continued to contribute to the Nazi war effort but on the other developed concrete ideas that were independent of the Third Reich. This attitude allowed them to fit into a culture that was determined by destruction and which, in practice, reacted defensively and with piecemeal solutions. The bombing war and the Allied invasion pulled the rug from under the cultural synthesis that had formed in the mid-1930s and had become more radical after the outbreak of war. In view of the hopeless military situation only a minority of Germans were convinced by a revival of the rhetoric of decision and renewal familiar from 1933/34. Even so, Nazi ideology, though often blended with bourgeois traditions and consumerist trends, was still in evidence up to the end of the Third Reich. It could survive because it had been mediated through a variety of channels and had also been absorbed by the Germans. On the other hand, it met with strong reservations among those for whom Imperial Germany and the Weimar Republic rather than National Socialism had been the major influences. But, under the conditions of a dictatorship with broad support among the population, these reservations could not find public expression. An alternative consciousness to National Socialism could only be preserved or nurtured in very restricted circles, such as in the family of the young Berlin soldier and later deserter Hans Stock, who told his parents about the pillaging of Slovenian villages and shooting of alleged partisans: 'It was an indescribable image of our "culture", though I've almost got used to it.'[60]

CONCLUSION

After the Nazi Dream

As the Third Reich crumbled, so did its culture. In the last months of the war stolen works of art were taken to bunkers and mines. Concerts, film production, and theatrical life came to an almost complete halt. Like all other Germans, musicians and actors were at risk of injury or death from air raids, and had to fight in the Wehrmacht or the Volkssturm (a national militia called into being in the final months of the war). Even the Berlin Philharmonic, who, as standard-bearers of German musical life, were classified to the end of the war as being in a reserved occupation, could virtually never perform. Their final concerts before the surrender were held at makeshift venues before untypical audiences such as the Hitler Youth, Wehrmacht soldiers, and leading Nazi functionaries. On 11 April 1945 they gave a private concert for Albert Speer, though with reduced numbers as some members had taken flight and others had committed suicide. Thus the Armaments Minister could enjoy Beethoven, Bruckner, and Wagner, while the Red Army was already setting about taking Berlin. Wilhelm Furtwängler, the orchestra's resident conductor, who had given such a boost to the cultural prestige of the Third

Reich, was, however, no longer there. To Goebbels's annoyance, he preferred to wait in Switzerland for the war to end.

After twelve years German culture and Nazi dominance parted company. Something that had been 'like a dream' for millions of people and had won them over could not survive without dictatorial power and military success. Hitler barely mentioned culture in his last recorded comments. He was instead focusing on preserving his image as a political genius. As he became increasingly frail physically, the Führer invoked Frederick the Great, whose posture and gestures he imitated. Hitler presented the imperialist war and the mass murder of the European Jews as unavoidable, for he wanted to be seen after his death as carrying out '*völkische Realpolitik*': 'There are those who strive for the wellbeing of the individual as an abstract idea and chase the illusion of a universalist solution', he dictated to his loyal follower Martin Bormann. 'The others are those who are realistic and act. National Socialism recognizes only the ethnic German nation [*Volkstum*] and is concerned only with the welfare of the German people.'[1]

Hitler's appeal to hold fast to the Nazi vision of the world, especially in defeat, did not provoke a response from the majority of his national comrades. Foreign observers who arrived in Germany with the Allied armies were struck by something else, namely the tendency on the one hand to adopt a defiant and defensive attitude to justify the Third Reich and on the other to deny any shared responsibility for its policies. The American officer Saul K. Padover had the task of conducting detailed interviews with the population to gain a clear impression of their attitude. Because he was a native of Vienna, he had no language difficulties. The interviews provided him with insights that were as disconcerting as they were telling. Particularly well-educated Germans were 'possessed of arrogant pride in German *Kultur*', which had legitimized their participation in the National Socialist project and, even after the latter's collapse, was not called into question. One philosopher and art historian refused to see any connection between his support for Hitler and the destruction of his beloved Aachen. 'Politics I do not understand', he mumbled, and repeated to Padover the typical excuse of the educated middle class: 'My preoccupation is with the beautiful and the true.' When speaking to a retired military man who made reference to Germany as a '*Kultur* state', the American officer finally lost his temper: 'Herr General, you speak of *Kultur*. Do you know of the murder factories, do you know what the Germans have done in Europe?'[2]

However justified Padover's criticism of the idea of German culture was, it quickly appeared unlikely that the latter would ever again be associated with total war and racially motivated murder. After May 1945 a new incarnation of the Third Reich was impossible, both because of Allied control and because the consequences of its policies for the Germans had become evident. The destructive dynamic of the Nazi regime with its dire effects on German and European culture had come to an end.

Culture in the Third Reich had depended on a specific constellation. Hitler's political goals and cultural preferences had given rise to permanent rivalry among his followers. The enmity between Rosenberg, who had support from his *völkisch* activists and later his task force, and Goebbels, who controlled the Propaganda Ministry and the system of Reich Chambers of Culture, had spurred them both on to keep launching new initiatives. The cult of the Teutons for Himmler and city planning for Speer had given both men their own cultural domains. Göring had retained cultural influence through his oversight of the Prussian state theatres, which also helped him project the image of a Renaissance man. Like Hitler, all these prominent Third Reich figures had aimed to acquire prestigious works of art and committed theft on a grand scale. And, in spite of making many pragmatic decisions in individual cases, they had all taken pains to appear to their Führer as radical and antisemitic.

The effects of this constellation had spread to the individual Nazi Party administrative districts of the Reich (the Gaus) and later even to the occupied territories in Europe. Personal ambitions, bureaucratic energy, and dictatorial powers had been mobilized in aid of cultural 'purification'. By such means racist ideas had been able to develop and blend with other tendencies. German culture had expanded and, notwithstanding some transient attractiveness, had done so by the use of force and at the expense of other cultures. Only total military defeat put an end to this. The leaders of the Third Reich committed suicide (with the exception of Speer, who for many years was a prisoner in Spandau and later earned a large amount of money by publishing his memoirs), and the institutions they had established were abolished. After 1945 it was again possible to distinguish between German and National Socialist culture: this was beneficial to former national comrades keen to exculpate themselves, as well as to the occupying powers as a means of reconnecting with German traditions.

Even so, the impact of the Third Reich on German culture was still felt beyond its demise. Its rule robbed millions of people of their capacity to express themselves politically and culturally. Social Democrats and Communists had at best been able to sing their songs in private. Anti-fascist humanism had survived only in exile and been in no position to exercise any influence on the attitudes of Germans within the Reich. After 1945 it was still marginalized in the Federal Republic and soon also in the German Democratic Republic, which exerted more and more rigid control over cultural life. Jews had been banned since 1933 from concert halls and theatres, from the auditorium as well as the stage. Under increasingly difficult conditions they had fought to maintain some cultural space and freedom, from the Cultural Associations of the pre-war years to the ghettos of the war period, through making music, reading, and writing diaries. After the Holocaust, Jewish culture, most of whose practitioners had perished, could revive at best through small beginnings.

The marginalization of minorities and political opponents in Germany would not have been possible if the Third Reich had not simultaneously been so successful in winning the support of the national comrades. It had created a culture in which specifically Nazi components overlapped and blended with bourgeois and nationalist traditions, as well as with popular entertainment. After the war, however, it was very simple to block out this synthesis and conjure up the impression of a cultural continuity that tran-scended the regime's collapse. For a long time the erstwhile critics of the Third Reich were thus in a difficult position in western Germany. That was one reason why, after his return from California in 1952, Thomas Mann lived for the rest of his life in Kilchberg in Switzerland rather than in places he knew well, such as Munich and Lübeck. Victor Klemperer, on the other hand, remained in the Soviet zone of occupation, in spite of his strongly bourgeois outlook. He later even became a member of the GDR national assembly, the *Volkskammer*. Convinced right-wing intel-lectuals could also find themselves at odds with the cultural life of the Federal Republic, even though they were regarded with a cer-tain fascination for that very reason. Both Carl Schmitt and Ernst

Jünger lived away from the public eye, though they maintained many contacts and were widely read. By contrast, those performers involved in light entertainment, who had contributed so much to the popularity of the Third Reich, could not complain about being marginalized. Their seemingly unpolitical hit songs and comedies remained popular and, like Heinz Rühmann for example, they were able to carry on seamlessly with their careers.

Although the culture of the Third Reich came to an end in 1945 it nevertheless still impacts on the present time, however profound the rupture marked by Hitler's death and however little the names Arno Breker, Wilhelm Furtwängler, or Zarah Leander may mean to younger Germans. Even in the twenty-first century we are still repeatedly being confronted with the legacy of this culture. Nazi art or art works stolen by Nazis surface in unexpected places, for example in Bad Dürckheim where, in May 2015, police made a sensational discovery, unearthing Josef Thorak's bronze horses that had once stood outside the New Reich Chancellery and a large-scale relief by Arno Breker destined for the triumphal arch in the new capital. Television documentaries show again and again how much our present view of National Socialism is still shaped by photos and films commissioned by the Nazis themselves for propaganda purposes. Random elements belonging to the culture of the Third Reich are still being used, whether without any recognizable political purpose in popular culture or very consciously by right-wing extremist movements in Germany and elsewhere.

A key factor in the rise of the Third Reich was the Germans' nationalistic claim to cultural superiority in the first third of the twentieth century. It arose during the imperial period, grew more intense during the First World War, and continued during the Weimar Republic, despite all that era's modernist and democratic tendencies. The visions that resulted from it were incompatible both with cultural diversity within Germany and with the right of other cultures to exist. Since 1945 the great range of transnational influences acting on German culture have made this claim to superiority far less plausible. Even so, what Thomas Mann told the Germans in a radio talk a year before the end of the war is still important: 'German culture is not the highest and only true culture, but rather one among others, and its deepest impulse was always admiration; arrogance will kill it. The world does not revolve around Germany; it is only a small part of this vast world, and there are more pressing issues to tackle than the problems of the German soul.'[3]

NOTES

Introduction: 'Like a Dream'

1. *Die Tagebücher von Joseph Goebbels*, Part I: 1923–1941, ed. by Elke Fröhlich (Munich, 1998–2006), vol. 8, 200 (1/2 July 1940).
2. See the classic studies by George Mosse, *Nazi Culture: Intellectual, Cultural and Social Life in the Third Reich* (New York, 1966); Peter Gay, *Weimar Culture: The Outsider as Insider* (New York, 1968); and most recently, Jost Hermand, *Culture in Dark Times: Nazi Fascism, Inner Emigration, and Exile* (New York, 2012), part I.
3. Peter Reichel, *Der schöne Schein des Dritten Reiches: Gewalt und Faszination des Faschismus* (Munich, 1991).
4. In contrast to Hermand, *Culture in Dark Times*, Michael Kater's Culture in Nazi Germany (New Haven, 2019) provides full coverage of the war years and Jews' cultural activities. However, while the book stands out for its immensely knowledgeable discussion of numerous individual trajectories, it never quite explains why the incoherent and mediocre culture of the Third Reich appealed to so many Germans and helped to create such a ferocious dynamic.

1. From Weimar Culture to 'German' Culture

1. *Deutsche Illustrierte*, 23 October 1928, 28 February 1928.
2. *Daheim*, 21 April 1928, 28 July 1928.
3. Hedda Kalshoven, *Ich denk so viel an Euch: Ein deutsch–holländischer Briefwechsel 1920–1949* (Munich, 1995), 93 (21 January 1930).
4. Ibid., 71 (19 August 1924).
5. Ibid., 108 (22 June 1931).
6. Peter Longerich, *Heinrich Himmler* (Oxford, 2012); Robert Gerwarth, *Hitler's Hangman: The Life of Heydrich* (New Haven, 2012).
7. Kalshoven, *Ich denk so viel an Euch*, 101 (21 February 1931).
8. *Berliner Zeitung*, midday edition, 7 May 1932.
9. Kalshoven, *Ich denk so viel an Euch*, 106 (15 April 1931), 132 (18 January 1932).

10. David Imhoof, 'Blue Angel, Brown Culture: The Politics of Film Reception in Göttingen', in John Alexander Williams (ed.), *Weimar Culture Revisited* (New York, 2011), 49–72 (64).

11. *Die Tat*, 23 (1931/32), 928.

12. Mathias Rösch, *Die Münchner NSDAP 1925–1933: Eine Untersuchung zur inneren Struktur der NSDAP in der Weimarer Republik* (Munich, 2002), 156, 292–4.

13. *Völkischer Beobachter*, 1/2 March 1931, 29/30 March 1931, 22 August 1931.

14. *Der Angriff*, 2 May 1931, 12 January 1931.

15. *Völkischer Beobachter*, 11 March 1931, 13 March 1931.

16. Ibid., 20 November 1931.

17. Diaries of Luise Solmitz, 4 February 1932, 16 February 1932, 28 August 1932, Archiv der Forschungsstelle für Zeitgeschichte Hamburg, 11/S11.

18. Victor Klemperer, *I Shall Bear Witness: The Diaries of Victor Klemperer 1933–1941* (London, 1999), 28–9.

19. Victor Klemperer, *Leben sammeln, nicht fragen wozu und warum: Tagebücher 1925–1932*, ed. by Walter Nojowski (Berlin, 1996), vol. 2, 525 (19 May 1929), 620 (20 December 1929), 717 (21 June 1931).

20. Klemperer, *I Shall Bear Witness*, 33 (28 July 1933), 40 (6 September 1933), 86 (13 June 1934), 76 (5 April 1934).

21. Ibid., 8 (17 March 1933), 10 (21 March 1933), 10 (22 March 1933).

22. On what follows, see Peter Jelavich, *Berlin Alexanderplatz: Radio, Film, and the Death of Weimar Culture* (Berkeley, 2006), 62–92, 126–90.

23. Bärbel Schrader (ed.), *Der Fall Remarque: Im Westen nichts Neues. Eine Dokumentation* (Leipzig, 1992), 167, 161, 167, emphases in the original.

24. *Tempo*, 1 July 1931.

25. Thomas Balistier, *Gewalt und Ordnung: Kalkül und Faszination der SA* (Münster, 1989), 141.

26. 'Hass und Begeisterung bilden Spalier': Die politische Autobiografie von Horst Wessel, ed. by Manfred Gailus and Daniel Siemens (Berlin-Brandenburg, 2011), 109–11.

27. Daniel Siemens, *The Making of a Nazi Hero: The Murder and Myth of Horst Wessel* (London, 2013), 15, 109.

28. Gerhard Paul, *Aufstand der Bilder: Die NS-Propaganda vor 1933* (Bonn, 1990), 240.

29. Kurt Kreiler, 'Vom zufälligen Tod eines Anarchisten: Leben und Tod des Schriftstellers Erich Mühsam', in Günter Morsch (ed.), *Konzentrationslager Oranienburg* (Berlin, 1994), 95–107.

30. Norbert Frei and Johannes Schmitz, *Journalismus im Dritten Reich* (3rd ed., Munich, 1999), 30.

31. '*Schreiben, wie es wirklich war…*' *Aufzeichnungen Karl Dürkefäldens aus den Jahren 1933–1945*, ed. by Herbert und Sibylle Obenaus (Hannover, 1985), 35 (12 March 1933), 51 (12 May 1933).

32. Kalshoven, *Ich denk so viel an Euch*, 175–6, 177 (14 March 1933).

33. Ibid., 190 (6 April 1933), 199 (17 May 1933), emphasis in the original.

34. Solmitz diaries, 6 February 1933, 16 March 1933, 1 March 1933.

35. Carl Schmitt, *Tagebücher 1930 bis 1934*, ed. by Wolfgang Schuller (Berlin, 2010), 257 (31 January 1933), 271 (19 March 1933).

36. Raphael Gross, *Carl Schmitt und die Juden: Eine deutsche Rechtslehre* (Frankfurt, 2000), 49, 60, 62, 65.

37. Schmitt, *Tagebücher*, 287 (29 April 1933).

38. Dirk Blasius, *Carl Schmitt: Preußischer Staatsrat in Hitlers Reich* (Göttingen, 2001), 89, 110–1.

39. Carl Schmitt, 'Reich – Staat – Bund' (1933), in Schmitt, *Positionen und Begriffe im Kampf mit Weimar—Genf—Versailles 1923–1939* (Berlin, 1988), 190–8 (198).

40. Martin Heidegger, 'The Self-Assertion of the German University: Address, Delivered on the Solemn Assumption of the Rectorate of the University Freiburg. The Rectorate 1933/34: Facts and Thoughts', *Review of Metaphysics*, 38 (March 1985), pp. 467–502, 474, 476, 479 [emphases in original].

41. Albrecht Schöne, *Göttinger Bücherverbrennung 1933* (Göttingen, 1983), 19.

42. Manfred Gailus, '1933 als protestantisches Erlebnis: emphatische Selbsttransformation und Spaltung', *Geschichte und Gesellschaft*, 29 (2003), 481–511 (484–5, 494–5).

43. Doris Bergen, 'Die "Deutschen Christen" 1933–1945: ganz normale Gläubige und eifrige Komplizen?', *Geschichte und Gesellschaft*, 29 (2003), 542–74 (561).

44. Bernhard Fulda and Aya Soika, 'Emil Nolde and the National Socialist Dictatorship', in Olaf Peters and the Neue Galerie (eds), *Degenerate Art: The Attack on Modern Art in Nazi Germany* (Munich, 2014), 184–93.

45. Joachim Dyck, *Der Zeitzeuge: Gottfried Benn 1929–1949* (Göttingen, 2006), 20, 27, 84, 110.

46. '*Schreiben, wie es wirklich war…*', 53 (24 May 1933), 66 (end of August 1933).

47. Kalshoven, *Ich denk so viel an Euch*, 196 (4 May 1933), 199 (17 May 1933), 215 (18 October 1933).

48. Solmitz diaries, 28 February 1933, 4 July 1933, 8 April 1933, 8 June 1933. The last two quotations are missing from the typescript Solmitz made in the 1950s but are now accessible in Frank Bajohr, Beate Meyer, and Joachim Szodrynski (eds), *Bedrohung, Hoffnung, Skepsis: Vier Tagebücher des Jahres 1933* (Göttingen, 2013), 189, 215.
49. Martin Heidegger, *Überlegungen II–VI (Schwarze Hefte 1931–1938)*, ed. by Peter Trawny (Frankfurt, 2014), 111.

2. National Socialism as a Cultural Synthesis

1. Angela Schwarz, *Reisen ins Dritte Reich: Britische Augenzeugen im national-sozialistischen Deutschland (1933–39)* (Göttingen, 1993), 97.
2. *Die Tagebücher von Joseph Goebbels*, Part I, vol. 3/I, 170 (20 January 1935), 173 (24 January 1935).
3. Ibid., vol. 3/I, 164 (6 January 1935), 177 (31 January 1935).
4. Ibid., vol. 3/I, 177 (31 January 1935), 165 (8 January 1935), 173, 170 (18 January 1935).
5. Ibid., vol. 3/I, 55 (30 May 1934); ibid., vol. 4, 90 (13 April 1937).
6. Ibid., vol. 3/II, 250 (21 November 1936); vol. 4, 71 (29 March 1937), 57 (18 March 1937).
7. Ibid., vol. 3/II, 250 (14 November 1936); vol. 3/I, 292 (13 September 1935).
8. Ibid., vol. 3/II, 251 (15 November 1936); vol. 3/I, 366 (21 January 1936); vol. 4, 194 (24 June 1937).
9. Ibid., vol. 3/II, 229 (28 October 1936).
10. Michael H. Kater, *The Twisted Muse: Musicians and their Music in the Third Reich* (New York, 1997), 19.
11. All quotations from *Alfred Rosenberg: Die Tagebücher von 1934 bis 1944*, ed. by Jürgen Matthäus and Frank Bajohr (Frankfurt, 2015), 133 (5 June 1934).
12. *Die Tagebücher von Joseph Goebbels*, Part I, vol. 4, 32 (3 March 1937).
13. Joseph Wulf, *Theater und Film im Dritten Reich: Eine Dokumentation* (Gütersloh, 1963), 77.
14. Jan-Pieter Barbian, *Literaturpolitik im 'Dritten Reich': Institutionen, Kompetenzen, Betätigungsfelder* (Munich, 1995), 429.
15. Jenny Williams, *Mehr Leben als eins: Hans Fallada. Biographie* (Berlin, 2011), 237. This book originally appeared in English as *More Lives than One: A Biography of Hans Fallada* (London, 1998).
16. Ernst Wiechert, *Der Totenwald/Eine Mauer um uns bauen/Tagebuchnotizen und Briefe* (Munich, 1979), 36, 37, 46.

17. *Die Tagebücher von Joseph Goebbels*, Part I, vol. 6, 522 (30 August 1938).
18. Solmitz diaries, 28 February 1935.
19. Kalshoven, *Ich denk so viel an Euch*, 238 (6 August 1934).
20. *Völkischer Beobachter*, 10 September 1936.
21. *Die Tagebücher von Joseph Goebbels*, Part I, vol. 4, 32 (3 March 1937).
22. Franz Josef Görtz and Hans Sarkowicz, *Heinz Rühmann 1902–1994: Der Schauspieler und sein Jahrhundert* (Munich, 2001), 189, 164, 172.
23. Heinz Rühmann, *Das war's: Erinnerungen* (Berlin, 1982), 146.
24. Clemens Zimmermann, 'Landkino im Nationalsozialismus', *Archiv für Sozialgeschichte* 41 (2001), 231–43 (240–2).
25. Florian Cebulla, *Rundfunk und ländliche Gesellschaft 1924–1945* (Göttingen, 2004) 51, 210.
26. *Berliner Lokal-Anzeiger*, 31 March 1935 (Sunday edition).
27. Ibid., 20 March 1935 (evening edition), 16 July 1935 (evening edition), 17 July 1935 (evening edition), 2 November 1935 (morning edition).
28. Klemperer, *I Shall Bear Witness*, 273 (22 May 1937).
29. *Deutschland-Berichte der Sozialdemokratischen Partei Deutschlands (Sopade)* (Salzhausen, 1982⁶), 2 (1935), 1075, 1459, 1456.
30. Solmitz diaries, 11 August 1935.
31. Wilhelm Henze, *'Hochverräter raus!' Geschichte, Gedichte und Zeichnungen eines Moorsoldaten*, ed. by Habbo Knoch (Bremen, 1992), 17, 130.
32. Ibid., 107, 154, 208 (15 July 1934).
33. Ibid., 133, 135, 65.
34. Habbo Knoch, 'Schreiben im Verborgenen: Ein biographischer Versuch über Wilhelm Henze', in ibid., 247–83 (265–6, 268).
35. Guido Fackler, 'Cultural Behaviour and the Invention of Traditions: Music and Musical Practices in the Early Concentration Camps, 1933–6/7', *Journal of Contemporary History*, 45 (2010), 601–27.
36. Henze, *'Hochverräter raus!'*, 245 (29 November 1935).
37. *Sopade-Berichte* 2 (1935), 422–3.
38. Ibid., 664, 666.
39. Joachim Fest, *Ich nicht: Erinnerungen an eine Kindheit und Jugend* (Reinbek bei Hamburg, 2006), 73–101.
40. Charlotte Beradt, *Das Dritte Reich des Traums* (Frankfurt, 1994), 21–2.
41. Henze: *'Hochverräter raus!'*, 275.
42. Irmgard Keun, *Ich lebe in einem wilden Wirbel: Briefe an Arnold Strauss 1933 bis 1947*, ed. by Gabriele Kreis and Marjory S. Strauss (Düsseldorf, 1988), 165–6 (5 May 1936).
43. Ibid., 169 (6 May 1936), 183 (11 August 1936), 248–9 (28 July 1938).

44. Dan Stone, *Responses to Nazism in Britain, 1933–1939: Before War and the Holocaust* (Basingstoke, 2003), 115.

45. John F. Kennedy, *Unter Deutschen: Reisetagebücher und Briefe 1937–1945*, ed. by Oliver Lubrich (Berlin, 2013), 106 (18 August 1937). My thanks to the editor for providing me with the original quotations.

3. Towards a 'Pure' Culture

1. Stefan Schweizer, *'Unserer Weltanschauung sichtbaren Ausdruck geben': Nationalsozialistische Geschichtsbilder in historischen Festzügen zum 'Tag der deutschen Kunst'* (Göttingen, 2007), 143–4.

2. Ibid., 146, 206.

3. Ibid., 250, 240.

4. *Die Tagebücher von Joseph Goebbels*, Part I, vol. 3, 245 (10 January 1936).

5. *Himmler privat: Briefe eines Massenmörders*, ed. by Katrin Himmler and Michael Wildt (Munich, 2014), 201 (16 November 1937), 191 (8 January 1938 und 4 April 1939), 207 (3 July 1938).

6. Ibid., 207 (3 July 1938), 210 (14 November/3 December 1938).

7. Longerich, *Himmler*, 243, 224, 235, 236.

8. Ibid., 267–8.

9. Uta Halle, 'Ur- und Frühgeschichte', in Jürgen Elvert and Jürgen Nielsen-Sikora (eds), *Kulturwissenschaften und Nationalsozialismus* (Stuttgart, 2008), 109–66 (quotation 144).

10. Michael Zimmermann, *Rassenutopie und Genozid: Die nationalsozialistische 'Lösung der Zigeunerfrage'* (Hamburg, 1996), quotations 132, 134, 138.

11. Peter-Heinz Seraphim, *Das Judentum im osteuropäischen Raum* (Essen, 1938), 14, 673, emphases in the original.

12. *Die Tagebücher von Joseph Goebbels*, Part I, vol. 4, 306 (18 May 1938).

13. Klemperer, *I Shall Bear Witness*, 319 (12 July 1938), 362 (7 April 1939).

14. Alon Confino, *A World without Jews: The Nazi Imagination from Persecution to Genocide* (New Haven, 2014), 62.

15. Michael Wildt, *Volksgemeinschaft and the Dynamics of Racial Exclusion: Violence against Jews in Provincial Germany, 1919–1939* (New York, 2012), 125, 230, 242.

16. Printed in Peter-Klaus Schuster (ed.), *Nationalsozialismus und 'Entartete Kunst': Die 'Kunststadt' München 1937* (Munich, 1987), 242–52.

17. William Gould, *Hindu Nationalism and the Language of Politics in Late Colonial India* (Cambridge, 2004), 158.

18. Olaf Gaudig and Peter Veit, *Der Widerschein des Nazismus: Das Bild des Nationalsozialismus in der deutschsprachigen Presse Argentiniens, Brasiliens und Chiles 1932–1945* (Berlin, 1997), 188, 249.

19. Gitta Sereny, *Albert Speer: His Battle with Truth* (London, 1995), 106.

20. Albert Speer, *Erinnerungen* (Frankfurt, 1969), 149.

21. Ibid., 83.

22. Helmut Weihsmann, *Bauen unterm Hakenkreuz: Architektur des Untergangs* (Vienna, 1998), 19.

23. Dieter Bartetzko, *Illusionen in Stein: Stimmungsarchitektur im deutschen Faschismus. Ihre Vorgeschichte in Theater- und Filmbauten* (Reinbek, 1985), 11.

24. *Sopade-Berichte*, 4 (1938), 970.

25. Gisela Graichen and Horst Gründer, *Deutsche Kolonien: Traum und Trauma* (3rd, Berlin, 2005), 417–8.

26. Willi Oberkrome, *Volksgeschichte: Methodische Innovation und völkische Ideologisierung in der deutschen Geschichtswissenschaft 1918–1945* (Göttingen, 1993), 176, 178.

27. Frank Reichherzer, *'Alles ist Front!' Wehrwissenschaften in Deutschland und die Bellifizierung der Gesellschaft vom Ersten Weltkrieg bis in den Kalten Krieg* (Paderborn, 2012), 348.

28. Helmut Maier (ed.), *Gemeinschaftsforschung, Bevollmächtigte und der Wissenstransfer: Die Rolle der Kaiser-Wilhelm-Gesellschaft im System kriegsrelevanter Forschung des Nationalsozialismus* (Göttingen, 2007).

29. Alf Lüdtke, '"The Honor of Labor": Industrial Workers and the Power of Symbols under National Socialism', in David Crew (ed.), *Nazism and German Society, 1933–1945* (London, 1994), 67–109 (91).

30. *Sopade-Berichte*, 5 (1938), 277, 685.

31. Ibid., 421, 944, 262, 267.

32. Klemperer, *I Shall Bear Witness*, 304 (31 January 1938).

33. Josef Mooser, 'Die "Geistige Landesverteidigung" in den 1930er Jahren: Profile und Kontexte eines vielschichtigen Phänomens der schweizerischen politischen Kultur in der Zwischenkriegszeit', *Schweizerische Zeitschrift für Geschichte*, 47 (1997), 685–708 (690, 697).

34. Ira Katznelson, *Fear Itself: The New Deal and the Origins of Our Time* (New York, 2013), 281–91.

35. On this subject see Maurice Friedman, *Martin Buber's Life and Work: The Middle Years 1923–1945* (New York, 1983), 157–294.

36. Martin Buber to Eduard Strauss, 31 July 1938, in Buber, *Briefwechsel aus sieben Jahrzehnten*, ed. by Grete Schaeder, vol. 3: *1938–1965* (Heidelberg, 1975), 13.

37. Martin Buber, 'Das Ende der deutsch-jüdischen Symbiose (January 1939)', in Buber, *Der Jude und sein Judentum: Gesammelte Aufsätze und Reden* (Cologne, 1963), 644–7.

38. Martin Buber, 'Die Kinder', in Buber, *Der Jude*, 583–5.

39. Martin Buber to Otto Hirsch, 5 December 1933, in Buber, *Briefwechsel aus sieben Jahrzehnten*, vol. 2: *1918–1938*, ed. by Grete Schaeder (Heidelberg, 1973), 508.

40. Martin Buber, 'Die Frage an den Einzelnen', in Buber, *Werke*, vol. 1: *Schriften zur Philosophie* (Munich, 1962), 215–65 (250).

41. Klemperer, *I Shall Bear Witness*, 147 (2 May 1935).

42. *Das Tagebuch der Hertha Nathorff: Berlin–New York. Aufzeichnungen 1933–1945*, ed. by Wolfgang Benz (Frankfurt, 1988), 86 (8 August 1936).

43. Marcel Reich-Ranicki, *Mein Leben* (Stuttgart, 1999), 111.

44. Saul Friedländer, *Nazi Germany and the Jews*, vol. 1: *The Years of Persecution, 1933–1939* (New York, 1997), 67–8.

45. Eike Geisel and Henryk M. Broder, *Premiere und Pogrom: Der Jüdische Kulturbund 1933–1941* (Berlin, 1992), 80, 91, 177.

46. *Jüdische Rundschau*, 10 January 1936.

47. *C.[entral]V.[erein]-Zeitung*, 3 March 1938.

48. Klemperer, *I Shall Bear Witness*, 338 (3 December 1938), 347 (New Year's Eve 1938).

49. *Das Tagebuch der Hertha Nathorff*, 161 (27/28 April 1939).

4. Cultures at War

1. Hans-Eugen Bühler and Edelgard Bühler, *Der Frontbuchhandel 1939–1945: Organisationen, Kompetenzen, Verlage, Bücher* (Frankfurt, 2002), 51–2.

2. Laura Fahnenbruck, *Ein(ver)nehmen: Sexualität und Alltag von Wehrmachtsoldaten in den besetzten Niederlanden* (Göttingen, 2018), 86–7.

3. Die Tagebücher von Joseph Goebbels, Part II: Diktate 1941–1945, ed. by Elke Fröhlich (Munich, 1993–1996), vol. 3, 377 (26 February 1942).

4. Jana Bruns, Nazi Cinema's New Women (Cambridge, 2009), 109–70.

5. Zarah Leander, Es war so wunderbar! Mein Leben (Hamburg, 1973), 126, 14, 170.

6. Gerhard Stahr, Volksgemeinschaft vor der Leinwand? Der nationalsozialistische Film und sein Publikum (Berlin, 2001), 210.

7. Sopade-Berichte, 7 (1940), 97, 221.

8. *Völkischer Beobachter*, 7 March 1940, 28 July 1940, 25 July 1940 (emphasis in original), 18 March 1940.

9. Alexander B. Rossino, Hitler Strikes Poland: Blitzkrieg, Ideology, and Atrocity (Lawrence, 2003), 191.

10. Ibid., 145–52, 187–90.

11. Karsten Linne, Deutschland jenseits des Äquators? Die NS-Kolonialplanungen für Afrika (Berlin, 2008), 79.

12. Klemperer, I Shall Bear Witness, 383 (6 October 1939), 415 (26 May 1940), 431 (30 August 1940), 471 (29 May 1941).

13. Solmitz diaries, 19 October 1939, 17 June 1940, 20 October 1940, 14 February 1941.

14. Karl Heinz Roth, ' "Ich klage an": Aus der Enstehungsgeschichte eines Propaganda-Filmes', in Götz Aly (ed.), Aktion T4 1939–1945: Die 'Euthanasie'-Zentrale in der Tiergartenstraße 4 (Berlin, 1989), 93–119 (93).

15. Christian Kuchler, 'Bischöflicher Protest gegen nationalsozialistische "Euthanasie"-Propaganda im Kino: "Ich klage an" ', Historisches Jahrbuch, 126 (2006), 269–94 (286).

16. Das Schwarze Korps, 20 February 1940, 2 May 1940, 25 July 1940.

17. Frank Bajohr and Christoph Strupp (eds), Fremde Blicke auf das 'Dritte Reich': Berichte ausländischer Diplomaten über Herrschaft und Gesellschaft in Deutschland 1933–1945 (Göttingen, 2011), 544.

18. Sopade-Berichte 7 (1940), 177.

19. Hans-Jörg Koch, Das Wunschkonzert im NS-Rundfunk (Cologne, 2003), 187–8.

20. Ernst Jünger, Tagebücher II: Strahlungen. Erster Teil (Stuttgart, n.d.), 256 (30 May 1941), 374 (2 August 1942).

21. Ibid., 240 (6 April 1941).

22. Ibid., 293 (8 December 1941), 384 (18 August 1942), 335 (15 March 1942).

23. Sven Olaf Berggötz, 'Ernst Jünger und die Geiseln: Die Denkschrift von Ernst Jünger über die Geiselerschießungen in Frankreich 1941/42', Vierteljahrshefte für Zeitgeschichte, 51 (2003), 405–72.

24. Jünger, Tagebücher II, 293 (8 December 1941).

25. Allan Mitchell, Nazi Paris: The History of an Occupation (New York, 2008), 27–34, 44 (photos).

26. Franka Maubach, Die Stellung halten: Kriegserfahrungen und Lebensgeschichten von Wehrmachthelferinnen (Göttingen, 2009), 121, 112.

27. Heinrich Böll to his fiancée, later his wife, Annemarie, in Heinrich Böll, Briefe aus dem Krieg 1939–1945, ed. by Jochen Schubert (Cologne, 2001), vol. 1, 250 (12 September 1941), 280–1 (1 January 1942), 353 (28 May 1942), 464 (9 September 1942).

28. Ibid., 205 (29 June 1941).

29. Jünger, *Tagebücher II*, 440 (22 November 1942), 441 (23 November 1942).

30. Sven Oliver Müller, *Deutsche Soldaten und ihre Feinde: Nationalismus an Front und Heimatfront im Zweiten Weltkrieg* (Frankfurt, 2007), 190, 187.

31. Arthur Greiser, *Der Aufbau im Osten* (Jena, 1942), 8, 9, 15.

32. Catherine Epstein, *Model Nazi: Arthur Greiser and the Occupation of Western Poland* (Oxford, 2010), 242–4, 247–8.

33. Ibid., 235, 269.

34. *Alfred Rosenberg: Die Tagebücher* 336 (6 September 1940).

35. Ibid., 372 (2 April 1941), 598 (16 May 1942).

36. *Völkischer Beobachter*, 5 July 1940.

37. R. S. Tazelaar, *Prof. dr. Willem Mengelberg: Het tragische Heldenleben van een dirigent 1871–1951*, Master's dissertation, University of Amsterdam, 2014, quotation 77.

38. *Das Reich*, 7 July 1940.

39. On what follows see Julian Jackson, *France: The Dark Years 1940–1944* (Oxford, 2001), 190–212, 300–26.

40. Jacques Chardonne, *Voir la figure* (Paris, 1941), 13, 14–5.

41. Lucien Rebatet, *Les mémoires d'un fasciste I: Les Décombres 1938–1940* (Paris, 1976), 532, 588.

42. François Dufay, *Die Herbstreise: Französische Schriftsteller im Oktober 1941 in Deutschland* (Berlin, 2001), 48.

43. *Die Tagebücher von Joseph Goebbels*, Part II, vol. 3, 317 (15 February 1942).

44. *Alfred Rosenberg: Die Tagebücher*, 359 (2 February 1941).

45. Aneta Mihaylova 'Right-Wing Ideology and the Intellectuals in Romania during the Second World War', *New Europe College Yearbook*, 9 (2001/2), 107–37 (121).

46. *Das Reich*, 26 May 1940, 16 June 1940, 14 July 1940.

47. Ibid., 8 September 1940, 9 June 1940, 25 August 1940, 6 April 1941.

48. Ibid., 3 August 1941, 17 August 1941, 30 November 1941.

49. Benjamin George Martin, ' "European Literature" in the Nazi New Order: The Cultural Politics of the European Writers' Union, 1941–3', *Journal of Contemporary History*, 48 (2013), 486–508.

50. *Signal*, beginning of June 1941, beginning of February 1942, end of May 1942.

51. Mark Walker, 'Eine Waffenschmiede? Kernwaffen- und Reaktorforschung am Kaiser-Wilhelm-Institut für Physik', in Maier (ed.), *Gemeinschaftsforschung*, 352–94 (369).

NOTES

5. Culture of Destruction

1. *Die Tagebücher* von Joseph Goebbels, Part II, vol. 11, 62 (7 January 1944), 184 (28 January 1944), 229 (13 February 1944).
2. Misha Ashter, 'Das Reichsorchester': Die Berliner Philharmoniker und der Nationalsozialismus (Munich, 2007), 130.
3. Philipp Manes, As If It Were Life: A WW II Diary from the Theresienstadt Ghetto, ed. Ben Barkow and Klaus Leist (New York, 2009), 58, 85, emphasis in the original.
4. Ibid., 93–94, 71, 103; Manes, Als ob's ein Leben wär: Tatsachenbericht Theresienstadt 1942–1944, ed. Ben Barkow and Klaus Leist (Berlin, 2005), 193.
5. Manes, As If It Were Life, 178, 179.
6. Ibid., 221 (quotation), 263–6.
7. On what follows see Andrea Löw, Juden im Getto Litzmannstadt: Lebensbedingungen, Selbstwahrnehmung, Verhalten (Göttingen, 2006), 194–223, 393–442; Markus Roth and Löw, Das Warschauer Getto: Alltag und Widerstand im Angesicht der Vernichtung (Munich, 2013), 52–64, 130–51.
8. Reich-Ranicki, Mein Leben, 219.
9. Löw, Juden, 210.
10. Saul Friedländer, *The Years of Extermination: Nazi Germany and the Jews, 1939–1945* (New York, 2007), 395.
11. Reich-Ranicki, *Mein Leben*, 259.
12. Löw, Juden, 418.
13. Victor Klemperer, *To the Bitter End: The Diaries of Victor Klemperer 1942–1945* (London, 2000), 163 (29 August 1942) emphasis in the original.
14. Ibid., 133 (26 July 1942), 8 (17 January 1942), 91 (11 June 1942).
15. Ibid., 84 (11 May 1942), 140–1 (23 June 1942), emphases in the original.
16. *The Diary of Anne Frank: The Critical Edition.* Prepared by the Netherlands State Institute for War Documentation (New York, 1989], 290 (29 October 1942), 314 (17 November 1942), 601 (11 April 1944).
17. Willy Lindwer, *The Last Seven Months of Anne Frank* (New York, 1992).
18. Ana Novac, *Die schönen Tage meiner Jugend* (Munich, 2010), 23, 45.
19. Gabriele Knapp, '"Befohlene Musik": Musik und Musikmißbrauch im Frauenlager von Auschwitz-Birkenau', Acta Musicologica 68 (1996), 149–66.

20. Max Domarus, *Hitler: Reden und Proklamationen 1932–1945*, vol. 2 (Neustadt a. d. Aisch, 1963), 1867.

21. Müller, *Deutsche Soldaten*, 148–9.

22. Mechtild Rössler and Sabine Schleiermacher (eds), *Der 'Generalplan Ost': Hauptlinien der nationalsozialistischen Planungs- und Vernichtungspolitik* (Berlin, 1993), 263.

23. Longerich, *Himmler*, 660–1.

24. Thomas Mann, *Tagebücher 1940–1943*, ed. by Peter de Mendelssohn (Frankfurt, 1982), 394 (18 February 1942), 430 (16 May 1942).

25. Ibid., 440 (12 June 1942), 476 (21 September 1942), 534 (8 February 1943).

26. Thomas Mann and Agnes E. Meyer, *Briefwechsel 1937–1955*, ed. by Hans Rudolf Vaget (Frankfurt, 1992), 353 (11 January 1942), emphasis in the original, 367–8 (16 February 1942).

27. Jochen Strobel, *Entzauberung der Nation: Die Repräsentation Deutschlands im Werk Thomas Manns* (Dresden, 2000), quotations 232 footnote 270, 233–4.

28. Wendy L. Wall, *Inventing the 'American Way': The Politics of Consensus from the New Deal to the Civil Rights Movement* (Oxford, 2008), 101–59 (quotation 115).

29. Michaela Hoenicke Moore, *Know Your Enemy: The American Debate on Nazism, 1933–1945* (New York, 2010), 169, emphasis in the original.

30. Erich Fromm, *The Fear of Freedom* (1941) (London, 1960), 204.

31. Wendy Webster, '"The Whim of Foreigners": Language, Speech, and Sound in Second World War British Film and Radio', *Twentieth Century British History* 23 (2012), 359–82 (372–4).

32. *Vrij Nederland*, 21 March 1943.

33. *Albert Camus à Combat: Éditoriaux et articles d'Albert Camus 1944–1947*, ed. by Jacqueline Lévi-Valensi (Paris, 2002), 157–8.

34. Jochen Hellbeck, *Stalingrad: The City that Defeated the Third Reich* (New York, 2015), 137, 394.

35. Geoffrey Hosking, 'The Second World War and Russian National Consciousness', *Past and Present*, 175 (May 2002), 162–87 (168–9).

36. *Völkischer Beobachter*, 27 June 1943, emphasis in the original.

37. Mann, *Tagebücher*, 594 (29 June 1943).

38. *Völkischer Beobachter*, 30 June 1943.

39. Hagen Fleischer, 'Die "Viehmenschen" und das "Sauvolk": Feindbilder einer dreifachen Okkupation: der Fall Griechenland', in

Wolfgang Benz, Gerhard Otto, and Anabella Weismann (eds), *Kultur—Propaganda—Öffentlichkeit: Intentionen deutscher Besatzungspolitik und Reaktionen auf die Okkupation* (Berlin, 1998), 135–69 (157).

40. Domarus, *Hitler*, vol. 2, 2083 (30 January 1944), 2072 (1 January 1944).

41. *Adolf Hitler: Monologe im Führerhauptquartier 1941–1944*, ed. by Werner Jochmann (Hamburg, 1980), 398 (13 June 1943).

42. On what follows see Bernd Wegner, 'The Ideology of Self-Destruction: Hitler and the Choreography of Defeat', *German Historical Institute London Bulletin*, 26 (2004), no. 2, 18–33.

43. Michael Geyer, '"There is a Land Where Everything is Pure: Its Name Is Land of Death": Some Observations on Catastrophic Nationalism', in Greg Eghigian and Matthew Paul Berg (eds), *Sacrifice and National Belonging in Twentieth-Century Germany* (College Station, 2002), 118–47.

44. Thomas Mann, *Deutsche Hörer! 55 Radiosendungen nach Deutschland* (2nd ed., Stockholm, 1945), 104 (31 December 1943).

45. Wolfram Pyta, *Hitler: Der Künstler als Politiker und Feldherr: Eine Herrschaftsanalyse* (Munich, 2015), 434–5.

46. *Das Reich*, 12 December 1943.

47. *Deutsche Allgemeine Zeitung*, 26 July 1943.

48. *Berliner Lokal-Anzeiger*, 2 July 1943, emphasis in the original.

49. *Deutsche Allgemeine Zeitung*, 25 July 1943, emphasis in the original, 22 February 1944.

50. Ibid., 12 March 1944, 12 July 1944.

51. Günther Krenzin to his wife, 17 June 1944, 21 June 1944, 12 July 1944, Feldpostarchiv in the Museum für Kommunikation Berlin, 3.2002.858.2.

52. Hans-Joachim S. to his wife, Feldpostarchiv in the Museum für Kommunikation Berlin, 3.2002.1214.0, 25 June 1942, 26 July 1942, 3 October 1942.

53. Ibid., 31 January 1943, 8 May 1943, 14 May 1943, 22 June 1943.

54. Ibid., 16 October 1944.

55. Lutz Raumer to his parents, 29 March 1944, Feldpostarchiv in the Museum für Kommunikation Berlin, 3.2002.7404, http://www.museumsstiftung.de/briefsammlung/feldpost-zweiter-weltkrieg/brief.html?action=detail&what=letter&id=362 &le_ fulltext=Lutz Raumer [accessed 25 August 2015].

56. Wolfgang Panzer an seine Frau, 5 August 1944, Feldpostarchiv in the Museum für Kommunikation Berlin, 3.2013.355, http://www.

museumsstiftung.de/briefsammlung/feldpost-zweiter-weltkrieg/
brief.html?action=detail&what=letter&id=1593&le_keyword=USA
[accessed 25 August 2015].

57. Theo Findahl, 'Teppichangriff', in Oliver Lubrich (ed.), *Reisen ins Reich 1933 bis 1945: Ausländische Autoren berichten aus Deutschland* (Munich, 2009), 362–6 (365: 22 November 1943), emphasis in the original.

58. *Die Tagebücher von Joseph Goebbels*, Part II, vol. 11, 448 (10 March 1944); vol. 12, 59 (6 April 1944); vol. 13, 81 (10 July 1944).

59. Werner Durth and Niels Gutschow, *Träume in Trümmern: Stadtplanung 1940–1950* (Munich, 1993), 53.

60. Jens Ebert and Thomas Jander (eds), *Endlich wieder Mensch sein: Feldpostbriefe und Gefangenenpost des Deserteurs Hans Stock 1943/1944* (Berlin, 2009), 165 (29 September 1943).

Conclusion: After the Nazi Dream

1. *Hitlers politisches Testament: Die Bormann Diktate vom Februar und April 1945* (Hamburg, 1981), 98 (21 February 1945).

2. Saul K. Padover, Psychologist in Germany: The Story of an American Intelligence Officer (London: Phoenix House, 1946), 128, 120, 289.

3. Mann, Deutsche Hörer, 112 (1 May 1944).

GLOSSARY

Brecht, Bertolt (1898–1956) A playwright, theatre director, and Communist intellectual. Originally from Bavaria, Brecht rose to prominence in Berlin during the 1920s. His plays first reflected expressionist influences but were then increasingly written and staged to popularize Communist views in a didactic style known as 'epic theatre'. In a similar vein, Brecht wrote *The Threepenny Opera* and the script of the film *Kuhle Wampe or Who Owns the World?*. From 1933 he was an exile in various European countries and the United States, before returning to Berlin in 1949 to continue his theatrical work and support the Communist regime in East Germany.

Breker, Arno (1900–1991) A sculptor and artistic representative of the Third Reich. Before 1933, Breker did not adopt clear political positions and even betrayed some cosmopolitan inclinations, spending a couple of years in Paris and Rome. But, once his neoclassical style had caught Hitler's and Speer's attention, he received lucrative commissions for statues at the Reich Chancellery and numerous other public buildings. During the war, Breker successfully exhibited his sculptures in Paris. While most of his public work was destroyed by the Allies, he continued to make sculptures for private patrons and to be admired in some quarters, culminating in the opening of a museum dedicated to him in 1985.

bürgerlich Middle-class or bourgeois, although neither fully captures the meanings of *bürgerlich*, which encompass economic status, political citizenship, and cultural ambition. Inseparable from education (*Bildung*), *bürgerlich* culture enriched the German middle class's life, while also justifying its claim to authority over workers, the rural population, and Catholics. It laid a strong emphasis on music, literature, and the visual arts as canonized in the nineteenth century. From around 1900, cultural modernism divided the German middle classes: some of their members, especially in the big cities, were open to new developments; others staunchly defended their heritage. This division was skilfully exploited by the Nazi movement, which at times claimed to transcend *bürgerlich* culture and at others posed as its defender.

Combat League for German Culture (Kampfbund für deutsche Kultur) An association of National Socialists and, initially, other right-wingers aiming to restore Germanness to German culture by defending it against left-wing, Jewish, and modernist influences. Founded in 1928 in Munich by Alfred Rosenberg and others, the Combat League simultaneously campaigned against currents and events that it despised and offered an alternative programme of lectures, film screenings, and musical performances. In 1933 its *völkisch* activists took over various cultural organizations and institutions across Germany, but their influence was soon countered by that of Goebbels's more pragmatic and institutionalized Propaganda Ministry and Reich Chamber for Culture. In 1934 the Combat League merged into the National Socialist Cultural Community, until that organization was, in turn, taken over by Strength through Joy in 1937. Despite this decline, former Combat League members occupied important positions within the cultural universe of the Third Reich.

Expressionism A broad and multi-faceted artistic movement of the early twentieth century. From 1900, various visual artists and literary writers started a mainly German variant of modernism. Reflecting both a grim fascination with the turmoil of the big city and a love for idyllic landscapes, expressionism was politically ambivalent. Among its practitioners were radical leftists as well as ardent nationalists, the latter enabling certain overlaps with National Socialism. However, Hitler's hatred of the movement soon put an end to these, leading to the expressionist Emil Nolde being the painter with the largest number of works on show at the 1937 Degenerate Art exhibition despite his initial sympathies for the regime.

Furtwängler, Wilhelm (1886–1954) A world-famous conductor and, as such, of great value for the Third Reich's national and international image. In 1922 Furtwängler took over Germany's foremost orchestra, the Berlin Philharmonic. Owing to his prominence, as well as his opulent conducting style, he was courted by the new regime. Furtwängler expressed a certain distance and tried to defend some Jews and modernists; in the case of the composer Paul Hindemith he even did so publicly. When these attempts proved unsuccessful and attracted the ire of several leading Nazis, he backpedalled, accepting a role as a seemingly unpolitical musician though in reality acting as an important provider of cultural legitimacy.

Goebbels, Joseph (1897–1945) The Third Reich's propaganda minister and a key figure in German cultural life. Exempt from serving in the First World War due to a disability and unsuccessful as a literary writer, Goebbels joined the Nazi Party in 1924. He soon became a loyal follower of Adolf Hitler, who entrusted him with the leadership of the Berlin district (*Gau*) and then, in 1933, with the new Ministry of Propaganda. From this position, Goebbels exercised a major influence on the German film industry and frequently intervened in theatrical, musical, and literary affairs. His ministry's increasing control of the Reich Chamber of Culture reinforced his power. While always having to fend off competing individuals and institutions, Goebbels maintained a strong position, marshalling his propagandistic energy for the defence of the Third Reich during its final years.

Göring, Hermann (1893–1946) An ace pilot during the First World War, ardent right-winger, and leading National Socialist from 1922. Responsible mainly for rearmament, he was initially deemed the second man in the Third Reich. However, his status declined during the war owing to the rise of Himmler and his own unconvincing record as organizer of armament production and aerial defence. Göring intervened in cultural life by protecting certain artists, most prominently the gay actor Gustav Gründgens at the Preußische Staatstheater in Berlin. He also saw himself as a Renaissance man and underscored this self-image through a luxurious lifestyle that included the acquisition and display of works of art. Benefiting from his key role in the exploitation of occupied Europe, he was able to purchase numerous paintings very cheaply or simply loot them.

Heidegger, Martin (1889–1976) A highly influential philosopher in Germany and internationally, as well as an intellectual supporter of National Socialism. Heidegger became prominent with his book *Being and Time* (1927) and also for his rejection of the offer of a professorial chair at the University of Berlin in favour of remaining at the University of Freiburg in his native Black Forest. After being elected as rector of the University, he publicly expressed his admiration for the advent of the Third Reich. More withdrawn after the end of his tenure in 1934, he continued to developed his critique of modernity, which enabled him to retain his prominence in West Germany after 1945 as well as among French postmodernist thinkers of the 1970s and 1980s. In recent years, the publication of his *Black Notebooks* has led to renewed debates owing to the antisemitic statements contained in them.

Himmler, Heinrich (1900–1945) The leader of the SS and as such the organizer of the concentration camp universe and later the Holocaust. Having narrowly missed battlefield experience in the First World War, Himmler joined the extreme-right movement as a student of agriculture and the Nazi Party in 1923. He soon took control of, and then rapidly expanded, the Schutzstaffel (SS), thus advancing to a key position within the Third Reich. Himmler took *völkisch* thought to its extreme conclusion, applied it to various realms, and commissioned 'scientific' work underpinning the predominance of the Germanic race. Employing numerous university graduates, his SS funded archaeological, prehistorical, and medical projects as well as 'research into Jewishness'.

Jünger, Ernst (1895–1998) Arguably the most significant right-wing literary writer and intellectual in twentieth-century Germany. A repeatedly injured and highly decorated officer, Jünger turned his experiences of the First World War into the memoir *Storm of Steel* (first published in 1920), before working to undermine the Weimar Republic under the banner of 'soldierly nationalism'. However, Jünger increasingly became a cool observer of his time rather than an activist aiming to change it. Keeping his distance from the Nazi regime and implicitly criticizing it in *On the Marble Cliffs* (1939), he served as an army captain during the war and in this capacity was involved in the intellectual life of occupied Paris. After 1945, he remained a prolific novelist, having withdrawn from public life while cultivating a following in both Germany and France.

Klemperer, Victor (1881–1960) A professor of Romance languages and literatures who stemmed from a Jewish family but had converted to Protestantism before the First World War. Long known for *LTI*, a seminal book on Nazi language that first appeared in 1947, Klemperer acquired additional prominence after his extensive diaries were found and published in the 1990s. These diaries give profound insights into Munich after 1918, Dresden from the 1920s to the end of the Third Reich, and East Germany after 1945, when Klemperer opted to serve the Communist regime. They also compellingly reflect the perspective of a *bürgerlich* war veteran, who wanted nothing more than to be German and despised Zionism but had to realize that antisemites were hell-bent on excluding and persecuting him. Klemperer had to live in a 'Jewish house' and carry out forced labour during the war—but without ever being deported, thanks to his loyal non-Jewish wife, Eva.

Lang, Fritz (1890–1976) One of the most influential film directors of the twentieth century. Hailing from Vienna, Lang embarked on a spectacular career after moving to Berlin in 1919. He excelled at adopting major cultural currents such as expressionism (*Dr Mabuse, the Gambler*), the interest in Teutonic myths (*The Nibelungs*), modernism (*Metropolis*), and the fascination with crime (*M*). These qualities made Lang attractive to Goebbels but, after some initial hesitation, Lang decided to pursue his career in Hollywood instead. There, he made compelling anti-fascist films (*Hangmen Also Die!*; *Ministry of Fear*) as well as major *film noir* thrillers (*The Big Heat*).

Mann, Thomas (1875–1955) Perhaps the most significant literary writer in twentieth-century Germany and an outspoken opponent of the Third Reich. Mann hailed from a *bürgerlich* family in the Northern German city of Lübeck, which he immortalized in his first novel *The Buddenbrooks* (1901), but soon moved to Munich. A cultural nationalist during the First World War, he later became a defender of the Weimar Republic. Mann's second major novel *The Magic Mountain* (1924), which looked back to pre-war Europe from the vantage point of an alpine sanatorium, and the Nobel Prize for Literature awarded to him in 1929 further increased his status and prominence. From his Swiss and then American exile, he strove to fight Hitler's dictatorship by intellectual means, most importantly in speeches that were broadcast by the BBC. However, his influence within Germany remained limited, a bitter experience that militated against his returning to his country after 1945.

Reich Chamber of Culture (Reichskammer für Kultur) A heavily controlled professional organization of artists in Germany as well as the occupied Netherlands. The Reich Chamber of Culture was founded in November 1933, at the behest of Goebbels, who thus resisted the efforts of his rival Robert Ley to integrate cultural life in the German Labour Front. It was divided into the Reich Chambers of Literature, Theatre, Film, Music, the Visual Arts, Radio, and the Press, which worked to improve conditions for their members through rules pertaining to wages, honoraria, and copyright, the introduction of a social insurance system, and the regulation of admission to the profession in question. The latter increasingly led to the exclusion of Jews from cultural life. While there was initially a degree of corporate self-governance and artistic autonomy, in the mid-1930s the Reich Chamber of Culture came fully under the Ministry of Propaganda's rigid control.

Riefenstahl, Leni (1902–2003) An actor and film director who made important contributions to Nazi propaganda. Beginning in the late 1920s with a series of dramas set in the Alpine mountains, Riefenstahl's career received a boost in the Third Reich, when Hitler and Goebbels made ample use of her talents. She directed compelling documentaries celebrating the 1934 Nazi Party Rally in Nuremberg (*Triumph of the Will*) and the 1936 Olympics in Berlin (*Olympia*), before the war narrowed the space for such extravagant propaganda. Riefenstahl was shocked to witness a shooting of Jews while filming in Poland, although she did not have any qualms about using concentration camp inmates as extras for another project. Tainted by her role in the Third Reich, Riefenstahl did not complete any further films after 1945 but turned her attention to photography, most prominently of the Nuba tribes in Sudan.

Rosenberg, Alfred(1893–1946) A Baltic German émigré, *völkisch* ideologue, and ardent National Socialist from the party's beginnings in postwar Munich. While his lengthy book *The Myth of the Twentieth Century* (1930) was more quoted than actually read, Rosenberg exerted significant influence by editing the party newspaper, the *Völkischer Beobachter*, and heading the Combat League for German Culture. This league fought modernist and left-wing culture and was staunchly antisemitic. In the Third Reich, the role of the league declined in favour of Goebbels's propaganda ministry and Reich Chamber of Culture, although Rosenberg and his followers still made a sizeable impact through numerous specific interventions. During the war, Rosenberg became an important figure again owing to his role in occupied Europe, especially the Soviet Union, where he led his own task force in looting artworks, books, and manuscripts.

Rühmann, Heinz (1902–1994) A highly popular film actor whose career spanned the twentieth century. Beginning on the stage, Rühmann rose to prominence in the cinema around 1930, when the introduction of sound increased the demand for domestic stars. His films, mostly resembling Hollywood's screwball comedies, continued to attract a large audience after 1933. While he protected his Jewish ex-wife by arranging for her marriage to a neutral foreigner, Rühmann cultivated good relations with Nazi leaders and later offered his audience humorous and sentimental escapes from the war. In West Germany, some of his previous films remained much-loved and he continued his career by increasingly developing into a character actor.

Speer, Albert (1905–1981) An ambitious architect, dedicated bringer into being of Hitler's visions, and organizer of the war economy. Speer's career took off from 1931, allowing him to renovate party-owned buildings, remodel ministries and official residences, and design the settings for the 1 May 1933 demonstration in Berlin and the Nazi Party rally in Nuremberg. Speer soon became close to Hitler, sharing and refining his Führer's visions and implementing them as Berlin's General Building Inspector. Although little of the vast 'Reich Capital of Germania' ever materialized, the project had devastating consequences for evicted Jewish tenants and concentration camp inmates working in quarries. After his release from an allied prison in 1966, Speer wrote memoirs in which he omitted these aspects of his activities and overstated his achievements as an organizer of the economy during the second half of the war, while accepting partial responsibility for the Third Reich.

Strength through Joy (Kraft durch Freude) The leisure organization of the German Labour Front and, as such, an important factor in German cultural life. Founded in 1933 and modelled on its Italian equivalent Opera Nazionale Dopolavoro, Strength through Joy aimed at integrating industrial workers and white-collar employees in the Third Reich. The day trips and holidays it offered were a spectacular propaganda success, even if cruises to Norway or Madeira were more often imagined than actually experienced. It also published books and journals and organized tens of thousands of opera and theatre performances, concerts, and variety shows. Strength through Joy thus made cultural events accessible to new audiences and, in doing so, provided employment for numerous actors, singers, and musicians.

völkisch Typical of an extreme-right intellectual current and social movement that emerged in the late nineteenth century. *Völkisch* writers were obsessed with an existential struggle between peoples (*Völker*) and consequently with Germans' ethnic homogeneity. They saw this homogeneity as an original state that had been diluted by modern developments such as urbanization, the rise of mass consumption, and the emancipation of the Jewish minority. Hence their yearning to revive a mythical past in which Teutonic tribes defeated the Romans or medieval kings expanded their realms into Eastern Europe. In the Third Reich the *völkisch* movement enjoyed more power than ever, albeit without being able to dominate cultural life on account of the parallel importance given by the Nazis to pragmatic considerations, *bürgerlich* traditions, and popular culture.

Wagner, Richard (1813–1883) A writer and composer of operas who rose to fame in the nineteenth century and was celebrated in the Third Reich. Wagner mostly adopted Teutonic or medieval sagas, turning them into musically innovative and emotionally captivating works, for which he built his own theatre in Bayreuth in the 1870s. Because he had been a revolutionary in 1848/49, but made no secret of his antisemitic views, the political implications of his work were equivocal. Although he did have admirers on the left and outside Germany, his daughter-in-law Winifred laid the groundwork for an extreme-right cult. Her circle offered the avid Wagner fan Adolf Hitler a chance to acquire cultural legitimacy and influential friends in post-1918 Bavaria.

SELECT BIBLIOGRAPHY

This book is based on the studies listed below, though not all have been cited individually in the notes, which have been kept short. As well as giving the sources of quotations, the notes provide references for material drawn from specialized studies and research that supplements already-established knowledge.

Adam, Christian, *Lesen unter Hitler: Autoren, Bestseller, Leser im Dritten Reich* (Frankfurt, 2013)

Ashter, Misha, *'Das Reichsorchester': Die Berliner Philharmoniker und der Nationalsozialismus* (Munich, 2007)

Baranowski, Shelley, *Strength through Joy: Consumerism and Mass Tourism in the Third Reich* (Cambridge, 2004)

Barbian, Jan-Pieter, *Literaturpolitik im 'Dritten Reich': Institutionen, Kompetenzen, Betätigungsfelder* (Munich, 1995)

Barron, Stephanie (ed.), *'Entartete Kunst': Das Schicksal der Avantgarde im Nazi-Deutschland* (Munich, 1992)

Behrenbeck, Sabine, *Der Kult um die toten Helden: Nationalsozialistische Mythen, Rituale und Symbole 1923 bis 1945* (Vierow bei Greifswald, 1996)

Benz, Wolfgang, Gerhard Otto, and Anabella Weismann (eds), *Kultur—Propaganda–Öffentlichkeit: Intentionen deutscher Besatzungspolitik und Reaktionen auf die Okkupation* (Berlin, 1998)

Bergen, Doris, *Twisted Cross: The German Christian Movement in the Third Reich* (Chapel Hill, 1996)

Birdsall, Carolyn, *Nazi Soundscapes: Sound, Technology and Urban Space in Germany, 1933–1945* (Amsterdam, 2012)

Bollenbeck, Georg, 'German *Kultur*, the *Bildungsbürgertum*, and its Susceptibility to National Socialism', *German Quarterly*, 73 (Winter 2000), 67–83

Bollmus, Reinhard, *Das Amt Rosenberg und seine Gegner: Studien zum Machtkampf im nationalsozialistischen Herrschaftssystem* (2nd ed., Munich, 2006)

Brenner, Hildegard, *Die Kunstpolitik des Nationalsozialismus* (Reinbek bei Hamburg, 1963)

Brockhaus, Gudrun, *Schauder und Idylle: Faschismus als Erlebnisangebot* (Munich, 1997)

Brockhaus, Gudrun (ed.), *Attraktion der NS-Bewegung* (Essen, 2014)

Carter, Erica, *Dietrich's Ghosts: The Sublime and the Beautiful in Third Reich Film* (London, 2004)

Confino, Alon, *A World without Jews: The Nazi Imagination from Persecution to Genocide* (New Haven, 2014)

Dahm, Volker, *Das jüdische Buch im Dritten Reich*, 2 vols (Frankfurt, 1979–1981)

Dietmar, Carl, and Marcus Leifeld, *Alaaf und Heil Hitler: Karneval im Dritten Reich* (Munich, 2010)

Engel, Kathrin, *Deutsche Kulturpolitik im besetzten Paris 1940–1944: Film und Theater* (Munich, 2003)

Föllmer, Moritz, and Rüdiger Graf (eds), *Die 'Krise' der Weimarer Republik: Zur Kritik eines Deutungsmusters* (Frankfurt, 2005)

Frei, Norbert, and Johannes Schmitz, *Journalismus im Dritten Reich* (3rd ed., Munich, 1999)

Friedländer, Saul, *Nazi Germany and the Jews* (New York, 1997), vol. 1: *The Years of Persecution, 1933–1939*; vol. 2: *The Years of Extermination, 1939–1945*

Friedländer, Saul, and Jörn Rüsen (eds), *Richard Wagner im Dritten Reich* (Munich, 2000)

Fritzsche, Peter, 'Nazi Modern', *Modernism/Modernity*, 3/1 (1996), 1–22

Fritzsche, Peter, *Germans into Nazis* (Cambridge, Mass., 1998)

Fritzsche, Peter, *Life and Death in the Third Reich* (Cambridge, Mass., 2008)

Führer, Karl Christian, *Medienmetropole Hamburg: Mediale Öffentlichkeiten 1930–1960* (Hamburg, 2008)

Führer, Karl Christian, 'High Brow and Low Brow Culture', in Anthony McElligott (ed.), *Weimar Germany* (Oxford, 2009), 260–81

Gay, Peter, *Weimar Culture: The Outsider as Insider* (New York, 1968)

Graf, Rüdiger, *Die Zukunft der Weimarer Republik: Krisen und Zukunftsaneignungen in Deutschland 1918–1933* (Munich, 2008)

Hake, Sabine, *Popular Cinema of the Third Reich* (Austin, 2000)

Hausmann, Frank-Rutger, *Die Geisteswissenschaften im 'Dritten Reich'* (Frankfurt, 2011)

Heinrich, Anselm, 'Brüche und Kontinuitäten: Theater im 'Dritten Reich' und in der Bundesrepublik', *Zeitgeschichte online* (December 2012), https://zeitgeschichte-online.de/themen/bruche-und-kontinuitaten

Herf, Jeffrey, *Reactionary Modernism: Technology, Culture, and Politics in Weimar and the Third Reich* (Cambridge, 1984)

Hermand, Jost, *Old Dreams of a New Reich: Volkish Utopias and National Socialism* (Bloomington, 1992)

Hermand, Jost, *Culture in Dark Times: Nazi Fascism, Inner Emigration, and Exile* (New York, 2012)

Heuss, Anja, *Kunst- und Kulturgutraub: Eine vergleichende Studie zur Besatzungspolitik der Nationalsozialisten in Frankreich und der Sowjetunion* (Heidelberg, 2000)

Hirsch, Lilly E., *A Jewish Orchestra in Nazi Germany: Musical Politics and the Berlin Jewish Cultural League* (Ann Arbor, 2010)

Hoenicke Moore, Michaela, *Know Your Enemy: The American Debate on Nazism, 1933–1945* (New York, 2010)

Hoffend, Andrea, *Zwischen Kultur-Achse und Kulturkampf: Die Beziehungen zwischen 'Drittem Reich' und faschistischem Italien in den Bereichen Medien, Kunst, Wissenschaft und Rassenpolitik* (Frankfurt, 1998)

Hummel, Karl-Joseph, and Michael Kißener (eds), *Die Katholiken und das Dritte Reich: Kontroversen und Debatten* (Paderborn, 2009)

Imhoof, David M., *Becoming a Nazi Town: Culture and Politics in Göttingen during the Weimar and Nazi Eras* (Ann Arbor, 2013)

Jaskot, Paul B., *The Architecture of Oppression: The SS, Forced Labor and the Nazi Monumental Building Economy* (London, 2000)

Jelavich, Peter, *Berlin Alexanderplatz: Radio, Film, and the Death of Weimar Culture* (Berkeley, 2006)

Kater, Michael H., *Different Drummers: Jazz in the Culture of Nazi Germany* (New York, 1992)

Kater, Michael H., *The Twisted Muse: Musicians and their Music in the Third Reich* (New York, 1997)

Kater, Michael H., *Composers of the Nazi Era: Eight Portraits* (New York, 2000)

Kater, Michael H., *Das 'Ahnenerbe' der SS 1935–1945: Ein Beitrag zur Kulturpolitik des Dritten Reiches* (4th ed., Munich, 2006)

Kater, Michael H., *Culture in Nazi Germany* (New Haven, 2019)

Koch, Hans-Jörg, *Das Wunschkonzert im NS-Rundfunk* (Cologne, 2003)

Krockow, Christian von, *Die Entscheidung: Eine Untersuchung über Ernst Jünger, Carl Schmitt, Martin Heidegger* (Stuttgart, 1958)

Kroll, Frank-Lothar, *Utopie als Ideologie: Geschichtsdenken und politisches Handeln im Dritten Reich* (2nd ed., Paderborn, 1999)

Krumeich, Gerd (ed.), *Nationalsozialismus und Erster Weltkrieg* (Essen, 2010)

Kundrus, Birthe, 'Total Entertainment? Cultural Warfare 1939-1945: Film, Radio, and Theatre', in Jörg Echternkamp (ed.), *Germany and the Second World War*, Vol. IX/II: *German Wartime Society 1939–1945: Exploitation, Interpretations, Exclusion* (Oxford, 2014), 95–162

Lane, Barbara Miller, *Architecture and Politics in Germany, 1918–1945* (Cambridge, Mass., 1968)

Large, David Clay, *Where Ghosts Walked: Munich's Road to the Third Reich* (London, 1997)

Latzel, Klaus, *Deutsche Soldaten—nationalsozialistischer Krieg? Kriegserlebnis— Kriegserfahrung 1939–1945* (Paderborn, 1998)

Leo, Per, *Der Wille zum Wesen: Weltanschauungskultur, charakterologisches Denken und Judenfeindschaft 1890–1940* (Berlin, 2013)

Löhr, Hanns Christian, *Hitlers Linz: Der 'Heimatgau des Führers'* (Berlin, 2013)

Longerich, Peter, *'Davon haben wir nichts gewusst!' Die Deutschen und die Judenverfolgung 1933–1945* (Berlin, 2006)

Longerich, Peter, *Heinrich Himmler* (Oxford, 2012)

Longerich, Peter, *Goebbels: A Biography* (New York, 2015)

Marßolek, Inge, and Adelheid von Saldern (eds), *Radiozeiten: Herrschaft, Alltag, Gesellschaft (1924–1960)* (Potsdam, 1999)

Martin, Benjamin G., *The Nazi-Fascist New Order for European Culture* (Cambridge, Mass., 2016)

Mathieu, Thomas, *Kunstauffassungen und Kulturpolitik im Nationalsozialismus: Studien zu Adolf Hitler, Joseph Goebbels, Alfred Rosenberg, Baldur von Schirach, Heinrich Himmler, Albert Speer, Wilhelm Frick* (Saarbrücken, 1997)

Moeller, Felix, *The Film Minister: Goebbels and the Cinema in the Third Reich* (Stuttgart, 2000)

Möller, Horst, *Exodus der Kultur: Schriftsteller, Wissenschaftler und Künstler in der Emigration nach 1933* (Munich, 1984)

Mosse, George, *Nazi Culture: Intellectual, Cultural and Social Life in the Third Reich* (New York, 1966)

Müller, Sven Oliver, *Deutsche Soldaten und ihre Feinde: Nationalismus an Front und Heimatfront im Zweiten Weltkrieg* (Frankfurt, 2007)

O'Brien, Mary-Elizabeth, *Nazi Cinema as Enchantment: The Politics of Entertainment in the Third Reich* (Rochester, 2004)

Oswald, Rudolf, *'Fußball-Volksgemeinschaft': Ideologie, Politik und Fanatismus im deutschen Fußball 1919–1964* (Frankfurt, 2008)

Paret, Peter, *An Artist against the Third Reich: Ernst Barlach, 1933–1938* (Cambridge, 2003)

Paul, Gerhard, *Aufstand der Bilder: Die NS-Propaganda vor 1933* (Bonn, 1990)

Petropoulos, Jonathan, *Art as Politics in the Third Reich* (Chapel Hill, 1996)

Petropoulos, Jonathan, *The Faustian Bargain: The Art World in Nazi Germany* (Oxford, 2000)

Petsch, Joachim, *Baukunst und Stadtplanung im Dritten Reich: Herleitung/ Bestandsaufnahme/Entwicklung/Nachfolge* (Munich, 1976)

Pine, Lisa, *Hitler's 'National Community': Society and Culture in Nazi Germany* (2nd ed., London, 2017)

Proctor, Robert, *Racial Hygiene: Medicine under the Nazis* (Cambridge, Mass., 1988)

Pyta, Wolfgang, *Hitler: Der Künstler als Politiker und Feldherr. Eine Herrschaftsanalyse* (Munich, 2015)

Raphael, Lutz, 'Radikales Ordnungsdenken und die Organisation totalitärer Herrschaft: Weltanschauungseliten und Humanwissenschaftler im NS-Regime', *Geschichte und Gesellschaft*, 27 (2001), 5–40

Reichel, Peter, *Der schöne Schein des Dritten Reiches: Gewalt und Faszination des Faschismus* (Munich, 1991)

Rentschler, Eric, *The Ministry of Illusion: Nazi Cinema and Its Afterlife* (Cambridge, Mass., 1996)

Reuveni, Gideon, *Reading Germany: Literature and Consumer Culture in Germany before 1933* (New York, 2005)

Ross, Corey, *Media and the Making of Modern Germany: Mass Communications, Society, and Politics from the Empire to the Third Reich* (Oxford, 2008)

Rovit, Rebecca, *The Jewish Kulturbund Theatre Company in Nazi Berlin* (Iowa City, 2012)

Rupnow, Dirk, *Täter, Gedächtnis, Opfer: Das 'Jüdische Zentralmuseum' in Prag 1942–1945* (Vienna, 2000)

Rutz, Rainer, *Signal: Eine deutsche Auslandsillustrierte als Propagandainstrument im Zweiten Weltkrieg* (Essen, 2007)

Sarkowicz, Hans (ed.), *Hitlers Künstler: Die Kultur im Dienst des Nationalsozialismus* (Frankfurt, 2004)

Schäfer, Hans Dieter, *Das gespaltene Bewusstsein: Vom Dritten Reich bis zu den langen Fünfziger Jahren* (Göttingen, 2009)

Schütz, Erhard, and Eckhard Gruber, *Mythos Reichsautobahn: Bau und Inszenierung der 'Straßen des Führers' 1933–1941* (2nd ed., Berlin, 2000)

Semmens, Kristin, *Seeing Hitler's Germany: Tourism in the Third Reich* (Basingstoke, 2005)

Stahr, Gerhard, *Volksgemeinschaft vor der Leinwand? Der nationalsozialistische Film und sein Publikum* (Berlin, 2001)

Steigmann-Gall, Richard, *The Holy Reich: Nazi Conceptions of Christianity, 1919–1945* (Cambridge, 2003)

Steinweis, Alan E., 'Weimar Culture and the Rise of National Socialism: The Kampfbund für deutsche Kultur', *Central European History*, 24 (1991), 402–23

Steinweis, Alan E., *Art, Ideology and Economics in Nazi Germany: The Reich Chambers of Music, Theater, and the Visual Arts* (Chapel Hill, 1993)

Steinweis, Alan E., *Studying the Jew: Scholarly Antisemitism in Nazi Germany* (Cambridge, Mass., 2006)

Strobl, Gerwin, *The Swastika and the Stage: German Theatre and Society, 1933–1945* (Cambridge, 2009)

Süß, Dietmar, *Death from the Skies: How the British and Germans Survived Bombing in World War II* (Oxford, 2014)

Swett, Pamela E., Corey Ross, and Fabrice d'Almeida (eds), *Pleasure and Power in Nazi Germany* (Basingstoke, 2011)

Urban, Markus, *Die Konsensfabrik: Funktion und Wahrnehmung der NS-Reichsparteitage, 1933–1941* (Göttingen, 2007)

Williams, John Alexander (ed.), *Weimar Culture Revisited* (New York, 2010)

Winkel, Roel Vande, and David Welch (eds), *Cinema and the Swastika: The International Expansion of Third Reich Cinema* (2nd ed., Basingstoke, 2011)

PICTURE CREDITS

ACKNOWLEDGEMENTS

This book originally appeared in German, as part of a new series on 'Die Deutschen und der Nationalsozialismus'. I should like to thank Norbert Frei, Chair of Modern and Contemporary History at the University of Jena, and Sebastian Ullrich, history editor at C.H. Beck, for the invitation to write it and invaluable advice along the way. Rüdiger Graf, Markus Roth, and Tim Schanetzky also read the manuscript and made numerous pertinent suggestions. Further thanks go to all who made the publication in English possible. At Oxford University Press, Matthew Cotton was welcoming and efficient at the initial stages, while Valliammai Krishnappan steered me through the production process. Two anonymous reviewers, who have subsequently identified themselves as Riccardo Bavaj and Matthew Stibbe, gently pointed out some room for improvement. Lesley Sharpe and Jeremy Noakes offered their expertise as translators of books on Nazi Germany, Stephen Curtis copy-edited the manuscript with his customary thoroughness, and Christine Brocks compiled the index with a sharp eye for any remaining inconsistencies. The original publication was dedicated to my mentor Wolfgang Hardtwig, and it is my pleasure to restate just how much my historical understanding of culture owes to him.

INDEX

INDEX

Himmler, Heinrich 13, 114, 116–19, 121–2, 196–7, 232, 244, 253, 259, 269
Himmler, Margarete 115
Hindemith, Paul 15, 73, 108
Hindenburg, Paul von 36, 137
Hinkel, Hans 155, 158, 160
Hirschfeld, Magnus 38
Hitchcock, Alfred 234, 238–9
Hitler putsch 111
Hitler salute 53, 111
Hitler Youth 67, 209, 259, 267
Hitler, Adolf:
    antisemitism 130
    death 272
    and Goebbels 62–4, 80, 129, 202, 264
    and NSDAP 9, 39
    opponents 76
    regime 105–6, 241, 246, 248
    rise 251
    and Rosenberg 67
    speeches 84
    and Speer 132
    success 241, 248
    taste 75
    views on art 144
Hofbräuhaus 108
Hoffmann, Heinrich 111
Hohenstaufen 115, 118
holidays 22, 58, 90–2, 182, 228
Hollywood 19, 23, 81–2, 92, 104, 107, 169, 178, 212, 236, 238–40
Holocaust 207, 271,
Homer 225
homosexuality 67, 240
Horst Wessel Song 39–40, 43
Hossenfelder, Joachim 48
Hotel Adlon 263
'House of German Art' 11, 128
Hubmann, Hanns 217
Huch, Ricarda 37
Hugenberg, Alfred 19–20
humanitarianism 240
Hungary 145, 211–12, 242
hyperinflation 70

I Accuse 179–81
'I'm dancing to heaven with you' 258
ideology 4, 21, 25, 48, 63, 79, 83, 92–3, 118–19, 237–8
    Communist 245

Nazi 3, 24, 71, 85, 87, 107, 240, 256, 265
    racist 120, 244
Imperial Germany 8, 15–16, 44, 55, 85, 123, 132, 265
imperialism 114, 118
Impressionism 75
'In Defence of Culture' 105
individualism 47, 79
individuality 79, 159, 178
inflation 7
Institute for Advanced Studies 104
International Chamber of Film 211
Intrigue and Love 188
Iron Gustav 71
isolation 59, 94–6, 100–1
Israel 104
Italy 114, 145–7, 153, 196, 207, 219, 242, 259

Jacobins 28
Jannings, Emil 20
Japan 145–6, 202, 212, 237
jazz 11, 14, 29, 83, 92, 154, 183, 225, 229, 259
Jerusalem 148, 213
Jeu de Paume 196
Jew Süss 176, 188
Jewish Central Museum 232
Jewish Council 224
Jewishness 122–3, 150, 232
Jews:
    assimilated 42
    baptized 49
    Berlin 220
    deportation of 223
    European 219, 221–2, 229, 233, 250, 256, 268
    exclusion of 42, 76, 130, 157, 177, 190, 211, 222
    extermination of 206, 232
    'free of Jews' 122
    French 186
    'half-Jews' 71, 117, 122
    influence of 40, 122, 128, 230–1
    left-wingers 46, 69
    marginalization of 130, 148, 152–3, 201, 222
    middle-class 159
    naturalized 31
    Polish 174
    'quarter-Jews' 122